Worke~
Work~ ~es

Workers after Workers' States

Labor and Politics in Postcommunist Eastern Europe

Edited by
Stephen Crowley and David Ost

ROWMAN & LITTLEFIELD PUBLISHERS, INC.
Lanham • Boulder • New York • Oxford

ROWMAN & LITTLEFIELD PUBLISHERS, INC.

Published in the United States of America
by Rowman & Littlefield Publishers, Inc.
4720 Boston Way, Lanham, Maryland 20706
www.rowmanlittlefield.com

12 Hid's Copse Road, Cumnor Hill, Oxford OX2 9JJ, England

British Library Cataloguing in Publication Information Available

Library of Congress Cataloging-in-Publication Data

Workers after workers' states : labor and politics in postcommunist Eastern Europe /
edited by Stephen Crowley and David Ost.
    p. cm.
  Includes bibliographical references and index.
  ISBN 0-7425-0998-2 (alk. paper)—ISBN 0-7425-0999-0 (pbk. : alk. paper)
  1. Labor movement—Europe, Eastern.   2. Post-communism—Europe, Eastern.
3. Labor union—Europe, Eastern—Political activity.   4. Industrial relations—Europe,
Eastern.   5. Europe, Eastern—Economic conditions—1989–   6. Europe, Eastern—
Social conditions—1989– I. Crowley, Stephen, 1960–   II. Ost, David.
HD8380.7 .W67   2001
322'.2'0947—dc21   2001019531

Printed in the United States of America

♾ ™ The paper used in this publication meets the minimum requirements of American
National Standard for Information Sciences—Permanence of Paper for Printed Library
Materials, ANSI/NISO Z39.48–1992.

To my parents, Joan and Richard, for everything
S. C.

To Carola Frege, for her companionship and support
D. O.

Contents

Acknowledgments

This project was made possible through a research grant provided by the National Council for Eurasian and East European Research (NCEEER), under authority of a Title VIII grant from the U.S. Department of State. (Needless to say, neither NCEEER nor the U.S. Government is responsible for the views expressed in this volume.) Assistance in preparing and administering the grant was provided by Oberlin College, especially by Joe Fetsic, David Love, and Pam Snyder.

First drafts of the essays in this volume were presented at a conference held in Warsaw in June 1999. The conference was held jointly with, and graciously hosted by, the Institute of Public Affairs, Warsaw. Particular thanks go to the institute's very capable organizer, Dr. Tomasz Kozłowski, and to its director, Lena Kolarska-Bobińska. Thanks also to Joanna Chmielecka for helping arrange conference logistics, and to Jadwiga Gryczyńska for organizing accommodations. David Ost wishes to thank the American Fulbright Program, Central European University, and Warsaw University for supporting his stay in Warsaw. The AFL-CIO's Solidarity Center provided help in enlisting collaborators for this project; in particular, we would like to thank Adrian Dougherty, Rudy Porter, and Dick Wilson. Finally, thanks to Susan McEachern at Rowman & Littlefield for her interest in our project and to the comments of an anonymous reviewer.

Introduction

The Surprise of Labor Weakness in Postcommunist Society

David Ost and Stephen Crowley

There are two questions that motivate this book. First, given unprecedented political freedoms coupled with truly painful economic change, why has labor been so quiescent in postcommunist Europe? There have been varying degrees of protest, which we explore in the various chapters, but the widely predicted "social explosion" of labor fighting against the effects of radical market reform simply never happened. Second, why has labor remained, more than a decade after the start of the "transition," a weak social and political actor throughout the region? Contrary to what so many expected, unions seem to be among the weakest institutions of the new civil society—weak in terms of gaining influence over policy making and securing material rewards for workers. Our aim, in presenting these ten studies of different Eastern European nations, is to understand how this happened and why.

While labor decline in the era of globalization is a familiar theme,[1] the situation in the postcommunist world is particularly acute. First, its recent economic depression is without parallel. According to one recent account of what we might call the "transition depression," the total value of goods and services produced by "transition economies" declined by at least 25 percent in real terms from 1989 to 1997.[2] After the Great Depression, this is the largest peacetime contraction in world output. The decline in Poland was almost as severe as that of Germany in the four years preceding Hitler's rise to power. In Russia, even before the 1998 collapse of the ruble, the trough was even deeper. As for wages, the cuts have been "larger than those experienced by labor in major countries during the Great Depression."[3] To put it mildly, this drastic economic decline created some significant grievances among workers in the region; intuitively at least, one would expect to see some significant protest as a result.

1

The specifics, of course, are different for each country. (See tables 1, 2, and 3.) However, regardless of the country (whether former Soviet or Central European) and regardless of the path taken (whether shock therapy or gradualist[4]), the post-1989 period saw a dramatic wage decline, a sudden precariousness of employment, and an unsettling of the entire welfare structure. Even when they did not lose their jobs, workers now feared they could. In the meantime, they suffered as prices escalated out of control, their savings wiped out from inflation. Past benefits distributed through the workplace, such as housing, were now jettisoned as "unproductive"; markets rose to provide these goods and services but at prices not even imaginable on factory wages.

Besides material benefits, workers lost prestige. The new system was explicitly aimed at building a propertied class (or "middle class," as it was called). Working-class mores were seen as decidedly passé, their protests interpreted through a newly pervasive neoliberal lens as an outmoded defense of outmoded particular interests, the satisfaction of which would harm the economy as a whole.

Objectively and subjectively, workers took a beating. And as the chapters in this book demonstrate, labor's response has been almost universally minimal. If this seems obvious and unsurprising in retrospect, it certainly was not so in the early 1990s, when most social scientists were predicting extensive labor protest, not quiescence. This was certainly true of those studying the political economy of transitions. As Haggard and Kaufman concluded in their widely noted study, "In general, organized workers, both public and private, are best positioned to act politically against stabilization and devaluation. . . . Other things being equal, one would expect the degree of unionization and

Table 1   Real GDP 1989–1999 (1989 = 100)

	1990	1991	1992	1993	1994	1995	1996	1997	1998	1999
Bulgaria	90.9	83.3	77.2	76.1	77.5	79.7	71.6	66.6	68.9	70.6
Croatia	92.9	73.3	64.7	59.5	63.0	67.3	71.3	76.2	78.1	77.9
Czech Rep.	98.8	87.3	86.9	86.9	88.8	94.1	98.7	97.7	95.5	95.3
Hungary	96.5	85.0	82.4	81.9	84.4	85.6	86.8	90.7	95.1	99.4
Poland	88.4	82.2	84.4	87.6	92.1	98.6	104.5	111.7	117.1	121.9
Romania	94.4	82.2	75.0	76.2	79.2	84.8	88.2	82.8	78.3	75.8
Russia	97.0	92.2	78.8	71.9	62.8	60.2	58.2	58.7	55.8	57.6
Slovakia	97.5	83.3	77.9	75.1	78.7	84.0	89.2	94.8	98.6	100.5
Ukraine	96.4	88.0	79.2	68.0	52.4	46.1	41.5	40.1	39.4	39.3
Yugoslavia	92.1	81.4	58.7	40.6	41.7	44.2	46.8	50.3	51.5	41.6

Source: Economic Survey of Europe, No. 2/3 (New York & Geneva: United Nations, 2000).
Note: Yugoslavia includes Serbia and Montenegro.

Table 2   Registered Unemployment (percentage of labor force)

	1990	1991	1992	1993	1994	1995	1996	1997	1998	1999
Bulgaria	1.8	11.1	15.3	16.4	12.8	11.1	12.5	13.7	12.2	16.0
Croatia	—	14.1	17.8	16.6	17.3	17.6	15.9	17.6	18.6	20.8
Czech Rep.	0.7	4.1	2.6	3.5	3.2	2.9	3.5	5.2	7.5	9.4
Hungary	1.7	7.4	12.3	12.1	10.9	10.4	10.5	10.4	9.1	9.6
Poland	6.5	12.2	14.3	16.4	16.0	14.9	13.2	10.3	10.4	13.0
Romania	1.3	3.0	8.2	10.4	10.9	9.5	6.6	8.8	10.3	11.5
Russia	—	—	4.7	5.5	7.5	8.9	10.0	11.2	13.3	12.2
Slovakia	1.6	11.8	10.4	14.4	14.8	13.1	12.8	12.5	15.6	19.2
Ukraine	—	—	0.3	0.4	0.3	0.6	1.5	2.8	4.3	4.3
Yugoslavia	—	21.0	24.6	24.0	23.9	24.7	26.1	25.6	27.2	27.4

Source: Economic Survey of Europe, No. 2/3 (New York & Geneva: United Nations, 2000).
Note: Yugoslavia includes Serbia and Montenegro.

Table 3   Consumer Prices (annual average, percentage change over previous year)[a]

	1989	1990	1991	1992	1993	1994	1995	1996	1997	1998	1999
Bulgaria	6.4	23.8	338.5	91.3	72.9	96.2	62.1	123.1	1082.6	22.2	0.4
Croatia	1200.0	609.5	123.0	663.6	1516.6	97.5	2.0	3.6	3.7	5.9	4.3
Czech Rep.	1.4	9.9	56.7	11.1	20.8	10.0	9.1	8.9	8.4	10.6	2.1
Hungary	17.0	28.9	35.0	23.0	22.6	19.1	28.5	23.6	18.4	14.2	10.1
Poland	264.3	585.8	70.3	45.4	36.9	33.2	28.1	19.8	15.1	11.7	7.4
Romania	1.1	5.1	170.2	210.7	256.2	137.1	32.2	38.8	154.9	59.3	45.9
Russia	2.5	5.3	100.3	1528.7	875.0	309.0	197.4	47.8	14.7	27.8	85.7
Slovakia	1.3	10.4	61.2	10.2	23.1	13.4	10.0	6.1	6.1	6.7	10.5
Ukraine	2.0	5.4	94.0	1209.6	4734.9	891.2	376.7	80.2	15.9	10.6	22.7
Yugoslavia	1265.0	580.0	122.0	8926.0	2.2E+14	7.9E+10	71.8	90.5	23.2	30.4	44.1

Source: Economic Survey of Europe: No. 2/3 (New York & Geneva: United Nations, 2000).
Note: Yugoslavia includes Serbia and Montenegro.
[a]1989 figures for Bulgaria, Russia, and Ukraine are retail prices; all figures for Croatia are retail prices.

the likelihood of adopting and sustaining orthodox stabilization and structural adjustment measures to be inversely correlated."[5] Likewise, Przeworski argued, "In sum, to advance reforms, governments must either seek the broadest support from unions, . . . or they must work to weaken these organizations and try to make their opposition ineffective."[6] Democratization scholars and specialists on postcommunist countries made similar arguments.[7] The economic hardship following the end of communism has been much greater than almost anyone expected, yet the response from Eastern Europe's workers has been, to say the least, quite limited.

Workers entered the new era in a weak position and have never recovered a position of strength. How might we know that labor is indeed weak? The following chapters attempt to capture the extent of this weakness through a variety of indicators:

- levels of union membership
- styles of management
- strength of collective bargaining
- number and impact of strikes
- nature of political alliances
- union impact on public policy
- material well-being of workers

These we will return to in the conclusion. What is the situation like today? More than a decade into the postcommunist transformations, trade unions have reconstituted themselves. However, as continued downsizing, increased wage differentials, increasingly authoritarian management, and the almost complete absence of unions in the new private sector make clear, they have been unable to bring about an inclusive form of capitalism.

Before discussing possible explanations for labor weakness, there is perhaps a prior question. Why write a book on labor? The topic is certainly not a fashionable one. With the downfall of regimes that claimed to rule on behalf of the working class, attention has turned to traditional political science concerns such as party formation[8] or economic issues like privatization.[9] When social scientists look at civil society, they tend to look at NGOs, or new forms of protest,[10] or the emergence of a new elite.[11] It is indicative of our times that so much has been written about new elite formation and so little about working-class formation. Yet to consider labor, strike activity, and trade unions peripheral matters best left to industrial-relations specialists is to forget that labor has been central to the fate of advanced capitalist democracies. This is especially true of Western Europe, to which the postcommunist countries so ardently aspire. Historically, unions have been important vehicles for expressing workers' grievances and also for structuring them. Trade unions have been essential to democratic stability because they channel the inchoate social anger that comes from being a subordinate into a formal economic grievance capable of being redressed. As a number of recent works have shown, labor was central to the democratization of Western Europe and critical to the formation of the welfare states that have maintained social peace since World War II.[12] That this West European model of labor relations and class compromise is itself being transformed just as Eastern European countries are attempting to adopt it is but one of the many challenges faced by postcommunist labor movements. Labor weakness in initial stages of democratization in Eastern Europe, therefore, may have profound political implications, for it means that the anger that trade unions have traditionally funneled into class cleavages can get diverted into nationalist, fundamentalist, and other illiberal directions. If this is so, far from helping consolidate liberal capitalist democracy—as some democratization theorists have theorized—labor weakness may threaten it.[13]

The crisis of the postcommunist labor movement does not mean the diminution of class anger; workers regularly express the highest levels of rejection of the present order. It means only that that anger hovers unstructured and immobilized—yet eminently structurable and mobilizable. With weak unions matched by weak parties, labor can be particularly open to mobilization by nationalism or other illiberal programs. It is because of this hypothesized link between class anger and political outcomes that we were especially interested in including chapters on Serbia and Croatia. It is unfortunate for social science—as well as intellectually inexcusable—that the former Yugoslav republics have been largely excluded from the comparative analysis of postcommunist societies, as if the outbreak of war were an indicator that these societies were simply outside the pale, rather than being extreme examples of processes occurring elsewhere in the region.[14] For it is precisely here that the link between unorganized economic anger and illiberal political outcomes appears to be most clear.[15]

Many of the following chapters will return to these questions. Ost, for example, argues that union weakness and the pro-market ideology of Solidarity has led to illiberal, fundamentalist tendencies in Polish politics. One hypothesis, therefore, is that the mobilization of anger along ethnic and nationalist lines is a result of the inability to mobilize anger along economic and class lines. Extreme nationalism, in other words, might be a by-product of labor's identity crisis. The study of labor in postcommunism is thus very much a study of comparative democracy.

How, then, does one explain labor weakness? There are, of course, various possible explanations. One view focuses on economic conditions. Russia, for example, has seen its gross domestic product decline by roughly half in an economic collapse that by most indicators is more severe than America's Great Depression. Among other problems, huge numbers of workers are simply not being paid, often for several months at a time, leading some to fear an uncontrollable social outburst. Yet the fact that there have been few protests over such dire conditions can perhaps be explained by the conditions themselves. With production falling and workplaces downsizing, the situation might just be too precarious for union organizing. Strikes are difficult to stage when factories have stopped production and a real threat of unemployment looms. Rational individuals and organizations will refrain from militant action in tough economic times, especially when there seems to be little alternative.

While this explanation might help explain union weakness in Russia or Ukraine, however, how can the inactivity and declining membership of labor unions be understood in countries such as Hungary, where conditions are much better? Having started reforms quite early, Hungary made rapid strides in economic transformation, achieved a growing economy with low inflation, received much of the area's foreign investment, and is well positioned to enter the European Union in the not-too-distant future. In this case, one could argue that there is little reason for an active labor movement because conditions are relatively good, but then we have a contradictory and ultimately useless explanation: Unions are weak when the economy is bad and weak when the economy is good. Clearly, economic conditions alone will not explain union weakness.

Another possible explanation that focuses on the problem of collective action comes from resource-mobilization theory. According to this view, collective-action problems result from institutions having poor access to mobilizable and intangible resources. Dawson has argued that communist societies, like resource-poor communities elsewhere, leave groups outside official frameworks with a legacy of inadequate communications systems, low funds, poor organizational skills, a lack of expertise, and a paucity of activists, which in turn leads potential movement organizers to an overreliance on volunteer staff, weak linkages between and within units, and unstable group membership.[16] The state of union activity in the postcommunist world does seem to resemble this predicted outcome. Activists are few, local unions remain isolated from each other, and membership is erratic and declining. The problem with this approach, however, is that trade unions were always particularly *privileged* with regard to resources in communist societies. Even after the old party-affiliated union elites were toppled, trade unions were guaranteed access to crucial mobilizable resources such as property, funds, factory radio systems, newsletters, and even newspapers. They had the right to make legally binding agreements and a staff paid by factory management. The resources exist, but still the activists and commitment do not.

Resources might, however, help explain the predicament of postcommunist unions in other ways. Under communism, workers looked to trade unions not as defenders of their interests but as providers of in-kind benefits and social services provided through the workplace.[17] With the collapse of communism, formerly official trade unions focused on retaining their property and right to distribute benefits—rather than defending workers against management— because benefits were seen as the key to retaining members. It might therefore be difficult for unions to take a combative stance against management and the state, because those institutions ultimately provide the resources and define property rights. This legacy may help explain a curious paradox alluded to above. Throughout the region, the formerly official trade union remains the largest union, despite the perception of members that these organizations do not effectively represent their interests. Union weakness, in other words, may result from continued union reliance on resources provided by the old state enterprises.

Finally, one explanation for union weakness that seems particularly fruitful holds that the problem derives not from institutions or resources but from ideas and identity. Identity theorists of collective action argue that people become involved with organizations to find meaning in their lives.[18] Trade unions have certainly served this function in a wide variety of contexts, from early French unions[19] through German social-democratic unions[20] to Solidarity in Poland.[21] The studies here and elsewhere suggest, however, that unions in the postcommunist world do not seem to be playing that role. Activists are dropping out, membership is dwindling, and labor organizations do not seem relevant as an important collective identity.[22] Interests do not seem clear, and ideas seem vitally important.[23] By the late communist period, for example, many workers had eagerly embraced capitalism as the putative alternative, and they understood a good society to mean one with unfettered ownership rights. In the former Soviet Union, coal miners went on strike demanding the market economy that would ruin them.[24] In Poland, even Solidarity activists have often treated unions as a relic of communism rather than as an important institution of capitalism.[25] The following chapters show other ways in which ideas shape outcomes. These cases suggest that it is labor's own antiunion ideas, or what might be called a crisis of class identity, that contributes powerfully to union weakness.

Weak union identities, of course, have their roots in the communist past, where unions were authoritarian institutions officially charged with helping management fulfill the plan. The chapters here point to the centrality of legacies in a wide context. Arandarenko, for example, argues that labor weakness in Serbia stems from the way labor was integrated into the communist system, and he claims, provocatively, that self-management left a particularly negative legacy. Kideckel shows that the official valorization of labor in the old Romanian system and in the immediate aftermath of the fall of the Ceauşescus combined with what he calls a "structural denigration," leaving unions with illusions about working-class power that have contributed to their ultimate inefficacy. For Pollert, labor weakness in the Czech Republic is a result of a passive incorporation into the political sphere that began in the Habsburg era and survived into the late communist era, with relative prosperity reinforcing old traditions of compliance. Pańków and Kopatko, meanwhile, see the Soviet legacy as particularly burdensome for Ukrainian labor today.

The essays here also help us identify the particular features of the new market economy that work to the disadvantage of unions. The enormous growth of small, private firms is clearly a major factor. Unions find it difficult to organize small firms, and employees are reluctant to join. Of course, these are problems of small firms everywhere, but when combined with the pro-market ideas of many Central and Eastern European trade unionists, it is no surprise that membership has declined so dramatically. Indeed, one of the most important indicators of union decline in the region is the almost complete absence of unions from the burgeoning new private sphere. As for large enterprises, privatization seems to have a dual impact, facilitating both formal collective agreements and the lax enforcement of contracts. Of course, privatization is not the only factor. Kopatko and Pańków show us that even where the state remains the largest employer, unions are regularly ignored and overlooked. Their account also reminds us of the sources of union weakness in the old era, as they tell of Ukrainian unionists sent to jail for militant activities.

Significantly, while the studies point to institutional arrangements that damage labor's interests, they do not offer clear examples of those that can aid unions. It is typical to think of tripartite commissions as pro-labor institutions, but Pollert and Stein show that even where such bodies are firmly institutionalized—as in the Czech and Slovak republics—they have done little to empower labor. All the countries in the region now have some form of tripartism, but without binding power or strong unions behind them, the ensuing "corporatism" is more illusory than real.[26]

Does this mean that nothing can help and that unions are destined for marginalization? Is the weakness that unions experience in Eastern Europe merely a function of the new global economy that seems to have labor on the defensive throughout the world? Is labor's predicament in postcommunist societies really no different from that faced by workers elsewhere? While there is no question that international economic factors provide an important piece of the puzzle of labor's weakness in Eastern Europe—and we will return to these questions in the conclusion—the following chapters make clear that workers in postcommunist societies face unique dilemmas.

We have assembled here a set of ten essays by experts—several of whom are from the region, and all of whom have extensive experience in the region. Each essay focuses on the state of trade unions and the relationship between labor and politics in a particular postcommunist country. The ten countries are Bulgaria, Croatia, the Czech Republic, Hungary, Poland, Romania, Russia, Serbia, Slovakia, and Ukraine. These countries constitute a full array of postcommunist politics and polities, with a wide variation of labor institutions, economic policies, democratic institutions, political experiences, and economic outcomes. Besides the traditional countries of Eastern Europe, we include the two most industrialized former Soviet republics and the two most populous countries of the former Yugoslavia. While all the essays here address the same basic theme of labor weakness—and most do so through a historical excursion into the past decade—there are some differences. Arandarenko begins with union weakness in Serbia and focuses on explanations for the phenomenon. Kokanović tackles the Croatian situation through extensive use of recent economic figures and trends. Kopatko and Pańków turn to household surveys of the Donbass region to inquire what this tells us about labor in contemporary Ukraine.

We should note that in putting together this volume, we deliberately chose not to engage in a comparative study. Instead, we asked experts to write chapters on ten different countries. Current academic fashions tend to favor comparative over country-specific approaches, but we beg to differ. First of all, comparisons are impossible without a solid foundation of knowledge on which to build. In several of the cases that we discuss—such as Romania, Ukraine, Serbia, and Croatia—very little has appeared in English, especially concerning the relationship of labor and politics. Yet there is a further problem, quite common today, in the rush to offer comparisons. While much can be learned through the comparative method, hasty comparisons can obscure rather than reveal underlying trends. Comparative analysis can easily misidentify superficial institutional differences and policy outcomes as reflections of significant substantive variation. However, institutions or events that signify strength in one context might signify nothing more than legacy in another. Whether labor is weak or strong makes sense only in a particular national context. For example, we know that a single confederation dominates labor in the Czech Republic—compared to different degrees of pluralism in the other countries—and that centralization is typically associated with strength in the West. However, it is an empirical question that can only be answered in a Czech-specific context what such monopoly control really signifies and the extent to which it translates into pro-labor outcomes. Polish and Romanian union leaders have become prime ministers—something that would seem a natural signifier of strength to the comparative observer—but what this really means about the ability of unions to shape policy can only be answered by close analysis of the particular situations in those countries.

We ourselves certainly engage in comparative analysis, as we do in the conclusion to this volume, but we do so on the basis of the country-specific studies contained in these chapters. In this way, we avoid the inappropriate assumptions often made by those rushing to compare without having solid foundations in the particulars. Earlier predictions that labor would be an obstacle to reform assumed that "trade union" signified the same sort of organization in one context as in another.[27] Yet these predictions missed the essential point that the following case studies make clear: Unions in the post-communist context act quite differently from how unions are "supposed" to act.[28] Labor research, in particular, has been dominated by studies of labor in capitalist economies and has produced a powerful set of assumptions. Under-standing and comparing Eastern European labor must be based on different assumptions, the nature of which will only become clear in the course of concrete empirical investigations.

By bringing together these different countries, we hope to reach some general conclusions about labor and politics in the postcommunist context and to try to explain the origins and implications of apparent labor weakness. Our book aims not only to measure and explain labor's weakness in the postcommunist era but to explore the impact of that weakness on the consolidation of democracy.[29] If theories that proposed labor's centrality to democratization are at all correct, then the weakness of the labor movement in these societies signals serious trouble for the process of democratization. Conversely, if democratization proceeds without labor's active participation, then previous theories need to be revised. Will labor become securely integrated into the new capitalisms[30] emerging in Eastern Europe, or will its diminished status and reduced power—besides creating new forms of inequality—turn workers into the populists that liberal reformers still fear? These are some of the key questions we explore in the essays in this book. We will examine answers to these questions in the conclusion.

NOTES

1. William Greider, *One World, Ready or Not* (New York: Simon & Schuster, 1997); Jeremy Rifkin, *The End of Work* (New York: Touchstone, 1994).

2. Branko Milanovic, *Income, Inequality, and Poverty during the Transition from Planned to Market Economy* (Washington, D.C.: World Bank, 1998), 6.

3. Milanovic, *Income, Inequality,* 30.

4. See Beverley Crawford's distinction between these two paths in her introduction to *Markets, States, and Democracy: The Political Economy of Post-Communist Transformation* (Boulder: Westview Press, 1995).

5. Stephen Haggard and Robert Kaufman, *The Political Economy of Democratic Transitions* (Princeton: Princeton University Press, 1995), 269.

6. Adam Przeworski, *Democracy and the Market: Political and Economic Reforms in Latin America and Eastern Europe* (New York: Cambridge University Press, 1991), 182.

7. See also Giuseppe di Palma, *To Craft Democracies: An Essay on Democratic Transitions* (Berkeley: University of California Press, 1990); Ken Jowitt, "The Leninist Extinc-

tion," in *The Crisis of Leninism and the Decline of the Left,* Daniel Chirot, ed. (Seattle: University of Washington Press, 1991); and the critical discussion of what he terms the "breakdown of democracy thesis" in Bela Greskovits, *The Political Economy of Protest and Patience: East European and Latin American Transformations Compared,* (Budapest: Central European University Press, 1998).

8. Herbert Kitschelt, Zdenka Mansfeldova, Radoslaw Markowski, and Gabor Toka, *Post-Communist Party Systems: Competition, Representation, and Inter-Party Coopera-tion* (Cambridge: Cambridge University Press, 1999).

9. Roman Frydman and Andrzej Rapaczynski, *Privatization in Eastern Europe: Is the State Withering Away?* (Budapest: Central European University Press, 1994); David Stark and Laszlo Bruszt, *Postsocialist Pathways: Transforming Politics and Property in East Central Europe* (Cambridge: Cambridge University Press, 1998).

10. Grzegorz Ekiert and Jan Kubik, *Rebellious Civil Society: Popular Protest and Democratic Consolidation in Poland* (Ann Arbor: University of Michigan Press, 1999).

11. Gil Eyal, Ivan Szelenyi, and Eleanor Townsley, *Making Capitalism without Capi-talists: Class Formation and Elite Struggles in Post-Communist Central Europe* (London: Verso, 1998).

12. Gregory Luebbert, *Liberalism, Fascism, or Social Democracy: Social Classes and the Political Origins of Regimes in Interwar Europe* (New York: Oxford University Press, 1991); Dietrich Rueschemeyer, Evelyne Huber Stephens, and John D. Stephens, *Capitalist Development and Democracy* (Chicago: University of Chicago Press, 1992); Alexander Hicks, Joya Misra, and Tang Nah Ng, "The Programmatic Emergence of the Social Secur-ity State," in *American Sociological Review* 60, June 1995, 329–49.

13. For an elaboration of this argument see David Ost, "Is Latin America the Future of Eastern Europe?," in *Problems of Communism* 41:3, May–June 1992.

14. An excellent comparative book that *does* integrate Yugoslavia into a study of com-parative state socialism and its collapse is Valerie Bunce, *Subversive Institutions: The Design and the Destruction of Socialism and the State* (Cambridge: Cambridge University Press, 1999).

15. See Susan Woodward, *The Balkan Tragedy* (Washington, D.C.: Brookings Institute, 1995).

16. Jane Dawson, *Eco-Nationalism: Anti-Nuclear Movements in Lithuania, Ukraine, and Russia* (Durham, N.C.: Duke University Press, 1996).

17. See Stephen Crowley, *Hot Coal, Cold Steel: Russian and Ukrainian Workers from the End of the Soviet Union to the Post-Communist Transformations* (Ann Arbor: Univer-sity of Michigan Press, 1997).

18. See Alessandro Pizzorno, "Political Exchange and Collective Identity in Industrial Conflict," in *The Resurgence of Class Conflict,* Crouch and Pizzorno, eds. (London: Mac-millan, 1978); and Alberto Melucci, *Nomads of the Present* (Philadelphia: Temple Univer-sity Press, 1989).

19. William Sewell Jr., *Work and Revolution in France* (Cambridge: Cambridge Uni-versity Press, 1980).

20. Guenther Roth, *The Social Democrats in Imperial Germany* (New York: Putnam, 1959).

21. David Ost, *Solidarity and the Politics of Anti-Politics* (Philadelphia: Temple Uni-versity Press, 1990).

22. See also David Ost, "Labor, Class, and Democracy: Shaping Political Antagonisms in Post-Communist Society," in *Markets, States, and Democracy: The Political Economy of Post-Communist Transformation,* Beverley Crawford, ed. (Boulder: Westview Press, 1995); and David Ost and Marc Weinstein, "Unions against Unions: Towards Hierarchical Management in Post-Communist Poland," in *East European Politics and Societies* 13:1, Winter 1999.

23. On the lack of clarity of interests in postcommunism, see Valerie Bunce and Maria Csanadi, "Uncertainty in the Transition: Post-Communism in Hungary," in *East European Politics and Society* 7:2, Spring 1993, 240–75; and David Ost, "The Politics of Interest in Post-Communist East Europe," in *Theory and Society* 22, August 1993.

24. Crowley, *Hot Coal.*

25. See Julius Gardawski, *Poland's Industrial Workers on the Return to Democracy and Market Economy* (Warsaw: Friedrich Ebert Foundation, 1996); and Guglielmo Meardi, "Trade Union Consciousness, East and West: A Comparison of Fiat Factories in Poland and Italy," in *European Journal of Industrial Relations* 2:3, 1996, 275–302. Also Ost and Weinstein, "Unions against Unions."

26. David Ost, "Illusory Corporatism in Eastern Europe: Neoliberal Tripartism and Postcommunist Class Identities," in *Politics and Society* 28:4, December 2000, 503–30. For a statement on the legitimacy of corporatism in the region, see Elena A. Iankova, "The Transformative Corporatism of Eastern Europe," in *East European Politics and Society* 12:2, Spring 1998, 222–64.

27. See, for example, Przeworski, *Democracy and the Market.*

28. On how much comparative sociological analysis uses concepts culled from the Western capitalist experience that may not be appropriate for postcommunist systems, see Larry J. Ray, *Social Theory and the Crisis of State Socialism* (Cheltenham, U.K.: Edward Elgar, 1996).

29. It is in its effort to look specifically at the politics of labor relations that this book differs from others dealing with labor in Eastern Europe, most of which have focused either on enterprises (John Thirkell et al., *The Transformation of Labour Relations* [Oxford: Oxford University Press, 1998]); regional change (Jane Hardy and Al Rainnie, *Restructuring Krakow: Desperately Seeking Capitalism* [London: Mansell, 1996]); or legal frameworks (Hans Moerel, ed., *Labour Relations in Transition* [Netherlands: Institute for Applied Social Sciences, 1994]). Grzegorz Ekiert and Jan Kubik deal with labor protest (*Rebellious Civil Society* [Ann Arbor: University of Michigan, 1999]) but only in terms of understanding protests, not labor.

30. On the notion of plural capitalisms in postcommunist society rather than of a transition to a single capitalism, see David Stark and Laszlo Bruszt, *Postsocialist Pathways* (Cambridge: Cambridge University Press, 1998.)

Chapter One

Labor and Trade Unions in the Czech Republic, 1989–2000

Anna Pollert

UNION WEAKNESS OR STRENGTH: GLOBAL, POSTCOMMUNIST, AND NATIONAL QUESTIONS

Trade union weakness or strength in capitalist society—whether in mature or restored capitalism as in Central Eastern Europe (CEE)—needs to be understood in terms of the asymmetry of power relations between capital and labor. In the capitalist employment relationship, the employer has greater power than labor, even if the latter is organized. The employer can close down or move elsewhere. The employer has the support of the state and the media. Labor does not have this power. Trade union power (or lack of it) can be understood in terms of its ability to challenge this asymmetry and overcome opposition from the employer. Its potential strength resides in its capacity to organize and mobilize collectively to influence the terms under which labor power is sold, including the distribution of its product—primarily in wages. Trade union power thus involves both the practical capability to control workers' physical and social environment and the ideological sway to gain legitimacy as a social force.[1]

In addressing these questions in terms of any specific trade union movement at a point in time, both general issues of the balance of class forces and specific regional or national issues need to be explored. In the case of the Czech trade union movement ten years after the restoration of capitalism, how much is its experience unique, part of the wider experience of CEE, and wider still, another aspect of the general weakness of labor? To take the last question first, the crisis of the command economies of the Soviet bloc took place within a neoliberal revival in Western capitalism. The declining power

13

and legitimacy of organized labor has been almost universal in the final decades of the millennium. It would therefore be surprising if newly established trade unions adapting to global capitalism were in a strong position. Employers' and financial institutions' policies toward organized labor are, at best, tolerant of trade unions, at worst, hostile. International labor solidarity, always a difficult aim, is constantly undermined by multinational capital's mobility and divide-and-rule strategy.

The labor movements of CEE have the added difficulty of operating in economies that have become subordinate to the West.[2] They also are inexperienced in dealing with the capitalist employment relationship and its increasingly sophisticated management techniques. Other difficulties include a communist workplace tradition of atomization and individualism as well as an enterprise bargaining system in which unions and managers were partners. In the unprecedented historical transformation from communism (albeit distorted) to capitalism, the ideological problem of establishing the legitimacy of organized labor's pursuit of interests that are separate from capital's interests raises complex challenges for unions. It involves the relegitimization of trade unions as organs of genuine worker-interest representation rather than Communist Party conveyor belts. However, it also requires carving a space between opposing the old system and ambiguously both supporting and opposing the recently restored market economy.

There are thus broad organizational and ideological issues to address that relate to universal problems of labor within capitalism and to those associated with capitalist transformation—or restoration. In addition, the strength or weakness of any national labor movement is steeped in its history. The Czech labor movement, like many others in CEE, was formed in a period when the question of national self-determination had an uneasy relationship with the evolution of class-based organization. A further specifically national legacy is the relative affluence of Czech workers compared with less industrially advanced neighbors in the region. The significance of this for the character of trade unionism is also discussed.

The chapter reaches the present day and examines the implication for trade union strength or weakness of institutional developments, particularly of tripartism and collective bargaining. How far does collective bargaining, in terms of outcomes and process, demonstrate union strength or weakness? It may be that, as occurs in established capitalism, trade unions are primarily normalizing conflict in being the "management of discontent."[3] The degree of union strength can be gauged to some extent by the threat of the use of collective power, even in routine relations, so that "serious negotiations involve the overt or implicit threat of collective action, the mobilization of the power of the membership, if a satisfactory settlement is not achieved."[4]

In CEE, weakness is suggested by survey indications that much of what takes the form of "bargaining" masks the reality of simply endorsing legally stipulated minimum wages and conditions.[5] This chapter considers what has hindered trade union strength and how change has taken place in industrial relations developments—from passivity and consent to a sense of frustration and injustice. Throughout this, the difficulty considered is how to translate this into the exertion of power.

LABOR-MOVEMENT LEGACIES: CLASS, NATION, AND STATE

During the period when industrialization laid the foundations of union organization in CEE, nationalist rather than class struggles cut across history. The Czech labor movement's formative years were bound with the self-assertion of subordinate nations against the great European empires of Germany, Russia, or the Habsburgs.[6] The Habsburg response to the threat of Czech nationalism and the advanced working-class organization of its most industrialized parts established a distinctive tradition of state incorporation to win labor's consent. To induce nationalist loyalty, organized labor was given remarkable status in elected commissions of workers to run pension and social-insurance schemes.[7] Concessions to labor in this period left a legacy in that, on the one hand, institutional development of labor representation advanced, but on the other, the national question always remained a device to quell class radicalism. From the last decades of the nineteenth century into the First Republic of 1918–1938, a system of Habsburg-inherited centralized corporatism with authoritarian overtones persisted. This coexisted with a developing trade union system that was highly fragmented by craft, politics, and nationality.

Thus, the early Czech labor movement developed institutions of representation, but it had a tendency for national co-option coexisting with union fragmentation. In this, it differed from the Austrian labor movement from which it sprang. After World War I, the latter became more centralized and coordinated,[8] while the newly independent Czechoslovakia followed a different political and economic path. Older corporatist structures regulating insurance and unemployment remained, but unions continued to be divided by politics and ethnicity.[9] This arguably weakened labor's power. Corporatism became a form of central control over the rank and file, without a deepening of union organization on the ground. Patriotism, as before, kept class issues in check. Although Czech workers joined the post–World War I revolutionary wave—with a rapid increase in trade union membership, strikes demanding land distribution, and socialization of large enterprises and banks—labor radicalism was suppressed in the name of defending the new republic.[10] Concessions were won, including the eight-hour workday and extensive social reforms, but they were partly inspired by nationalism, with financing largely provided by the National Liberation Loan of 1918, a fund built by the patriotic contribution of the general population. The weakness of labor as an oppositional force was manifest when the general strike of December 1920 failed and trade union membership dropped.

Czech labor-movement history would be incomplete without a reference to the distinctive political history of parliamentary democracy. During the brief spell of independence from 1918 to 1938, the parliamentary democracy of the First Czechoslovak Republic was unique in CEE at the time, and it remains an important reference point in the collective memory. However, twenty years is arguably a very short time in which to deepen democratic traditions or to establish Parliament as a viable forum for labor representation. There was little real chance for the labor movement to challenge the much longer traditions of bureaucracy and authoritarianism. Democratic and liberal principles remained the domain of intellectuals and artists, and as during the Habsburg period, the middle classes led progressive movements.

Politically, however, the experience of parliamentary democracy allowed workers' parties to develop. The Communist Party (CP) had a much greater chance to grow in Czechoslovakia than in other CEE countries, which had authoritarian regimes in the interwar period. As a result, the CP has always had stronger electoral support than elsewhere in the region—not just in the interwar period but since 1989 also.[11] In the 1998 general election, the Communist Party of Bohemia and Moravia took 11 percent of the vote,[12] and with growing disillusion with the post-1998 government of the Social Democrats (ČSSD), it became the second-strongest party in July 1999.[13] Yet there is no necessary relationship between CP political support and leftist politics—the latter being a highly ambiguous concept in the context of the CP command economy legacy.

Nationalism, union division, authoritarian corporatism, parliamentary democracy, and the growth of the CP form part of the complex mosaic of experience. There is one further piece in the puzzle. Labor's apparent strength, as visible in its relative prosperity, also disarmed it ideologically. Throughout the imperial, interwar, and communist periods, material wealth proved to be the device that the state used to win labor's allegiance. It was largely available for historical reasons—the Czech lands were the most advanced industrially—but it also came after World War I from outside help, out of the allies' political expediency.[14] Some of the worst hardship after both world wars was mitigated. During the communist period, relative affluence[15] led some to argue that the bargaining of prosperity for political conformity created a "proletariat embourgeoise."[16] Although there was a workers revolt in Plzeň immediately after Stalin's death in 1953 that was met with Stalinist coercion, thereafter the CP under Novotny was never forced into reform by mass unrest. Revolt against the system only erupted again much later, in the Prague Spring of 1968.

The Prague Spring was undoubtedly a crucial experience in worker democracy, which should not now be overlooked in the emphasis on compliance. Workers councils were elected in the summer of 1968, and demands for self-management went far beyond the original intentions of limited workers' participation rights and continued after the August Soviet invasion in a "hot autumn." But the post-1968 "normalization" imposed tight bureaucratic control that neutralized them. Even after the 1988 State Enterprise Act reinvented enterprise councils, these were under the firm grip of the communist unions, the ROH (Revolutionary Trade Union Movement), and were dissolved again in April 1990. Cynicism about the "pseudo-participation" of workers councils, which went back to postwar factory councils as organs for raising "socialist consciousness"[17] and later exercises in incorporation,[18] now returned. After the imposition of post-1969 "normalization," this was combined again with providing relative economic prosperity. Political citizenship and opposition were harshly suppressed, but they were also exchanged for material well-being.

In sum, the economic prosperity of the highly industrialized Czech lands provided the state with the material means to offer concessions to neutralize potential opposition. Nationalism and union fragmentation had already weakened the labor movement. Moderation and state incorporation characterized the Czech labor leadership in the precommunist era. During communism, radicalism existed, but it was suppressed or bought off with relative affluence.

The advances enjoyed by the Czech workers were thus largely delivered by the enlightened self-interest of governments at different points in time, rather than won through union organization and mobilization against the power of capital. The Czech labor movement, when faced with restored capitalism, was ill prepared, both organizationally and ideologically, for struggle.

THE POSTCOMMUNIST LABOR
MOVEMENT IN ITS ECONOMY

What conditions did Czech workers face with the entry of their country into global capitalism? Today, they constitute almost a fifth of the four Visegrad countries' total workforce. Out of the Czech Republic's 10.3 million population, 4.9 million are employed—twice as many as in Slovakia, more than

Hungary's 4 million, but a small labor force compared with Poland's 14.5 million. The main industries are mining, chemicals, and manufacturing (of which transport equipment, electrical goods, and fuel processing are growth areas). Sectoral redistribution has followed other capitalist economies, with a decline in industry, mining, and agriculture and a growth in services. Western investment has been concentrated in the most promising sectors: telecommunications, automotives, petroleum, glass, tobacco, food and drink, retail, and banks.

Czech workers began this transition with material advantages. However, illusions in the free market and faith in their political leaders made this privilege more apparent than real, leaving the government largely unopposed as it wasted the opportunities of a country embarking on the capitalist road in much better economic shape than the other Visegrad countries. In 1989 the former Czech and Slovak Federative Republic (ČSFR) had low foreign debt, and the government was theoretically less in thrall to the IMF and the World Bank than elsewhere. In 1991, although the ČSFR suffered an almost 16 percent drop in GDP and a 25 percent fall in real wages, it started from much more prosperous beginnings, making its absolute misery less than Poland's or Hungary's.[19] Employment did decline—in 1995 employment was still 7 percent lower than in 1990—but this was less severe than in other Visegrad countries. Registered unemployment was low at around 3.5 percent in the first half of the 1990s,[20] although it climbed to 5 percent in 1997 and 9 percent by 2000.

But free-market policies, obsessed with formal privatization and rejecting a state industry policy, created an economic crisis in 1996 and 1997, from which there has been little recovery. GDP growth, which was 3.6 percent in 1996, was zero by 1999. Early economic advantage was both short-lived and uneven. Hardest hit were the monostructural regions dependent on one industry, such as the coal-mining areas of northwest Bohemia and north Moravia, the metallurgy area of north Moravia and the Kladno district west of Prague, and the electronics industry in northeast Moravia and parts of eastern Bohemia. In terms of growing unemployment, regional disparities are becoming more, rather than less, polarized with time.[21]

Workers' material advantage was whittled away. Consumption dropped drastically after the political and economic crisis of 1997, and growth in real wages almost halved from the previous year. The Czech Republic joined the downward path of Hungary, where living standards in terms of private consumption and real wages continued to fall until 1997, whereas they rose in Poland and Slovakia after 1996.[22]

In sum, after initial material and labor-market advantages in which relative falls in living standards were tolerated partly because they began at a higher

Table 1.1   Unemployment Rate, Czech Republic 1992–2000

Region	1992	1993	1994	1995	1996	1997	1998	1999	2000*
Prague	0.32	0.34	0.28	0.29	0.43	0.87	2.31	2.93	
Central	2.71	3.36	2.86	2.57	2.98	4.62	6.06	6.59	
Bohemia South	2.26	2.85	2.26	2.03	2.52	3.09	5.59	5.82	
Bohemia West	2.08	2.65	2.24	2.16	2.66	4.38	6.36	7.09	
Bohemia North	2.89	4.20	4.42	4.80	5.84	8.60	11.40	12.19	
Bohemia East	2.26	2.90	2.46	2.3	2.93	4.37	6.30	6.91	
Moravia South	2.97	3.85	3.29	2.88	3.45	5.31	7.73	8.38	
Moravia North	3.98	6.16	5.61	4.84	5.60	7.74	11.00	12.03	
Total	2.57	3.52	3.19	2.93	3.52	5.23	7.48	9.0	8.5

Source: Czech Statistical Office, April 1999; April 2001
*Through the third quarter of 2000

level (and partly because of faith in the free market), the Czech working class faced disillusion in the second half of the decade. However, after a legacy of compliance and naked oppression, a short-lived, popular, but not very deeply rooted democracy (the First Republic), and after 1968, one of the tightest and most centralized regimes of the Soviet-bloc, struggle was not familiar. The subsequent economic crisis did, however, lead to some radicalization. Nevertheless, past legacies and organizational and ideological difficulties continued to weaken the union movement.

FROM FRAGILE TRIPARTISM TO UNION DECLINE

One could argue that the Czech labor movement faces the deterioration in its circumstances in a better-organized state than its CEE neighbors. Unlike those countries where "new" and "old" union federations fomented a system of entrenched union rivalry, in Czechoslovakia the old unions disbanded in 1989 and were immediately re-created in one major new confederation, the Czech and Slovak Trade Union Confederation (ČSKOS).[23] After the country's breakup in 1993, this unified structure continued in each of the two new states, with the Bohemian and Moravian Confederation of Trade Unions (ČMKOS) in the Czech Republic and the Slovak Confederation of Trade Unions in Slovakia. A further feature of the Czech union context, again different from Hungary and Poland,[24] was the politically nonaligned character of the unions. Although an informal alliance between the unions and ČSKOS and the Social Democratic Party soon developed, the tight interweaving of trade unionism with party politics did not apply in the Czech Republic, giving the unions greater independence than in neighboring Visegrad countries.

The Fragile Shell of Tripartism

Most of the early efforts of the new trade union movement took place on a national, tripartite level. Tripartism had not grown from below, with a mass base. So early on, bargaining was not supported by potential mass mobilization. Yet while labor was not a strong social partner, this is not to dismiss entirely some successes for the unions in early legislation. If ČSKOS, then ČMKOS, had been entirely accommodating, the tripartite Council for Economic and Social Agreement would have surrendered entirely to the government's policies to weaken labor. While there were no labor victories, compromises included the drafting of the law on collective bargaining, in which the unions managed to defeat government proposals for a works council system. In the context of removing union rights of codetermination and the abolition of enterprise councils in April 1990, works councils were viewed as mere consultation organs that would threaten union bargaining rights. However, in most other areas, including defense of the minimum wage, the unions were defeated.

ČMKOS recognized the need to involve union members in its campaigns, and it succeeded in holding major demonstrations over a combination of issues—cuts in pensions, labor-market deregulation measures, and the austerity program—in 1994, 1995, and 1997. However, this was a far cry from building on union organization at the workplace level and mobilizing from here, which would arguably have had an impact. Time and experience were too short at this stage. It was not until the union-membership decline became too acute to ignore that ČMKOS and its member unions began to turn their attention to the workplace as the locus to build trade unionism. For the first half of the decade, "mobilization" amounted to calling national rallies in Prague. Some regional union activity took place, particularly in the suffering mining areas of the north and east, but this was not encouraged by the national union authorities. As in the Habsburg era, the interwar period, and the communist years, centralized control from the top was the norm. However, the weakness of the trade unions cannot be blamed entirely on the labor leadership or on workers' faith in national-level political bargaining at the expense of dealing with management at the company or industry level. The 1992–1998 right-wing Civic Democratic Party (ODS) and Civic Democratic Association (ODA) coalition government, especially Prime Minister Klaus, were unequivocally hostile to labor. Tripartite annual general agreements, always only gentlemen's agreements, were increasingly broken and devoid of content. The last one signed was in 1994, after which tripartism became moribund. It never amounted to neocorporatist political exchange in the sense of articulation between the top, middle, and lower levels of interest representation among labor, capital, and the state, which in the German or Swedish neocorporatist context gave labor influence.[25]

There was no network of intermediate agreements between sector-level unions and employers associations. Industry bargaining began weakly primarily because of the lack of development of employers associations, and it has deteriorated further with time. Sectoral collective agreements declined from twenty-nine in 1997 to twenty-four in 1999 (below 20 percent of employees), and the extension to cover companies not affiliated with relevant employers associations slumped from 191 in 1993 to 12 in 1995, and by 1996 the practice was abandoned.[26] During the revision of the Labor Code in 1999 and 2000 (largely in preparation for accession to an enlarged European Union), the unions were concerned with further weakening of the legislation upholding higher- (sector-) level collective bargaining.[27]

In 1997 tripartism was revived as an instrument to contain rising industrial unrest in the deepening crisis. However, its function remained the same despite a change in name (the Council for Economic and Social Accord) and some structural changes.[28] Without foundations in a stronger system of bargaining at other levels, tripartism will be unable to reverse the decline in consumption and real wages—the major grievance of workers.

Declining Trade Unionism

Union organization in the Czech Republic suffers from the effects of structural economic change and management policies to marginalize trade unions, as experienced elsewhere in CEE. Union membership has drastically declined from the near 90 percent membership of the communist era. From 4 million members and forty affiliated unions in 1992, ČMKOS affiliation in 1995 consisted of thirty-six unions and membership of 2.6 million, which included retired workers. By 1998 it had dropped further to thirty unions and approximately 1.5 million members.[29] There is a growing nonunion sector and declining membership in the unionized sector. Structural change means that employment in the formerly well-unionized, large, state enterprises has been superseded by poorly organized, small and medium firms of twenty-five to five hundred workers. In 1996 almost half of its employees worked in medium-sized firms, a third in small companies, and fewer than one-fifth in large enterprises. Between 1994 and 1996 there was a 10 percent density drop in medium-sized firms, a 5 percent fall in large enterprises, and in small firms, the 16.2 percent membership dropped to 14.6 percent—not only because of new, nonunion firms but because nonmembership nearly doubled from 5.7 percent to 10.3 percent in unionized firms. Membership in the state sector is now the same as in privatized companies: 37 to 40 percent.[30]

THE WEAKNESS OF LABOR:
COLLECTIVISM, INDIVIDUALISM, AND
PROBLEMS OF MOBILIZATION

Industrial Relations Developments

In spite of the decline in union membership and the ineffectiveness of tripartism, the labor movement in the Czech Republic has not been static or permanently passive. Since 1989 industrial relations has broadly followed two phases. The initial five years witnessed apparent social peace with virtually no industrial conflict. However, to equate lack of action with social consent is misleading. The problem here, as for any labor movement, is transposing dissatisfaction into mobilization, and this was lacking. Case-study research indicated that optimism in the eventual success of transformation was already tainted with doubts about restructuring at the workplace level on 1993. For example, interviews with workers in the retail, food, and engineering industries revealed dissatisfaction with wages and, in the latter, with the restructuring process itself.[31]

After 1995 a second phase of more overt labor-movement opposition began. Explanations for more visible opposition must reside in a mixture of further disillusionment as economic circumstances deteriorated, a growing sense of injustice, and more active calls to action by the unions. ČMKOS became radicalized by the government's dismissive attitude toward the principle of social partnership. Its mass rallies in 1994 and 1995 against government social policy also testified to the fact that workers were now prepared to take to the streets. There was also an increase in official industrial action. This was concentrated in the public service sector—the railways, health, and education sectors—as in the rest of CEE, and it centered on low pay and poor restructuring. The results varied. Usually, there were pay concessions but no major changes in policy, and the grievances that originally activated workers merely resurfaced later.[32] While any collective mobilization is worthy of note and cautions against dismissing labor as passive, action has been defensive, moderate, and often symbolic. Token strikes and "warnings" were often as far as opposition went, as in the case of the one-hour stoppage in October 1994 by seven thousand of the seventeen thousand direct workers at Volkswagen-Škoda (Škoda is the name of the successful Czech auto plant that Volkswagen took over) against subcontracting and undercutting wages. This was defeated as the multinational threatened to relocate to another low-cost country.[33] However, professional workers succeeded in organizing campaigns against low public-sector wages and damage to the health service. Doctors issued strike threats, and nurses and ambulance workers joined strikes and demonstrations in 1996.[34]

ČMKOS's more radical role, however, remained confined to demonstrations and pleading with the government. When it came to industrial action, the traditions prioritizing respectability over militancy prevailed. When tripartism was restored in 1997, ČMKOS subdued growing calls for a general strike in favor of defending the economy.

Labor-movement weakness can thus partly be explained by a common phenomenon—that of its policing by its leadership. However, the problem also requires a deeper analysis below the surface appearances of consent, compliance, and more overt conflict. This involves examining the ideological problems shared by different levels of the labor movement (union leaders and rank and file workers) and differentiating between levels of the industrial relations process.

Ideological Problems of Labor in Transformation to Capitalism

At the ideological level, does the difficulty for labor lie in its ambiguous embrace of the transformation to capitalism? This is a general problem for the postcommunist labor movement. Any radicalism of the early dissident movement, which overthrew the CP, was occluded by free-market ideology. This was arguably hegemonic for some time and is hardly surprising, given the overarching strength of this worldview in the West. Even for those in the labor movement not committed to free-market policies, the ideological dilemma is the support for change that is in favor of building capital accumulation and a capitalist class. While the Czechoslovak unions were not mass movements whose *raison d'être* was the defeat of communism, the unions are "schizophrenic," as a leading member of ČMKOS put it,[35] in that they must "support the reform process" but "do not like certain aspects." For the union confederation itself, this became an added factor in its desire for respectable social partnership.

The re-formed old unions also had the problem of carving out a new identity, new language, and new aims.[36] The lack of a distinctive labor-movement project or vision creates a space for other ideologies that are not necessarily progressive for labor. In the Czech context, the bourgeois parliamentary democracy of the interwar First Republic has been an important reference point, and while democracy is a strong central value for trade unionism, identity with successful Czech capitalism (a common theme of pride) is arguably not an inspiration for resurrecting the labor movement. A dilemma shared by other postcommunist labor movements is that the term "socialism" is discredited. This leaves the chief aim of the labor movement to be a "decent" form of market economy, in which labor has a fair share—a social-democratic model on the lines of European "social partnership" or the current union-revival rallying cry in the United States of "dignity at work." Significantly, one of ČMKOS's slogans in its demonstration against social security cuts in 1995 was *Odbory za důstojný život* (Trade unions for a dignified life). Yet for those suffering from major disillusionment, particularly as political parties of apparent left and right produce the same policies, the door is wide open to the visceral calls of nationalism and xenophobia.[37] Signs of this danger are suggested by a recent poll finding that over three-quarters of Czech citizens did not think that building a wall between Roma and Czech inhabitants in a town in northern Bohemia was a racist move.[38]

A further ideological complication for labor is the belief that many of the problems of transformation are just a hangover from communism, rather than its mixture with the advent of capitalism. Dissatisfaction has been aimed at both the state and the old *nomenklatura*—at the former for the inadequacies of legislation that have allowed unbridled financial corruption and at the latter for profiteering from it. There are two consequences. The first is an overreliance on legislation as the solution to unfettered, and what are seen as illegitimate, profits—a reliance that ties into the history of Habsburg bureaucracy and the rules of the communist Labor Code. The second relates to how perceived collective injustice is directed.

Collective injustice or grievance exists at a general level and as a necessary component of how workers define their interests.[39] The Czechs cannot be superficially labelled as "conservative," as they were in some studies in the early 1990s.[40] However, current problems of capitalism are often perceived as the lack of a break from communism. While there is truth in the social process of continuity in the way the old *nomenklatura* appropriated the surplus in new capitalism, as they had in the command economy, the economic base of the new reality is misunderstood. This leads to a false diagnosis that it is communism, not capitalism, that is the problem. This also breeds illusions that once the latter is purged of the former, fair competition will prevail—an illusion fed by free-market ideology. Thus, an important element of interest definition for labor can be misdirected against the old regime, not the new. This also leads to a cynical *plus ça change, plus c'est la même chose* fatalism, which is ultimately disempowering. To give one example, a trade union leader disillusioned with the squandering of opportunity in the engineering company ČKD by political mishandling and nepotism blamed *staři communisti* (old communists) and attributed the fate of the enterprise to a country that was, and would continue to be, full of "scheming scoundrels."[41] This failed to identify the political and economic processes responsible for the sacrifice of his enterprise (and his members' employment) as targets for opposition.

THE WEAKNESS OF ENTERPRISE LEVEL BARGAINING AND THE "NEW" INDUSTRIAL RELATIONS

Most national union personnel have been recruited from outside ROH, the former communist union federation, and are free from former habits. This is not the case at the enterprise level, where most union chairs are former ROH functionaries. Yet both groups of unionists continue to deal with the state and employers in a way similar to the past tradition of enterprise unionism.

In the first few years of transformation the most common practice of unions was to join with management to bargain with the state to elicit concessions for the enterprise. Surveys suggest that since the mid-1990s, enterprise union leaders have begun to define independent labor interests and that union-management relations are developing along "partnership and opposition" lines.[42] However, it is not clear what this means, or whether union leaders are really beginning to bargain with management. Case studies suggest unevenness. Czech union leaders have not been incorporated as the "managers of change" found in some Polish enterprises,[43] but neither have they successfully opposed employment reduction or the drop in real wages. Where they have been successful, as in the department store Kotva, it has been in defending enterprise welfare, not shop-floor wages.[44] In other case studies (e.g., Kmart, ČKD, Staropramen breweries) union leaders have been unable to defend workers in terms of excessive working hours or of indexing wages to keep up with inflation.

A number of factors contribute to the lack of success. Inexperience combined with inadequate information from employers has led to poor bargaining. In some cases, what is reported as "bargaining" is little more than rubber-stamping labor law and/or management dictate (Kmart); in others, agreements were made and broken by management (ČKD); and in others still, the union chair began with an unrealistically high wage demand and then capitulated to a zero increase.

In examining the bargaining process, however, we need also to analyze the employer and the tactics available to suppress potential opposition. Management attacked trade unionism simply by marginalization and ignoring agreements (where these existed). An example was the series of broken agreements in ČKD. The promised 5 percent "stimulation fund" for productivity never materialized, and the promise in the 1993 collective agreement of pay indexation to inflation at quarterly intervals was ignored. Members of the union committee requested their chair to convene a meeting, but they were rebuffed with the reply that the company was losing money.

This highlights a central strategy in the "new" industrial relations, which is to undermine the collective worker by fostering a different form of collectivism—that of company identity. Such unitary models are part of a long tradition of capitalist control, yet are now called "new." The question of a separate worker identity from the success of the enterprise within capitalism is always ambiguous. On the one hand, employment is dependent on enterprise success. On the other, there is always conflict over distribution of the surplus. In the context of transformation, and especially of recession, there is further pressure for workers to support their enterprise. The ideology of unitary interests presented by contemporary human resource management strategies thus fell—initially at least—on fertile ground. It also drew on the old communist management-union partnership and placed responsibility for losing money or insolvency outside the enterprise.

The other aspect of this cultivation of corporate identity in the "new" industrial relations is the individualization of the employment relationship, particularly with the individualization of reward. In all of the case study enterprises, an increasing proportion of the payment system moved from collective grades (tariffs) to performance-related pay dependent on individual appraisal. Added to this was a clause on secrecy. Workers were forbidden to discuss their pay, and in Kmart, even the union was prevented from gaining access to information on employees' earnings. The tactical success of this individualization policy was in the confusion and division created among workers. It reinforced the previous legacy of workplace atomization, when the individual or small group had been the best means of bargaining.[45] With the end of communism, liberal individualism, not collective organization, was heralded as freedom. Hence, in the workplace, individual expression, behavior, and organization were more immediately familiar from the past and seemed more attractive for the future in terms of motivation and reward. Individual pay and bonuses seemed attractive to most workers because they appeared to be a break from the former nepotistic and politicized reward system. The new payment systems were further sweetened in some enterprises, such as ČKD, by being accompanied by a new time-based system that removed the uncertainty of payment-by-results, a system still plagued by poor and irregular supplies.

Yet disorientation did occur. Early on, Western human resource management strategies met with little opposition, but as they frequently unraveled—with wage funds insufficient to fulfill the principles of rewarding performance—workers became disillusioned. Transformation had inspired hopes for a new kind of fairness. A sense of injustice and betrayal flared when pay agreements were broken, or when restructuring strategies were adopted that were clearly seen as failures. However, these were not aggregated into collective-interest representation. While the union leadership continued to prefer compliance with management—no doubt also trapped by enterprise failure—workers became divided by a reward system that reverted to the criteria of age and experience rather than effort and output, as had been hoped. The process of division was often recognized, but there was neither the confidence nor the experience of democratic self-organization to harness dissatisfaction into a collective response. Cynicism grew about new fads as parallels were detected between the old and new regimes, and habits of fear led to passivity, or exiting, rather than giving voice to grievances.

ČKD is an illustration. A mere thirty workers out of the total of fifteen hundred initially voiced concern about departing from the tariff system. However, six months after the first case study visit in 1993, dissatisfaction had increased. Few workers could understand why piece rates had been abolished in the first place; personal reward for performance never materialized because there was never enough money, and motivation was now lacking. Young workers could not see why they should work flat-out if they were paid on what remained effectively a time basis. Older, time-serving workers complained about the upstart younger generation. Disillusionment set in. Performance rewards could only be given by taking away from others. Enforced secrecy became a grievance—but not one that was collectivized because individualism seemed legitimate. "We don't mind; the main thing is, we have to look after ourselves. Besides, envy isn't a good thing" (ČKD worker).

The sense of lack of change streaked opposition with cynicism. "I don't want to poke my nose into other people's business. But it's absurd to have such strict penalties for breaking the rules. It goes from extreme to extreme. Ten years ago, they put up who got what as premiums on the notice board—and they called it democracy. That just bred jealousy. And now . . . ?" (ČKD worker).

The system lowered morale without breaking the pervasive atomization of former workplace relations. "Rumors get going. Nobody in the Factory Union Committee suspected this new system would breed such bad feelings and mistrust" (ČKD union committee member). Intimidation was a further dimension of lack of opposition. As several workers said, people were used to being frightened, and the fear was still deep in them.

Fear was a key element of worker paralysis, particularly among the young and among women. At Čokoládovny, a Western confectionery joint venture employing mainly women, foremen instituted a system of placing "yellow cards" into workers' clocking-in boxes as warnings over timekeeping or speed. At Kmart, workers were pressured to work on state holidays by fear of victimization if they did not. The message to workers was, "If you don't like it, go somewhere else" (worker, Prague store); "We only protested in our collective, quietly, in the corner, but there's no point. It's always the same, 'If you don't like it here, go somewhere else' " (worker, Pardubice store).[46]

At ČKD, breach of the collective agreement created a sense of injustice but no serious opposition. Company insolvency, combined with individualization and secrecy, paralyzed the union. As union committee members told me, "The unions can only 'warn.' There is no strength. It's hard to mobilize because nobody knows what the next one earns"; "You can't fight a loss-making company"; "If we prospered, that might change things" (union committee members).

Together, worker isolation, division, and fear pose major problems for building a postcommunist collective trade union presence. However, these are not necessarily seen as problems by the trade unions themselves. In each case study, both workers and union chairs felt that the "effort bargain" and pay were not a matter for the union but a private issue for the workers and their *mistř* (foreman). There is fear that trade union control over the labor process will be a return to the old bureaucratic union role, where every change had to pass through the Communist Party union machine. Organization and mobilization is thus hindered by union members' own perceptions of what unions should do.

WORKERS AND THEIR UNIONS

Opinion polls have found that workers no longer distrust unions because of their discredited political past. Workers regard unions as important protection at work rather than as providers of welfare and holidays. Surveys show, however, that unions are failing to recruit new workers, with 70 percent of members over age forty and fewer than 7 percent of members recruited since 1989. In 1995, ČMKOS perceived this crisis of membership as a result of poor information and communication to members, who allegedly did not appreciate what unions did for them. Subsequent research commissioned to address these issues revealed deeper causes of union decline. These were associated with what unions did and the meaning of trade unionism to members.

A survey of union members and functionaries in 1996 showed that workers join unions for very similar reasons to those in Western Europe: for traditional workplace defense and pay.[47] However, the finding that workers joined unions for "support with problems at work" had a distinct meaning, dominated by a legalistic, individualistic approach to workplace protection rather than an appeal to collective workplace support. Eighty-five percent ranked advice and representation in handling legal disputes as the most important area of support, followed by 73 percent rating support on grievances as most important.[48] Dependence on the law could pose major problems for developing a collective base for worker representation. With a poorly developed legislative apparatus at every level of the transforming economy (including the privatization process, corporate governance, and labor law) and a weak intermediary level of collective bargaining, legal enforcement alone is unlikely to have muscle. Failure is likely to discredit the unions, and they themselves report very frequent breaches of the law. Conversely, juridical success does not necessarily strengthen the process of collective bargaining or encourage collective organization if it merely relies on applying legislation.

Currently, the evidence of national union mobilizations in demonstrations and even short strikes (mainly in the public sector), suggests a duality in trade union representation. At the national and campaigning levels, collective action has taken place, perhaps because mobilization at this level has resonance with past actions against the state—as in 1968 and the mass movement leading to the Velvet Revolution. However, this momentary political collective identity does not necessarily translate into broad collective union identity and organization at the workplace, where the "collective" still remains small workgroups. In mature capitalism, this took years to build. Here, there has been a gap since World War II.

The survey also investigated what trade unionists do and how this relates to workers' responses to changes at the workplace. Job insecurity and arbitrary treatment at work were key anxieties, with 43.7 percent of members not feeling secure at work. Even in the low-unemployment environment of the Czech Republic, this may be associated with the rise of vulnerable forms of work, casualization, and use of nonstandard employment.[49] Yet union functionaries' activities were not, in the main, focused on these changes.[50] Most of their time was spent speaking with members negotiating on the annual collective agreement. Committee work, advice, and representation on individual issues and welfare ranked next in importance.[51] Asked to list the grievances most commonly reported, functionaries mentioned pay as foremost, followed by management attitudes, welfare, grading, redundancies, health and safety, dismissals, and overtime. Twenty percent of functionaries reported that redundancy and dismissal were their members' gravest grievances, but these did not feature prominently in their activities. It thus appears that functionaries were only partially responding to members' needs, which left a gulf between union activity and key worker concerns.

In the end, if union officials were more responsive to their members' concerns at the workplace, unions might have been better able to deliver more concrete gains for workers. The leadership has blamed poor communication for union decline, but such a diagnosis could lead to efforts to reinforce the existing bureaucracy rather than efforts to build collective identity able to challenge the legacy of atomization and the advent of individualizing management strategies. Recruitment, retention, organization, democratization, and building a collective presence pose the major challenges at the workplace.

CONCLUSION

Despite the signs of growing opposition to the return of capitalism, the Czech trade union movement has been unable to prevent the deterioration in its conditions or to stamp its influence on the transformation process. In spite of the election of a Social Democratic government in 1998, the labor movement has failed to press for a course of restructuring fundamentally different from the free-market route implemented by the previous government. Disillusionment is expressed in oscillations in party support, together with the rising popularity of the CP, but there is no evidence that any political party has any real alternative. A menacing possibility of further disappointments could be the rise of xenophobic nationalism. Part of the labor movements' weakness is ideological: Labor has no alternative vision other than a more humane form of capitalism. In addition, as the experience elsewhere in CEE testifies, pressure by international capital leaves these economies subordinate in the world capitalist order and hems in governments' room to maneuver. National labor movements can do little to press for change without the development of international trade unionism.

As this chapter has argued, there are a number of levels of analysis that contribute to understanding what is distinctive and what is more general about the Czech trade union movement, its potential strengths, and its weaknesses. At each level, ideological and organization problems go hand in hand. Despite early national labor movement representation and trade union organization, union division and nationalism dampened the development of labor as a real power that challenged the state or employers. In the interwar period its potential strength, both organizational and ideological, was sapped by calls to patriotism, limited corporatism, and considerable material concessions.

During communism, material concessions again pacified labor, while naked repression and one of the most tightly controlled regimes of CEE quashed opposition.

In the aftermath of the Velvet Revolution, Czech trade unions experienced similar ideological and organizational difficulties as other postcommunist labor movements. These combined with distinctive national legacies. Conservatism, passivity, and illusory hopes for a return to the successful capitalism and the moderate bourgeois democracy of precommunist times prevailed. Apart from 1968, there was no tradition of struggle or bargaining during the communist period. Moderation had nearly always delivered some compromise, and with the early experience of corporatism, considerable faith was placed in tripartism. It required disillusionment and falling trade union membership to shift attention to lower levels of the developing industrial relations system—by which time much had been lost.

The union confederation remains committed to "responsible" social partnership. Locked within its "schizophrenic" stance toward building a successful national capitalism, it is unlikely to turn to industrial militancy. Industry-level bargaining remains a weak form of union power. So, despite the apparent advantage of a centralized trade union movement, things have not gone well for Czech labor. The difficulties of confronting an economy in crisis, the rigors of the "new" industrial relations system, and the legacies of workplace individualism have proved major obstacles to strengthening trade union power.

NOTES

1. R. Hyman, *Industrial Relations: A Marxist Introduction* (London: Macmillan, 1975), 26.

2. P. Gowan, "Neo-Liberal Theory and Practice for Eastern Europe," *New Left Review* 213, September-October 1995, 3–60.

3. Hyman, *Industrial Relations,* 194.

4. Hyman, *Industrial Relations*, 190.

5. G. Casale, "Collective Bargaining and the Law in Central and Eastern Europe: Some Comparative Issues," in *ILO-CEET Report No. 20* (Geneva and Budapest: ILO-CEET, International Labour Office, Central and Eastern European Team, Budapest, and Equality and Human Rights Coordination Branch, 1997), 2.

6. C. Crouch, *Industrial Relations and European State Traditions* (Oxford: Clarendon Press, 1993), 118. In fact, the late nineteenth-century Czech (and Austrian) labor movement was split between demands for national self-determination and support (by Austro-liberals and the left of Austrian Social Democracy) for the Habsburg empire as a multicultural entity (C. Schorske, *Fin-de-Siècle Vienna: Politics and Culture* [London: Weidenfeld and Nicholson, 1979], 118). Similarly, in Poland, the problem of the "national question"

in relation to class struggle and solidarity bedeviled German Social Democracy and preoccupied Rosa Luxemburg in her insistence on internationalism (P. Nettl, *Rosa Luxemburg*, abridged edition [Oxford: Oxford University Press, 1969]).

7. Crouch, *Industrial Relations*, 85.

8. By 1925, Austria (along with Norway) had one of the most centralized labor movements in Europe, with a "reduction in heterogeneity in the shift from Austria-Hungary to *Restosterreich*" although a weak shop-floor presence (Crouch, *Industrial Relations*, 134–36). After 1925, the Austrian state continued to rely heavily on the labor movement, although the political ambiguity of labor's main political organ, the Christian Social Party, allowed later disillusion during the Great Depression to spawn the far right, as Austrofascism in 1934, and then through the *Anschlus* (Crouch, *Industrial Relations*, 145, 153).

9. A. Teichova, *The Czechoslovak Economy 1918–1980* (London: Routledge, 1988), 14, 78.

10. Teichova, *The Czechoslovak Economy*, 65; J. Korbel, *Twentieth-Century Czechoslovakia: The Meaning of Its History* (New York: Columbia University Press, 1977), 50.

11. A. Pollert, *Transformation at Work in the New Market Economies of Central Eastern Europe* (London: Sage, 1999), 35.

12. K. Henderson, "Social Democracy Comes to Power: The 1998 Czech Elections," *Labour Focus on Eastern Europe* 60, 1998, 5–28, 7. This compares with 32.3 percent for the Social Democrats and a combined 45.3 percent of the three center-right parties.

13. In an opinion poll in July 1999, the right-wing ODS received 23.4 percent support, the KSCM 17.8 percent, and the ČSSD only 16.8 percent—half its 1998 election share of the vote (RFE/RL Newsline, July 23, 1999).

14. During the First Republic, cushioning from the Great Depression was aided by Czechoslovakia's economic and political separation from Austria-Hungary. While Austria experienced postwar inflation, Czechoslovakia avoided it with currency reform and monetary stabilization. The new state's increasing orientation toward the West, not Austria, also helped. The country's special geopolitical position as a buffer against revolutionary Russia gave it a privileged provision for other aid. Britain provided long-term credit for food, which allayed unrest due to food shortages, while France extended a loan for military purposes, which provided employment (Teichova, *The Czechoslovak Economy*, 74).

15. Until the early 1960s, exports of heavy industrial goods to Russia and its satellites paid for imports, which largely made up for falling food production experienced elsewhere; real wages grew by 60 percent from 1950 to 1960 (Chris Harman, *Bureaucracy and Revolution in Eastern Europe* [London: Pluto, 1974], 193).

16. J. Valenta, "Czechoslovakia: A Proletariat Embourgeoise?" in *Blue Collar Workers in Eastern Europe*, J. F. Triska and C. Gati, eds. (London: George, Allen and Unwin, 1981).

17. L. Cziria, "New Collective Forms of Work Organization in Czechoslovak Economic Practice," in *New Collective Forms of Work Organization in Eastern Europe*, L. Hethy, M. Lado, and J. E. M. Thirkell, eds. (Budapest: Institute of Labour Research, 1989), 83.

18. V. Fišera, ed., *Workers' Councils in Czechoslovakia 1968–9* (London: Allison and Busby, 1978), 11; J. Vlacil, "Brief History of Participation in Czechoslovakia" in *Social Problems of Participation in the Changing Czechoslovak Economy*, Mimeo, working paper, (Prague: Institute of Sociology, Czechoslovak Academy of Sciences, 1991).

19. A. H. Amsden, J. Kochanowicz, and L. Taylor, *The Market Meets Its Match:*

Restructuring the Economies of Eastern Europe (Cambridge, Mass.: Harvard University Press), 32–33.

20. The reasons include state intervention to delay bankruptcy, active labor market policies, availability of employment in Germany and Austria, and a hugely expanding service sector rooted especially in a burgeoning tourist trade, particularly in Prague.

21. M. Illner, and A. Andrle, "The Regional Aspects of Post-Communist Transformation in the Czech Republic," in *Czech Sociological Review* 2:1, 1994, 107–27, 118; Table 1. Among the unemployed, similar groups are disadvantaged as in Poland and Slovakia. Youth unemployment (those under twenty-five) is responsible for about one-third of the unemployed. Women are also disadvantaged. In the Czech Republic, they constitute 60 percent of the unemployed in 1996 but only around half of the employed. With almost twice the unemployment rate of men (for instance, 4.2 percent compared with 2.4 percent in 1996) their *relative* disadvantage was worse than in other Visegrad countries (United Nations Economic Commission for Europe, *United Nations Economic Commission for Europe, Economic Survey of Europe 1995–1996* [New York and Geneva: United Nations, 1996], Table 3.4.6, p. 89; United Nations Economic Commission for Europe, *United Nations Economic Commission for Europe, Economic Survey of Europe 1995–1996* [New York and Geneva: United Nations, 1996], Table 3.3.5, p. 118).

22. United Nations Economic Commission for Europe, *United Nations Economic Commission for Europe, Economic Survey of Europe 1995–1996* (New York and Geneva: United Nations, 1996), 75–76; United Nations Economic Commission for Europe, *United Nations Economic Commission for Europe, Economic Survey of Europe 1997–1998 Nos. 1 and 2* (New York and Geneva: United Nations, 1998), 100, 116.

23. In 1989, ČSKOS became the largest union body, consisting of sixty-three member organizations—twenty-one federal, twenty Czech-Moravian, and twenty-two Slovak unions on industrial or occupational lines. By 1992 this had been rationalized to forty trade unions covering 4 million members (1992 figures). Other minor associations included the fourteen-union Confederation of Art and Culture (KUK) with one hundred thousand members, the fifty-thousand strong Trade Union Association of Bohemia, Moravia, and Slovakia with old Communist Party leanings, a Christian Democratic grouping, and as in several other countries in CEE, autonomous unions for particularly powerful groups such as train drivers.

24. Elsewhere (particularly in Poland in the case of Solidarity but also in Hungary in terms of the sponsorship of the militant new unions—such as Liga—by a government keen to weaken the major "old" confederation), there was major ambiguity in terms of the political party and labor interest representation role of the unions. The process of party alliances was linked with the early mass movement character of the "new" unions. Each time a new political party came into office, the role of its union ally shifted from a "union role," to that of government partner (J. Thirkell, R. Scase, and S. Vickerstaff, "Changing Models of Labour Relations in Eastern Europe and Russia," in *Labour Relations and Political Change in Eastern Europe*, J. Thirkell, R. Scase, and S. Vickerstaff, eds. [London: UCL Press, 1995], 17). See also L. Andor, "Trade Unions in Hungary," in *Labour Focus on Eastern Europe* 54, 1996, 68–77; R. Deppe and M. Tatur, "Transformation Processes and Trade Union Configurations in Poland and Hungary," in *Transfer* (Brussels) 3:2, 1997, 242–69; J. Hausner, "The State Enterprise Pact and the Potential for Tripartism in Poland," in *Tripartism on Trial*, R. Kyloh, ed. (Geneva: International Labour Organisa-

tion, 1995), 105–28; J. Bartosz, "Polish Trade Unions: Caught Up in the Political Battles," in *Labour Focus on Eastern Europe* 55, 1996, 38–47; and E. J. Dittrich and M. Haferkemper, "Labour Relations in the Making—Bulgaria, Hungary and the Czech Republic," in *Industrial Transformation in Europe: Process and Contexts*, E. J. Dittrich, G. Schmidt, and R. Whitley, eds. (London: Sage, 1995), 137–63.

25. Crouch, *Industrial Relations,* 53–55.

26. A. Pollert, "The Czech Republic: Industrial Relations Background," in *European Industrial Relations Review* 296, September 1998, 19–25.

27. A. Pollert, "The Regulation of the Employment Relationship in the Visegrad Countries," paper for the IREC Conference, LEST-CNRS, Aix-en Provence, France, May 20–22, 1999.

28. There were four levels:

1. The Plenary Session, with the government, the unions, and the employers each with seven representatives. It meets every two months.
2. The Presidium of the Council—the executive—one for the government, one for the union confederations, and one for the employers' federations.
3. Working groups (teams, working parties) to discuss individual subjects, constituting nine members at most—one to three appointed by each delegation.
4. The Secretariat of the Council, consisting of the executive secretary and one administrative officer. It is responsible for administrative issues.

29. In 1997 the largest Czech unions were the metal workers union, OS KOVO, (459,736 members), the teachers and education workers union (173,259 members), the railway workers union association (114,356 members), the mining, geology, and oil workers union (100,804 members), and the building workers union (86,675 members). Most unions are medium-sized, such as the union of workers in woodwork, forestry, and management of water supplies (76,006 members), the union of health service and social care workers (65,372 members), the union of postal, telecommunications, and newspaper workers (63,528 members), the textile, clothing, and leather workers union (60,523 members), the chemical workers union (53,102 members), the union of food and allied trades workers (48,069 members), the general union, UNIOS, (43,522 members), the shop workers union (40,657 members), and the union of transportation workers (36,657 members). There are also several small unions, such as teachers in higher education (18,138 members), the union for hospitality, hotel, and the travel sector workers (6,069 members), the firefighters union (6,284 members), the police (4,023 members), and several even smaller unions.

30. Pollert, *Transformation at Work,* 133–56.

31. A. Pollert, "Women's Employment and Service Sector Transformation in Central Eastern Europe: Case Studies in Retail in the Czech Republic," in *Work, Employment and Society* 9:4, 1995, 629–57; Pollert, *Transformation at Work,* 177–226. The cases portrayed in the book included local and multinational companies between 1993 and 1997. The cases were ČKD, a company at the heart of both Czech engineering and command economy overdevelopment of heavy industry; Kotva and Kmart, which were taken over by Tesco and were involved in endogenous restructuring and foreign ownership in retail; and a brewery multinational joint venture, Staropramen, which had Bass as majority owner. Most cases were in Prague, although branches of Kmart were elsewhere.

32. A. Pollert, "The Transformation of Trade Unionism in the Capitalist and Democratic Restructuring of the Czech Republic," in *European Journal of Industrial Relations* 3:2, 1997, 203–28.

33. BCE (Business Central Europe), March 1995, 8.

34. Pollert, "The Transformation of Trade Unionism."

35. Personal interview, 1994.

36. D. MacShane, "The Changing Contours of Trade Unionism in Eastern Europe and the CIS," in *New Frontiers in European Industrial Relations,* R. Hyman and A. Ferner, eds. (Oxford, England: Blackwell, 1994), 337–67.

37. J. Sylwestrowicz, "Capitalist Restoration in Poland: A Balance Sheet," in *Labour Focus on Eastern Europe* 52, 1995, 31–39; M. Haynes, "Eastern European Transition: Some Practical and Theoretical Problems," in *Economic and Political Weekly*, February 24, 1996, 478; R. Deppe and M. Tatur, "Transformation Processes and Trade Union Configurations in Poland and Hungary," *Transfer* 3:2, 1997, 246.

38. RFE/RL Newsline, May 26, 1999.

39. J. Kelly, *Rethinking Industrial Relations: Mobilization, Collectivism and Long Waves* (London: Routledge, 1998), 27.

40. B. Miller, S. White, P. Heywood, and M. Wyman, "Democratic, Market and Nationalist Values in Russia and East Europe: December 1993," Paper prepared for the 1994 Annual Conference of the Political Studies Association, Swansea, March 1994.

41. Pollert, *Transformation at Work*, 205.

42. P. O. Aro and P. Repo, *Trade Union Experiences in Collective Bargaining in Central Europe* (Geneva: International Labour Organisation, 1997).

43. J. Hardy, and A. Rainnie, "Trade Unions, Direct Investment and the Restructuring of Polish State-Owned Enterprises," *Transfer* 3:2, 1997, 270–90.

44. Pollert, "Women's Employment and Service Sector Transformation," 643.

45. M. Burawoy, *The Politics of Production* (London: Verso, 1985); M. Burawoy and P. Krotov, "The Soviet Transition from Socialism to Capitalism: Worker Control and Economic Bargaining in the Wood Industry," *American Sociological Review* 57, February 1992, 16–38; D. Filtzer, "Economic Reform and Production Relations in Soviet Industry 1986–1990," in *Labour in Transition*, C. Smith and P. Thompson, eds. (London: Routledge, 1992), 110–48.

46. Pollert, "Women's Employment and Service Sector Transformation."

47. J. Waddington and A. Pollert, "The Uniform Information and Communication System" in *ČMKOS: Trade Unions in the Czech Republic: A Report of Survey Results* (Prague: ČMKOS, 1997). The survey also showed that in the context of transformation, the campaigning role of unions has been a further attraction, where this role has focused on pay, social issues, and trade union rights.

48. R. Hyman. "Institutional Transfer: Industrial Relations in Eastern Germany," *Work, Employment and Society* 10:4, 1996, 601–39. See page 614 for Germany's Eastern *lander*.

49. Between 1994 and 1996 use of agency labor had risen by 52 percent, contracting outside the Labour Code by 49 percent, recruitment of rural labor by 47 percent, part-time labor by 24 percent, and foreign labor by 21 percent.

50. C. Mako, P. Novoszath, and A. Vereb, *Hungarian National Report: Changing Patterns of Job Structure, Worker Attitudes and Trade Union Activities at Firm Level: The*

Hungarian Case. (Budapest: Mimeo, Communication and Consultation Co. Ltd., and Centre for Social Conflict Research, 1995). This work shows similarities in Hungary.

51. Issues raised more than once a month featured grievances for 35 percent of representatives, pay problems for 27 percent, and health and safety issues for 15 percent. Overtime issues occurred monthly for only 7.6 percent, grading for 5.7 percent, shift work for 2.8 percent, and staffing levels for 4.4 percent.

Chapter Two

The Failure of Social-Democratic Unionism in Hungary

András Tóth

With the initial steps toward a new capitalist and democratic Hungary, all major political parties and trade unions envisioned a social-market economy, involving national-level tripartite concertation and a regulating role for unions in the economy through collective bargaining. The last decade, however, has seen a rather different development. While there was an expansion of neocorporatist institution building at the national level, unions, especially in the private sector, suffered a contraction in their ability to regulate the economy.

Meanwhile, a controversy has developed in the academic literature over the assessment of the strength and impact of unions within the new economy. Some observers have pointed out the weaknesses of tripartite institutions in regulating the economy.[1] However, others have stressed the importance of social and economic packages reached at the tripartite level.[2] For example, in 1991, under a right-wing government coalition, and in 1995, under a social-democratic government coalition, government policies pushed tripartism to the verge of collapse. Both times, union-led strikes forced the government to return to the bargaining table, revive tripartism, and reach consensus with social partners.[3] Further, finance ministers regularly accuse unions of blocking the implementation of neoliberal fiscal policies. However, Hungary is widely acclaimed by the international press as having one of the most liberal economic policies in the region. The quality of collective bargaining is low, and the coverage of agreements is shrinking continuously.[4] Nevertheless, proponents of labor's strength can argue that unions seemingly had power at major companies to shape privatization efforts, and in certain companies unions are successfully bargaining on behalf of workers.[5] In the constantly changing environment of postcommunist Hungary, unions seemed to have the strength to block government measures and change government policies at certain moments, just to be seen a year later as powerless giants accepting whatever measures the government put forth.

This chapter seeks to explain the controversy over the assessment of union power in Hungary today. In measuring trade union power, the chapter identifies two distinct sources of strength: the unions' mobilization power in the economy and the unions' influence on the political system through party linkages. The chapter assesses union power based on the configuration of these two power resources. Given the pluralist union structure, it also evaluates the constellation of power among different union tendencies and confederations, and it analyzes the nature of the emerging industrial relations system as a result of the constellation of power among union confederations.

To grasp the dynamics of change, the chapter distinguishes various developmental possibilities within the industrial relations system. Toward this aim, the chapter builds on a typology constructed by Valenzuela, who was interested in how unions were shaped by their organizational consolidation in the economy and their insertion into political systems.[6] Valenzuela identified three types of union insertion into democratic regimes: social democratic, contestatory, and pressure group. Unions of the social-democratic type are relatively strong unions with a high degree of affiliation and a solid plant-level presence. Generally, there is only one significant national union confederation (though there can be a certain fragmentation based on the professions of members, with little local competition between the different unions with different constituencies). The social-democratic union connects itself closely with a single, relatively strong social-democratic party.

In the contestatory model the labor movement is divided into different ideological tendencies, and each union is inserted into a different political camp. Union membership, to a significant extent, is a matter of political sympathy, identity, and choice. This model is characteristic of southern European countries, where the sharp ideological divisions facilitated the emergence of a divided union movement. The political and ideological divisions lead to competition among the different unions. In this case, interunion competition makes it difficult to reach a neocorporatist compromise. Rather, unions linked to governing parties use their contacts to ensure specific advantages for their constituencies.

Unions belonging to the third type, the pressure-group model, link themselves with preexisting parties or factions of political parties, and thus unionization does not entail the formation of a working-class party. Leaders of these types of unions, already having well-established bargaining practices, are not forced into a strategy of building political support for a party in exchange for policy measures that would help consolidate union organizations. Consequently, union leaders of this type do not have a firm party commitment. Rather, they rely on their ability to pressure whatever party is in power to achieve their organizational goals, and they are likely to avoid engaging in political exchange to do so.

This chapter, building on Valenzuela's model, classifies Hungarian unions along this typology, revealing the changing tendencies of union development. The conclusion identifies five paradoxes, which determine the features and dynamics of union power and explain the strengths and weaknesses of unions.

THE DECOMPOSITION OF THE STATE-SOCIALIST INDUSTRIAL RELATIONS SYSTEM (1987–1990)

Birth of New Unions

Politically active intellectual groups and a few similar, small, white-collar, independent unions set up the first pro-democratic union confederation, the democratic League of Independent Unions (*Független Szakszervezetek Demokratikus Ligája*—hereafter LIGA) in December 1988. The key leadership group of LIGA was formed by social-democratic intellectuals, who were committed to democratic rule and a social-market economy, which would secure the institutionalized voice of employees at the national and workplace level. LIGA aimed to deconstruct the state-socialist trade union system by encouraging employees to build new independent unions at the grassroots level. It asked workers to leave union organizations belonging to the once-official National Council of Trade Unions (*Szakszervezetek Országos Tanácsa*—hereafter SZOT) and organize their own unions to engage in "real" collective bargaining. LIGA, following the example of the Polish *Solidarność*, consciously built a decentralized civil-society-type union structure, which was based on consensual decision making as opposed to the democratic centralism of SZOT. The authorities did not ban the independent unions, but the last communist government did not invite LIGA to participate in negotiations that were held regularly with SZOT. LIGA proclaimed itself a politically independent union, but it had a close relationship with the new pro-democratic parties. Its key leadership group, however, had close connections to one of the most radical pro-democratic parties, the Alliance of Free Democrats (*Szabad Demokraták Szövetsége*—hereafter SZDSZ). LIGA became a founding member of the forum of pro-democratic organizations, the opposition roundtable (*Ellenzéki Kerekasztal* or EKA) set up in March 1989. As a member organization of EKA, it participated in the negotiations between the EKA and the ruling Hungarian Socialist Workers' Party (*Magyar Szocialista Munkáspárt*—hereafter MSZMP) to design the rules of the democratic transition between June and September 1989. During the negotiations LIGA adopted a strategy of self-restraint and did not raise demands for improving terms and conditions of employment. Consequently, one of the associated member organizations of LIGA, the Solidarity Independent Workers Union (*Szolidaritás Független Munkás Szakszervezet*—hereafter Szolidaritás), which had a more militant stance, left LIGA and declared itself an independent confederation.[7]

A further cleavage emerged among new independent unions because of the breakup of the EKA in September 1989. The moderate wing of the EKA, led by the Christian-Democratic Hungarian Democratic Forum (*Magyar Demokrata Fórum*—hereafter MDF), signed a compromise with the MSZMP, which was rejected by the radical parties led by SZDSZ. LIGA sided with SZDSZ, while the MDF sought to set up an alternative workers movement independent of LIGA. Under the tutelage of MDF, a new independent confederation called the National Association of Workers' Councils (*Munkástanácsok Országos Szövetsége*—hereafter MOSZ) was formed in summer 1990. MOSZ, beyond acting as a union, also promoted the dismantling of state ownership by means of employees' collective ownership through workers councils.[8]

While three different confederations emerged with distinct programs and ties to different cleavages of the emerging party system, none of the newly established unions had success attracting members in great numbers or in penetrating workplaces. Alternative unions were set up at only a few hundred workplaces, most seeking solutions to particular local problems. Most of these workplace organizations were small but fairly militant unions opposed to the SZOT locals. In most cases, these new local organizations met with the resistance of employers and the SZOT locals. There are different estimates on the membership size of the new unions. In the summer of 1989, LIGA had only ten thousand members.[9] Most likely, none of the new confederations had more than fifty thousand to seventy thousand members scattered in small workplace-level organizations throughout the country.[10]

On the other hand, the new unions had a political significance far above their membership size. Their emergence signaled the extent of social tensions and contributed to the pressure on the state-socialist elite for full democratization. The weak mobilization capacity of the new unions, however, did not force their allied parties or the government to take their economic demands into account. Nor was there a spontaneous outbreak of workers' anger that would have strengthened the capacity of the new unions.

Internal Reform and Decomposition of SZOT

The decomposition of the state-socialist regime and the emergence of independent unions inevitably put democratization on the agenda. The defeat of the conservative wing of the MSZMP triggered the removal of the old-guard SZOT leadership and put reforms into the hands of second- and third-layer union leaders. The opening of the internal competition for leadership positions propelled the decentralization and fragmentation of the centralized union. Namely, second- and third-layer union leaders—heads of union sections, subsectional associations, or major enterprise union sections—rather than compete for the top leadership of SZOT sought instead to convert their constituency into an autonomous union, so as to become the top leader of that. The resulting fragmentation did not stop at the federal level. SZOT had split into four confederations by the early summer of 1990. The *Magyar Szakszervezetek Országos Szövetsége* (National Confederation of Hungarian Trade Unions—hereafter MSZOSZ) was made up of union federations active in industry and the private-service sector. The *Autonóm Szakszervezetek Szövetsége* (Federation of Autonomous Unions—hereafter ASZSZ) was based on the Union of Chemical Workers and on a number of important public-utility unions. The *Szakszervezetek Együttmuködési Fóruma* (Cooperative Forum of Trade Unions—hereafter SZEF) was established by the public-service employees and civil servants unions. The *Értelmiségi Szakszervezetek Szövetsége* (Association of Academic Employees' Unions—hereafter ÉSZT) consisted of unions in academic and higher-education institutions. Among the four confederations, MSZOSZ was seen as the successor of SZOT, as it had inherited its assets and was led by the last top leader of SZOT.

Organizational fragmentation went hand in hand with decentralization. Amendments of union bylaws, influenced by the model of LIGA, introduced consensual and decentralized decision making. Unions once belonging to SZOT enjoyed stability at the workplace level. Only at a few workplaces did local union sections break up or an alternative independent union emerge. Unions emerging from SZOT largely maintained their membership of 4 million strong.

Alongside internal reforms, SZOT increasingly cut its ties to the ruling MSZMP. Each of the four successor confederations claimed to be a politically independent organization without any party linkages. During the transition period (and before it fragmented), SZOT maintained its position as the sole negotiating partner recognized by the government. However, there was a growing gap between SZOT, which argued for anticyclical government spending, and the government, which increasingly adopted neoliberal fiscal rigor. SZOT argued for increased social and public spending, and member unions of SZOT, led by the public-service unions, began to demand substantial wage increases to arrest the declining standard of living. However, none of these unions ventured to mobilize members for major strike action.

The Parallel Formation of Contestatory and Business-Type Unions

One of the key characteristics of the transition period was the lack of working-class militancy, partly due to the state-socialist development of Hungary and partly due to the negotiated nature of the transition.[11] Barely two dozen workplace stoppages broke out, and none of them spilled over to the regional or sectoral level. This phenomenon undermined the ability of unions to force their demands through mobilization. Moreover, with the lack of rank-and-file mobilization, union bureaucrats enjoyed an exceptional opportunity to design union strategies to fit their own political views and personal career paths.

Following Valenzuela's schema, the emerging pro-democratic unions can be characterized as contestatory unions. These unions had an overriding political goal of democratization and fit into distinct cleavages of the party system by building close ties to pro-democratic political parties. New unions gained national importance as part of the pro-democratic political bloc, but they had difficulty penetrating into workplaces. In other words, they had symbolic power by being part of the pro-democratic bloc, but they lacked industrial relations power. Their symbolic power was sufficient to reach their political ends—the transition—but due to their weak mobilization capacity, they coud not achieve their major economic and industrial relations demands.

The once-official unions, on the other hand, shifted toward pressure-type unionism. They cut their connections to MSZMP and did not establish any connections to pro-democratic political parties. Thus, they had no connection to any political parties in the emerging political system. At the same time, they were able to retain much of their membership and continue negotiating at workplaces. They shifted toward demanding improvements in the terms and conditions of employment and thus prepared themselves for a future based solely on the backing of their membership.

The formation of two distinct types of unionism, however, planted seeds for future trouble. The struggle over which type of unionism would be the major driving force in shaping the postsocialist industrial relations system heightened interunion conflicts during the period of the first democratic government.

Further hampering the future of unionism was the widely held belief that trade union practices and legal rights in the workplace were remnants of the old regime. The Constitutional Court reflected this opinion by repealing a series of union privileges.[12] These judgments explicitly stated that the previous right of unions to control the individual employment relationship was against freedom of contract. These judgments forecasted future legislation that sought to strengthen individual, as opposed to collective, rights.[13]

THE TRANSITION TOWARD A SOCIAL-DEMOCRATIC INDUSTRIAL RELATIONS SYSTEM (1990–1994)

The first democratic election, held in May 1990, was won by MDF, which formed a right-wing, Christian-democratic government in coalition with two smaller parties. The major opposition party became SZDSZ. The Hungarian Socialist Party (*Magyar Szocialista Párt*—hereafter the Socialist Party), the successor party of the former ruling MSZMP, received only 8 percent of the votes. The Socialist Party, however, successfully reconstructed itself as a Western European–style social-democratic and pro-worker party, and it was admitted to the Socialist International. The Socialist Party became the only major party on the left in the Hungarian party system, and from 1993 onward it became the major alternative to the right-wing government coalition.

The MDF government based its economic policy on three main pillars: liberalization, the privatization and restructuring of large state-owned companies, and stabilization. Price and trade liberalization was virtually finished by 1991. In conjunction with a drastic cut in subsidies for domestic companies, it created a competitive open market. Due to determined policies, privatization made great advances. The preferred method of privatization was selling companies outright, which facilitated the influx of foreign direct investment (FDI). Besides privatization, an increasing amount of foreign capital was invested into greenfield projects. By 1993, companies with foreign participation produced about half of all manufacturing value added, and they employed one-quarter of all private-sector workers. Some industrial sub-branches—such as auto and electrical-component manufacturing, breweries, and tobacco factories—became almost exclusively foreign-owned.[14] Concomitantly, small-business activity and self-employment were expanding rapidly. There was a considerable increase in productivity, which combined with a tightening of managerial control over the work process, the intensification of work, and increased flexibility.[15] Multinational companies (MNCs) pioneered Japanese-style work-organization practices. On the other hand, several case studies indicated the survival of paternalistic relationships and informal bargaining at the shop-floor level in domestic enterprises.[16] Despite successes, during the first years of transformation, the economy went through a "transition recession," aggravated by restrictive monetary policies through which the government tried to promote economic stabilization. The decline in GDP and a 20–30 percent inflation rate meant a deterioration in real wages. Sectors like coal mining, metallurgy, and textiles virtually disappeared. Unemployment peaked at 13.6 percent in February 1993. There has also been a marked decrease in economic activity of the working-age population.[17]

Concerning industrial relations, the government proposed a scheme that outlined the construction of a Continental European–style system. First, the government reestablished the national tripartite council, and it invited all seven union confederations to participate.[18] The new tripartite council, *Érdekegyezteto Tanács* (Interest Reconciliation Council—ÉT) soon became important. After a sudden hike of gasoline prices, a protest blockade by taxi drivers that was accompanied by widespread popular sympathy paralyzed the country in the autumn of 1990. The compromise that solved the crisis was worked out at a televised emergency meeting of the ÉT, and the responsible behavior of unions greatly contributed to the deal. After the events, all the political parties drew the conclusion that it was advisable to work out compromises over economic measures with social partners, and the best forum for such a negotiation was the ÉT. The increase of the social status of tripartite consultation opened a channel for negotiations between the government and unions over socioeconomic measures.

Second, the government drafted a new Labor Code, which envisioned a German-style reshaping of collective bargaining. The draft scheme proposed to lift the locus of collective bargaining to the sectoral level and, at the same time, introduce elected works' councils to conclude workplace-level agreements. The draft, however, planned only to grant information and consultation rights to works' councils.[19]

All the union confederations considered the proposal a threat because it would repeal workplace-level bargaining, which was the key bargaining level for the decentralized Hungarian unions. In the ÉT a compromise was worked out that was heavily influenced by interunion conflicts. Namely, employers wanted to establish a membership threshold for union representation to avoid chaotic multiunionism and the emergence of rival unions. The once-official unions were interested in a regulation that gave bargaining rights to the major union at the workplace, while new unions argued for bargaining rights exercised by a coalition of unions at each company. According to the eventual compromise, the institution of an elected works' council was introduced. Works' councils were given the right only to be informed and consulted by employers. In turn, local union sections retained their exclusive bargaining rights. However, to conduct a legally binding agreement, unions had to prove their representativeness by reaching certain thresholds of votes in the works' council elections. Moreover, the rights of local union sections were severely curtailed. The law based its perception of unions on the judgments of the Constitutional Court (referred to above). Specifically, the law recognized the role of collective bargaining in setting the terms and conditions of employment, but it did not allow unions to act as an intermediate organization between employee and employers if a breach of the agreement occurred or a dispute arose from it.[20]

Different regulations were legislated for public-service employees and public servants. Both the public-service-employee law and the public-administration-employee law established a rigid wage-tariff system that was based on education, seniority, and hierarchical position. A separate tripartite forum, *Költségvetési Intézmények Érdekegyezteto Tanácsa* (Interest Reconciliation Council for the Public Sector—KIÉT) was set up for consulting and negotiating the terms and conditions of work in the public sector.[21] The consequences of the new regulation will be discussed in the next section.

At the same time, the sharpening of interunion conflict between the new and the once-official unions became a major political issue. New unions claimed that their unsuccessful membership drives were due to the inertia of the past. They argued that the organizational survival of the successor unions was due to their inherited assets and the inertia of quasi-compulsory membership, which was still maintained by a coalition of management and "old" union leaders. Therefore, the new unions argued for "completing the transition" by redressing the inequalities in historical endowments. They lobbied successfully for a law on trade union membership renewal and for trade union elections that would be the basis for the redistribution of trade union assets. However, their lobbying was not accompanied by attempts to mobilize employees. Moreover, at the same time, they opted to support government policies and give up certain key points of their economic program. Parliament passed the requested laws, with the sole opposition of the Socialist Party, in the summer of 1991.

MSZOSZ, on the other hand, claimed that the new unions were small groups of politically active militants. At the same time, it renewed its campaign for anticyclical government policies and a wider social safety net by demanding the government "ease the burdens" of the transition. In July 1991, MSZOSZ called for national warning strikes against the worsening living conditions, and it demanded social policy measures to balance the impact of certain strict economic measures. At the same time, it accused the new unions of serving only government interests by seeking to demolish "real" unionism. MSZOSZ wisely adopted a combination of mobilization and compromise in its duel with the government. The government, fearing a disruption similar to the taxi blockade, ceded and reshuffled the state budget to cover certain social policy measures. Moreover, the government did not demand the strict application of the legislation aimed at breaking the organizational power of the once-official unions.

By reaching an agreement with the government, MSZOSZ gained a leading position among union confederations. In general, the once-official unions gained legitimacy by being accepted as the major negotiating partners of the government. The elections of pension and social security boards and the workplace-level works' councils in 1993 further underscored the dominant standing of the once-official unions.[22] The new unions, in turn, suffered a decisive setback, and they were never able to regain their previous symbolic power.

The crisis of 1991 further increased the role of the ÉT. The meetings of the ÉT discussed all major social-economic measures, including draft bills of the state budget, taxation, welfare services, labor-market policies, and labor-market institutions. Closely connected to macroeconomic negotiations, the ÉT became the locus of quasi-national collective bargaining by annually setting the national minimum wage and giving recommendations for the annual wage-bargaining rounds. Furthermore, a plethora of tripartite bodies developed, covering special issues like unemployment policies, vocational training, public-service employment regulation, privatization, and so on. These tripartite bodies were, in a formal sense, consultative bodies, but in actuality they worked as codecision-making bodies. In 1993 another set of tripartite governing bodies was set up for the national pension fund, the national health-insurance fund, and the national labor-market fund. These bodies, governing a sizable part of the state budget, had far-reaching implications on government policy. The tripartite bodies spread from the national level to the regional (that is, county and city) level, where there were tripartite bodies to handle local employment funds, devise local labor-market policies, and negotiate over local and regional development policies. At the same time, a slow rapprochement began between the successor union confederations. MSZOSZ and SZEF struck a cooperation agreement in 1993, and a similar agreement was struck between SZEF and ÉSZT.

The consequences of interunion warfare reshaped the party alliances of the major union confederations. The connections of LIGA and MOSZ to political parties evaporated. Both unions were too small to be a valuable partner for political parties. At the same time, both MDF and SZDSZ shifted toward more neoliberal economic thinking, and they dropped their earlier inclinations of supporting workers' grassroots reorganization. LIGA occupied a politically independent position. MOSZ shifted to a new niche of political unionism and converted itself into a Christian union, but it did not develop close linkages to any political party of the right. The third independent confederation, Szolidaritás, which shifted toward an ultra-right-wing political stance, was ostracized by all the other unions and was excluded from the ÉT. Contrary to the experience of the new unions, which lost their connections to the party system, MSZOSZ realigned itself with the Socialist Party, which was the only party that supported MSZOSZ during its duel with the government. Before the 1994 elections the Socialist Party and MSZOSZ made an electoral alliance, and some of the key leaders of MSZOSZ became candidates of the Socialist Party. The support of MSZOSZ, in turn, lent credibility to the leftist, pro-worker election campaign of the Socialist Party. The other three reformed union confederations—SZEF, ÉSZT, and ASZSZ—kept their distance from the Socialist Party. However, a few key union leaders of SZEF also became candidates of the Socialist Party.

The Height of Social-Democratic Industrial Relations

The posttransition period saw the failure of contestatory unions, which had close linkages to major parties of the former pro-democracy bloc. Starting with the transition period, new unions faced difficulties in penetrating workplaces. The end of the political transition and the ensuing transformation of the economy paralyzed their organizational growth. Furthermore, their support of the neoliberal policies of their allied political parties blocked their mobilization capacity after the political transition. Their organizational weaknesses came into play when they were unable to balance the pressure between MSZOSZ and the government. Their weakness in the field of industrial relations made them less valuable as political partners. After the compromise was struck between the government and MSZOSZ, their party connections evaporated, and thus they lost their power. The 1991 crisis again demonstrated that the party linkages of these unions were sufficient to achieve certain legislative measures, which suited the political needs of these parties, but they were not strong enough to survive a crisis. After the 1991 crisis, LIGA shifted toward a business unionism style by distancing itself from all political parties and concentrating on collective bargaining. MOSZ tried to find a new political niche, but it could not find a new political ally nor gain wide support for the Christian-union cause.

The uncontested driving force of the Hungarian union movement became the group of once-official unions. The pacesetter was MSZOSZ, which drove the tripartite-centered policy. Certainly, its institutional heritage—a politically minded leadership, an inclination toward an all-inclusive union, a staff accustomed to working on national-level policy—facilitated the development of the new strategy. Nevertheless, one of the key conditions of the smooth functioning of the ÉT lay in the responsible, consensus-seeking and self-restrained behavior of MSZOSZ. MSZOSZ adopted a policy of social partnership and pursued a strategy of representing all employees and pensioners, the lower two-thirds of society. In the context of neoliberal macroeconomic government policies and wave after wave of strict economic measures, MSZOSZ negotiated for social policy measures in the short term and for a Keynesian-type macroeconomic policy in the long term. Moreover, in the course of its duel with the government, it reestablished its relationship with the Socialist Party, which alone supported the cause of the successor unions. As a consequence of these processes, MSZOSZ shifted toward a social-democratic union type. The movement toward a social-democratic strategy was not confined to MSZOSZ because the successor unions largely cooperated with one another, which was made possible because their differences were based more on the different professions of their membership base than on the difference in political orientations.

In terms of institution building, the 1990–1994 period, however, saw a controversial development. Contrary to the tripartite institution-building processes, unions suffered a serious setback in the legal regulation of collective bargaining. The Labor Code of 1992 severely curtailed the rights of unions at the workplace level. The legislation, which is still in effect, confines unions' role to collective bargaining, and it does not allow for an intermediate role for unions in the control of managerial practices or in the grievance procedure. The doubling of workplace-level workers' representation with works' councils offered a new means for employers to substitute unions with a more docile institution.[23] The difficulties entailed by the new legislation, however, came to light only later.

The Socialist Party won the 1994 election. Its election program promised to further advance tripartite policy making and strengthen the regulating role of unions through collective bargaining and the empowerment of works' councils at the workplace. It seemed that the winning MSZOSZ-Socialist coalition would complete the construction of a social-democratic type of industrial relations system.

THE RUPTURE OF SOCIAL-DEMOCRATIC DEVELOPMENT (1995–1998)

After the elections, the Socialist Party, in coalition with SZDSZ, formed a social-democratic government. A former deputy secretary of SZOT became the minister of labor, and the government immediately began negotiations to conclude *Társadalmi-Gazdasági Megállapodás* (Social and Economic Pact—TGM) with social partners at the ÉT.[24] However, the relationship between the government and trade unions soon turned sour. The TGM negotiations suffered a failure in December 1994 as each of the three sides of the ÉT submitted such a long and diverse list of demands that they could not reach a workable compromise. In February 1995 the ÉT did not reach an agreement on wage recommendations for the annual bargaining round due to the unbridgeable differences in the positions of the government, the unions, and the employers. Finally, in March 1995, the government introduced a drastic package of economic measures to redress the budget deficit to avoid a Mexican-style financial crisis. The package, which involved cuts in several welfare benefits and caused a 12 percent drop in real wages in 1995 and an additional 5 percent in 1996, was introduced without prior consultation with the ÉT. MSZOSZ prepared an alternative economic program, but the finance minister rebuffed it at an emergency meeting of the ÉT. The ÉT had stalled. In the autumn of 1995, however, a strike and demonstration wave broke out that was led by unions of public-utility companies, belonging mostly to ASZSZ, and public-sector employees, belonging mostly to SZEF. The strikes forced the government to grant certain compromises to unions and to seek to reestablish social partnership through the reinvigoration of the ÉT.

The events of 1995 highlighted a shift in the mobilization power among the three major trade union confederations: MSZOSZ, SZEF, and ASZSZ. Economic restructuring, privatization, and legal regulations had differently shaped the space of union action in industry and private services (the private sector) versus public services and public utilities (the public sector). Drastic deunionization took place in the private sector. Company restructuring, privatization, outsourcing, and the closure of workplaces caused heavy losses in union membership at unionized companies. Management increasingly adopted a neutral, if not hostile, attitude toward unions and in most cases withdrew co-decision-making practices earlier enjoyed by unions. Consequently, the position of different union sections within the workplace has changed. Research in the auto and clothing industries shows that union membership is almost exclusively confined to production workers, while managerial, professional, and white-collar administrative staff left the unions; further, most union organizations consist of only a minority of employees. Besides deunionization in privatized plants, a nonunionized sector has emerged, consisting mainly of greenfield facilities of foreign investors and domestic entrepreneurs. As a consequence, MSZOSZ, which had 1.2 million members in 1993, had little more than half a million members in mid-1995. On the other hand, SZEF, ÉSZT, and ASZSZ were able to retain much of their membership because their constituencies were in relatively sheltered sectors of the economy. ASZSZ reportedly had 224,000 members, while SZEF had 380,000 in 1995, and ÉSZT 120,000 members.[25]

Not only did membership size became more balanced among the successor confederations, but collective bargaining figures also mirrored the emerging differences between unions in the different sectors. According to MSZOSZ, in 1995 local collective agreements covered 23–25 percent of employees of the private sector, and two years later the number declined to a mere 19.2 percent.[26] Recent research in the clothing industry showed that at many workplaces, unions were no longer able to conclude collective agreements, and there was a shift from collective bargaining to consultation and ad hoc problem solving. Only a few workplace-level work stoppages have broken out in the private sector every year, most of those with a defensive character. As a consequence of these processes, the ability of MSZOSZ to mobilize its members for a national action has evaporated. At the same time, 60–70 percent of public-utility companies are still covered by workplace collective agreements. Moreover, unions in this sector, especially in public-transportation companies, were able to regularly mobilize their members for wage demands. Successful strikes contributed to the cohesiveness of these unions, created commitment toward unions, and facilitated the emergence of solidarity among workers to support union demands. In the public-service sector the introduction of the wage-tariff system in 1992 led to centralized wage bargaining in the KIÉT, which in turn, stabilized the role and legitimacy of unions in these sectors. Consequently, pubic-sector unions also increasingly turned to organizing demonstrations and protests of their members to gain wage increases.

After the hot autumn of 1995, the reinvigorated ÉT returned to its consensus-making practice. The return to normality was helped by the economic recovery, achieved by the package of 1995, which reduced the budget deficit and foreign debt and introduced a predictable currency-devaluation regime. Moreover, the devaluation regime underpinned the export-led growth of the economy, which became the main pattern of the late 1990s. Since 1997, Hungary's economy has been growing steadily, reaching 4–5 percent growth in GDP annually. Unemployment has decreased to below 8 percent, and there has been a slow increase in real wages. The Hungarian recovery was underpinned by reindustrialization, mostly due to FDI in manufacturing. Despite the successes of stabilization and reindustrialization, the government remained fairly constrained due to the compelling tasks of reducing indebtedness, the budget deficit, and inflation to a level that would allow Hungary to have EU membership. Thus, cuts in welfare and public expenditures remained a central concern of the government after the successful stabilization.

Debates over the government budget strained the relationship among the major unions. SZEF believed that MSZOSZ fully backed the demands of public servants, while ASZSZ questioned the viability of strong ties between MSZOSZ and the Socialist Party. The changing power relations of union confederations further strained the relationship among them, as SZEF and ASZSZ were less ready to accept the tutelage of MSZOSZ. Strains increased because MSZOSZ was trying to become the representative for all of society, while SZEF and ASZSZ represented the sectional interest of their respective membership constituencies. As a result, the cooperation agreement between MSZOSZ and SZEF was not renewed after its expiration in 1997. Tensions among the major confederations were concealed, however, by the policy of the Socialist Party and the ÉT.

To secure the incorporation of unions, the Socialist Party further developed the web of neocorporatist institutions configured on the model of the ÉT. Moreover, it supported the reconfiguration of the employee side of the ÉT. In 1997, MSZOSZ, SZEF, ASZSZ, and ÉSZT agreed to a new voting system, which resulted in a new distribution of votes: MSZOSZ received eight votes, SZEF received six votes, ASZSZ received four votes, LIGA received two votes, ÉSZT received two votes, and MOSZ received one vote. The agreement also stipulated that only those confederations that received at least 10 percent of votes at the 1998 works' council elections could maintain membership in the ÉT.

Concerning labor law, no substantial changes were made in the legal position of local union sections or works' councils. Nor were measures taken to facilitate the extension of multiemployer collective bargaining. The controversial 1992 Labor Code actually increased in impact. The division of workers' representation between works' councils and unions allowed hostile management to favor works' councils and delegitimize unions. Moreover, the threshold the law set for unions to represent employees allowed management to not accept new unions as a legitimate negotiating partner at nonunionized plants. As a consequence, some federations—like the Metalworkers, which ventured an organizing campaign—faced major difficulties trying to organize nonorganized employees.[27]

Erosion of the Social-Democratic Industrial Relations Model

By all accounts, the Socialist Party government, in coalition with the major unions, should have led the construction of a social-democratic-style industrial relations system. However, the Socialist Party government repeated the controversial developments of the earlier right-wing government. To be sure, neocorporatist institution building, the 1995 crisis aside, continued. Also, the 1996 amendment of bylaws on the employee side of the ÉT prepared the exclusion of the former contestatory unions and allowed the further consolidation of the social-democratic set of unions. Yet these national-level developments were not accompanied by measures to strengthen the role of unions in the area of collective bargaining. This one-sided development especially hurt MSZOSZ, which ironically, was the main proponent of the social-democratic model. Together with membership losses, the weakening of the unions' position at the workplace level evaporated its mobilization power, which in 1991 it was able to use in its favor. Thus, MSZOSZ, the leading union, became more dependent on its political influence through the Socialist Party rather than on its mobilization power.

The coordination of industrial relations policies between the Socialist Party and MSZOSZ, to a certain extent, worked well, and MSZOSZ reached some of its organizational goals. However, the economic package of 1995 and the neoliberal economic policy of the government created trouble for MSZOSZ, which lost some of its credibility by not adopting a more openly critical attitude toward the government. Instead of MSZOSZ, unions belonging to SZEF and ASZSZ mobilized protests, demonstrations, and strikes to enforce the wage demands of their constituencies. The recurring mobilizations of these unions increased their cohesiveness and distanced them from the Socialist Party. Both unions began to shift back toward pressure-group unionism, underpinned by their strength in representing their constituencies. Moreover, the increasing strains and interest differentiation among these three major confederations led to the breakdown of amicable concertation among them.

In short, the 1995–1998 period saw a rupture in the development of a social-democratic industrial relations system. The Socialist Party hesitated in implementing a full-scale strengthening of union power, and it took only those measures that secured the integration of the top-level union leadership. The internal development of the union movement also led to a weakened MSZOSZ, the main mover of the social-democratic project. Until 1995 differences between the major successor unions seemed based on the different sectors and professions of their constituencies, and strains came from personal aspirations rather than real differences. However, 1995 was a turning point. Increasingly strategic differences emerged among the major confederations, and strains became unbridgeable. The disintegration of the social-democratic union bloc began. A halting move toward a pressure-group union model started.

The future of the industrial relations system depended on the outcome of the 1998 elections and whether the winning party (or parties) would further support the neocorporatist arrangement or, sensing the increasing weakness and divisions of trade unions, turn against it.

DISMANTLING OF POSTTRANSITION INDUSTRIAL RELATIONS SYSTEM

A coalition of right-wing parties headed by the Alliance of Young Democrats (FIDESZ), with the participation of MDF, won the 1998 election. The new government revived the attitude of the MDF-led government regarding the once-official unions as holdovers of the state-socialist elite. Further, none of the governing parties had close connections to LIGA or MOSZ. Thus, the government adopted a program of redrawing the industrial relations system, which involved rearranging and marginalizing the tripartite mechanism and weakening trade unions.

The government disbanded the ÉT and substituted it with two new bodies: *Szociális és Gazdasági Tanács* (Social and Economic Council—SZGT) and *Országos Munkaügyi Tanács* (National Labor Council—OMT). SZGT informs and consults with social partners and other civil society organizations about the economic programs of the government, and it meets twice a year. OMT is a tripartite body that consults over labor-market policies and labor law. The separation of the functions of the ÉT into two separate bodies ended the previous political exchanges over wage increases, tax law, pension and health contribution levies, and welfare benefit schemes. Moreover, in both bodies the government strictly adhered to the notion of consultation and refused to negotiate with the social partners. Meanwhile, the government repealed the major tripartite bodies set up during the 1990s to govern parts of the state budget, including those of the pension and health and safety funds. The government invited all union confederations to the new bodies, which effectively saved the national political role of LIGA and MOSZ, allowing the government to divide and rule.

The government also amended the Labor Code to authorize works' councils to conclude work agreements in place of collective agreements if there is no union at a workplace with which to bargain. This change further complicated the works' council-union relationship and hindered unions' attempts to organize nonunionized workplaces. The government abandoned centralized negotiations over annual wage increases in the public-service sector and intends to decentralize wage negotiations to the level of local governments. The separate tripartite body for the public sector, the KIÉT, was also disbanded. Decentralized wage negotiations coupled with an antiunion government policy might undermine the recently reinvigorated legitimacy of public-sector unions and result in a similar deunionization process as that which occurred in the private sector of the economy.

The initiatives of the government met with strong condemnations by trade unions (with the exception of MOSZ). Unions, however, were unable to form a common policy, nor were they able to coordinate their protest efforts to force the government to change its policy.

CONCLUSION: UNION STRENGTH AND BUILDING A NEW INDUSTRIAL RELATIONS

Hungary's negotiated transition from communism was not the result of a major popular protest movement, which might have led to a grassroots renewal of the union movement. Instead, the transition facilitated the emergence and consolidation of six union confederations that were centered in different segments of the economy and had widely different political orientations. The coexistence of different types of unions, in turn, opened various routes out of the ruins of the state-socialist industrial relations system.

This chapter, sketching the development of industrial relations in Hungary, revealed that there was momentum for the construction of a social-democratic type of industrial relations. However, this momentum broke down, and the Hungarian industrial relations system is again in transition, this time seemingly away from the practices of Continental Europe.

The major argument of this chapter is that at critical turning points, the union movement lacked sufficient strength and unity to force the consistent institutionalization of social regulation at the national and workplace level. The reasons for this union weakness can be found in five paradoxes.

First, each of the major union confederations had moments of strength due to the mobilization of workers and moments of political influence due to links with political parties. However, in no case did a union's mobilization strength coincide with a period of political influence through ties to governing parties. As a result, while each major union confederation achieved some of its demands, either through political ties or workplace power, no union combined political and industrial strength simultaneously to gain lasting achievements in politics and the economy.

Second, there was a constant fight among union confederations. Thus, the moments of a confederation's strength were to a great extent consumed by trying to gain advantages over rival confederations. The situation was further complicated by two major cleavages that divided unions. One cleavage was a political one and was between pro-democracy (or anticommunist) new unions and the once-official, former communist ones. The second cleavage emerged due to the fragmentation of SZOT primarily along professional lines, between once-official unions organizing industrial workers and unions organizing employees of public services and public utilities. While the first cleavage largely disappeared in the first half of the 1990s, this did not solve the problems of the second cleavage, which came into play in the second half of the decade. Consequently, there were only a few moments when unions reached unity of action, and the lack of durable strategic alliances seriously weakened unions' ability to promote a vision of a socially regulated society. In fact, just the opposite happened in most cases. When a union reached its peak of power, it was consumed with trying to achieve institutional changes to weaken rival confederations. Thus, rival unions blocked institutional changes that would have been favorable to all unions.

Third, in the context of widespread rank-and-file passivity, unions concentrated their efforts on achieving advantages over rival unions through legislation and politics. In turn, union headquarters paid little to no attention to organizing members or reorganizing the practices of interest representation, either of which might have led to an increase in the industrial relations power of unions.

Fourth, unions had political linkages to different political parties that in the end adopted very similar neoliberal economic programs. Thus, whenever these parties occupied governmental positions, tensions inevitably emerged between them and their allied unions. Both the first MFD-led government and the second Socialist Party–led government were ready to support those initiatives of their allied unions, which aimed at gaining advantages over rival unions but failed to deliver economic measures that would satisfy the constituencies of their allied unions. Thus, unions, constrained by the economic policies of their allies in power, experienced declines in their public support and finally could not make use of their political advantages to reinforce their industrial relations base. Two facts furthered the controversial relationship between unions and allied political parties. First, union formation and party formation were separate processes, or rather, unions enjoyed the tutelage of political parties. Thus, unions had ties to certain (leftist) factions within their allied parties but did not have decisive say in their formation of strategies. Second, the weak internal influence of unions on their allied parties was further weakened by the first paradox mentioned above. Namely, unions' mobilization power coincided with the periods when their allied parties were in opposition, but their mobilization power had already dissipated when allied parties took over governing positions. Thus, unions were not in a position to force their allied parties to carry out measures that would strengthen their mobilization power.

A final paradox is that the negotiated transition from the communist dictatorship bequeathed to the new regime a well-endowed union edifice with a membership of 4 million. Although the legitimacy of the old unions was widely questioned by pro-democratic political forces, the consideration of the leaders of the once-official unions on certain policy measures was unavoidable, thus spurring the development of the tripartite national forum, the ÉT. The establishment of the ÉT was further facilitated by external factors— namely, the importance of social concertation in most Continental European countries, the desire of the new governments to conform to EU practices, and the pressure of the ILO. On the other hand, the failure of new unions to become mass-membership organizations meant that interest-representation practices at the workplace level were not given a new legitimacy. Thus, the lack of a widely accepted union renewal allowed the legal regulation of workplace industrial relations to be recast in such a way as to curtail the legal rights of unions, making them less able to represent employees at the workplace effectively. This reshaping of national- and workplace-level regulation led to a weakening of union power in the workplace, which in turn undermined the unions' national representation.

The all-out attack of the current government on unions and the industrial relations system might suggest that in the following years unions will see a further erosion of their power and influence in Hungarian society. The abrupt change in the political climate, however, took place in a period of sustained growth. The new economic environment might create a space for a reorganizing drive for unions, which might rebuild their power base and thus secure their voice in national policy making. However, it remains to be seen what conclusions the major union confederations will draw from these recent developments. It would be difficult to find a union leader in Hungary today who would not admit that the union movement is too divided and therefore too weak to weather the unfavorable political and economic climate. However, it remains to be seen whether unions and their leaders will overcome the strains and bitter personal experiences of the last decade. Rather than uniting, it is just as likely that a major segment of the unions, building on their relatively strong constituencies, will opt for pressure-type unionism as the best way to maintain their organizational power, while the leaders of other unions will hope that their remaining membership, assets, and organizational power will last at least until they reach retirement age.

GLOSSARY OF COMMON ABBREVIATIONS

ASZSZ—Federation of Autonomous Unions, active chiefly in chemical and public-utility sectors

ÉSZT—Association of Academic Employees' Unions, the main union for academics

ÉT—Interest Reconciliation Council, or the tripartite commission, from 1990 to 1998

KIÉT—Interest Reconciliation Council for the Public Sector, a separate tripartite commission for the public sector

LIGA—The democratic League of Independent Unions, founded in late 1988 as the democratic opposition to the official communist unions, led mostly by intellectuals

MDF—Hungarian Democratic Forum, the conservative Christian party that led the first postcommunist government, from 1990 to 1994

MOSZ—The National Association of Workers' Councils, a trade union formed in summer 1990, allied with the MDF, favoring collective ownership through workers' councils

MSZMP—Hungarian Socialist Workers' Party, the ruling communist party until 1990

MSZOSZ—National Confederation of Hungarian Trade Unions, the main successor union to the once-official unions, made up chiefly of unions in the manufacturing and private-service sectors

SZDSZ—The Alliance of Free Democrats, the leading party of liberal oppositionists, founded in 1987 and initially affiliated with LIGA

SZEF—Cooperative Forum of Trade Unions, the main union federation for public and civil service employees

SZOT—The official communist-era National Council of Trade Unions

NOTES

1. András Tóth, "A munkaügyi kapcsolatok és szabályozásuk a Munka Törvénykönyvében," in *A munka világának szabályozása Nyugat-Európában és Magyarországon,* A. Varga, ed., Liga Akadémia Füzetek (Budapest: Friedrich Ebert Stiftung—Liga Akadémia, 1995), 139–59; C. Ory, "A munka hadának," in *Janus-arcú rendszerváltozás,* M. Schmidt, and G. L. Tóth, eds. (Martonvásár: Kairosz kiadó, 1998), 214–31.

2. Lajos Héthy, "Political Changes and the Transformation of Industrial Relations in Hungary," in *The Future of Industrial Relations: Global Change and Challenge,* J. R. Riland, R. D. Lansbury, and C. Verevis, eds. (Thousand Oaks, Calif.: Sage, 1994), 317–49.

3. Lajos Héthy, *Az érdekegyeztetés és a táguló világ* (Budapest: Friedrich Ebert Stiftung—Közösen a Jövo Munkahelyeiért Alapítvány, 2000).

4. András Tóth, "Multi-employer Collective Bargaining in Hungary," in *Transfer* 2, 1997; Lajos Bódis, "Informális alku a ruhaiparban" in *Közgazdasági Szemle* 7–8, 1997.

5. Lajos Héthy, "Hungary," in *Labour Relations and Political Change in Eastern Europe,* J. Thirkell, R. Scase, and S. Vickerstaff, eds. (Ithaca, N.Y.: Cornell University

Press, 1995), 81–109; László Neumann, "Company Restructuring and Industrial Relations in Privatised Telecommunication Services in Hungary," paper presented to the fifth IRRA Regional Industrial Relations Congress, Dublin, Ireland, August 26–29, 1997.

6. Samuel Valenzuela, "Labour Movements and Political Systems," in *The Future of the Labour Movement*, M. Regini, ed. (London: Sage 1991), 53–101.

7. A. Takács, *A szakszervezeti mozgalom alakulása 1988-tól napjainkig.* (Kézirat: Munkaügyi Kutató Intézet, 1992).

8. E. Szalai, *A civil társadalomtól a politikai társadalom felé, Munkástanácsok 1989–1993* (Budapest: T-Twins, 1994).

9. András Bozóki, *A rendszerváltás forgatókönyve. Kerekasztal tárgyalások 1989-ben. Dokumentumok* (Budapest: Magveto, 1999), 219.

10. Membership figures released by trade unions themselves were fairly unreliable during this period. The above estimations are those of the author, based on consulting union activists and internal documents.

11. L. Bruszt, "1989: Magyarország tárgyalásos forradalma," in *Magyarország politikai évkönyve* (Budapest: Aula-Omikk, 1990), 160–67.

12. Judgement 8/1989, IV.23 and Judgement 42/1990, VI.12.

13. C. Kollonay and M. Ladó, "Hungary," in *New Patterns of Collective Labour Law in Central Europe: Czech and Slovak Republics, Hungary, Poland*, U. Carabelli and S. Sciarra, eds. (Milano: Giuffre Editore, 1996), 101–61.

14. G. Hunya, "FDI in Hungary: A Key Element of Economic Modernization," in *WIIW* 226, February 1996.

15. R. Whitley and L. Czaban, "Ownership, Control and Authority in Emergent Capitalism: Changing Supervisory Relations in Hungarian Industry," in *The International Journal of Human Resource Management* 9:1, February 1998, 99–115.

16. Bódis, "Informális."

17. International Labor Organization, *Hungary: Sustainable Livelihood.* (Geneva: ILO-CEET, 1997).

18. The first tripartite forum was set up by the last communist government in December 1988, but it invited only SZOT to participate. This forum ceased to exist before the elections of 1990.

19. *Alapelvek a Munka Törvénykönyve újraalkotására* (Budapest: Munkaügyi Minisztérium, én.).

20. 1992/XXII. Act.

21. 1992/XXXIII. Act.

22. L. Somorai, "Az 1993. évi üzemi, közalkalmazotti tanács választások," in *Magyarország Politikai Évkönyve 1994*, S. Sándor Kurtán and L. P. Vass, eds. (Budapest: Demokrácia Kutatások Magyar Központja Alapítvány, 1994), 188–98.

23. András Tóth, "Invention of Works Councils in Hungary," in *European Journal of Industrial Relations* 3:3, 1997.

24. L. Héthy, "Siker vagy kudarc?," in *Figyel,* November 9, 1995, 61–68.

25. J. Borsik and L. Focze, "Autónóm Szakszervezetek Szövetsége," in *Forró Drót* 12, July 12, 1996; R. Girndt, "Hungary's Trade Unions: Division and Decline," in *Labour Focus on Eastern Europe* 55, autumn 1996, 47–59; Letter by the president of ÉSZT to the author, dated November 13, 1996.

26. NSZ. 1996. III. 25; *Népszabadság*, 1997.X.4.

27. A. Tóth, "Building Unions in Autotransplants in Hungary," in *Globalization of Work and Patterns of Labour Resistance,* J. Waddington, ed. (Mansell, 1997), 29–55.

Chapter Three

Neocorporatism in Slovakia: Formalizing Labor Weakness in a (Re)democratizing State

Jonathan Stein

With the enactment of the Law on Economic and Social Partnership in May 1999, Slovakia became one of few postcommunist states to legally require that the government regularly consult on key areas of social, economic, and employment policy with representatives of trade unions and employers. The law's adoption culminated efforts by the Slovak Confederation of Trade Unions (KOZ) to codify tripartite "social dialogue" within a formal and enforceable framework of rules rather than leaving its status prone, as it had been since 1990, to the shifting interests and political will of successive governments. Indeed, the legal institutionalization of tripartism was the central demand KOZ put to a broad coalition of political parties that in September 1998 defeated the corrupt and increasingly authoritarian government led by Vladimir Meciar's Movement for a Democratic Slovakia (HZDS).

The election was a milestone in Slovak politics. Up to that point, HZDS had never lost control of the government through electoral means. It had first come to power in 1992 on a populist-nationalist platform that led to the breakup of the Czechoslovak federation by the end of that year. The first post-independence government fell in March 1994 after more moderate HZDS cofounders, including the trade unions' second postcommunist president, Roman Kovac, broke with Meciar and subsequently joined a broad-based interim administration.[1] However, the election held later that year gave the HZDS 35 percent of the vote—more than three times the support of its nearest challenger.

In both elections, HZDS attracted significant working-class support by channeling economic fear and frustration into nationalist resentment directed against "anti-Slovak" influences: pro-federalists, the country's ethnic Hungarian minority, and liberal reformers portrayed as "selling out" the nation's interests and assets to foreigners. At the same time, its promise to steer privatization toward a "nationally conscious" class of industrial owners ensured strong support from communist-era enterprise managers. HZDS's Peronist cast—co-opting workers with the financial backing of industrialists—was particularly vivid in its decision to hire Silvio Berlusconi's Forza Italia campaign team to see it through the 1994 election.

The kitschy political spectacles that HZDS staged in that campaign were well suited to the changes in its electoral base that followed the resolution of the national question two years earlier. Older, less educated, and more rural than in 1992, HZDS voters in 1994 were united by little more than a crude psychological identification with the charismatic Meciar. However, his polarizing presence left HZDS isolated within the party system, forcing Meciar to form a government with the most reactionary forces on the political scene, the neocommunist Association of Slovak Workers and the extreme-right Slovak National Party. During the next four years, frequent breaches of the rule of law, erosion of democratic institutions, rampant clientelism, and outright thuggery directed against government opponents pushed the country into deepening international isolation.[2]

At first glance, KOZ's anti-Meciar position in 1998 and its successful push to institutionalize tripartism suggest the presence of a strong, politically effective labor movement in Slovakia. Yet its participation in the election campaign, while a departure from past practice, never included an official endorsement of any party. Instead, KOZ merely compiled individual parties' voting records on labor issues and published a critical analysis of the government's performance, subsuming its activities under a more explicitly partisan effort coordinated by a broad range of civil society organizations.[3] Moreover, its top-down, politically circumspect tactics were of a piece with its embrace of an essentially bureaucratic platform for labor. Rather than indicating a high degree of strength, tripartism has been a rearguard strategy enabling KOZ to preserve its organizational unity, identity, and prestige in the face of a declining membership that it remains unprepared to mobilize for industrial action.

This chapter argues that KOZ's neocorporatist approach has been sustained by the Slovak working class's legacy of dependent development, that is, its historical emergence through modernization processes—particularly industrialization and nation building—initiated and directed by the state. It should thus be viewed as an adaptive response to the structuring of long-term economic development and postcommunist social conflict in nationally inclusive rather than class-focused terms. On the one hand, this legacy has conferred on workers considerable symbolic esteem and formal rights, encouraging labor quiescence in exchange for the cultural trappings of public recognition. However, it has also left KOZ poorly equipped to defend workers' interests in a context of declining state influence over economic institutions and activities.

DEPENDENT WORKING-CLASS DEVELOPMENT

In her assessment of organized labor in the Czech Republic, Anna Pollert argues that a combination of nationalism, political and craft divisions, economic prosperity, and official repression thwarted class-based radicalism from Habsburg rule and the interwar Czechoslovak First Republic through the communist period. With the carryover of "traditions prioritizing respectability over militancy" into the postcommunist era, "the Czech labor movement, when faced with restored capitalism, was ill-prepared, both organizationally and ideologically, for struggle."[4]

Yet however enfeebling this legacy of repression, co-optation, and material concessions was for the Czech labor movement after 1989, the possibilities for independent working-class politics in Slovakia were far more constrained. As elsewhere in Eastern Europe, the industrial working class's very creation was largely the product of the communist party-state. Equally important, its emergence was closely bound ideologically with Slovak national identity and its political assertion.

Czech culture flourished under Vienna's liberal nationalities policy following the establishment of the Dual Monarchy in 1867, while the industrial working class joined mass political parties in droves. On the other hand, the first stirrings of Slovak nationalism after 1848 withered under Hungarian rule, with political mobilization exceptionally low due to the franchise's discrimination against national minorities and the working classes. While Slovaks accounted for around 10 percent of Hungary's population, they elected only three deputies to the 413-seat Parliament in 1910. Budapest's intensifying policy of cultural Magyarization led to large-scale Slovak emigration in the decades prior to Czechoslovakia's establishment in 1918 and exacerbated the already profound developmental discrepancies between the new state's titular nationalities. By the country's founding, only 390 Slovak teachers served a population of over 2 million, and adult illiteracy was more than five times higher than in the Czech lands.[5]

Slovakia's occupational structure, too, was much flatter than in Bohemia and Moravia. Employment in industry and crafts was just 17.4 percent in

1921 (compared with 40 percent in the Czech lands), while conditions for working-class organization were highly unfavorable. Industrialization was concentrated in geographically isolated pockets, and only 7.6 percent of industrial workers in 1926 were in companies with more than eighteen employees. Similarly, with subsistence agriculture sustaining a peasant-dominated agrarian sector that accounted for 60.6 percent of employment in 1921, the growth of cities lagged. Population density, at just seventy-two inhabitants per square kilometer in 1937, was only half the Czech level. Indeed, as Czech industrialists and financiers supplanted German and Hungarian economic control throughout the republic, "the structural changes in the interwar years emphasized the agricultural character of Slovakia," with the result that "the west-east gradient of industrialization was neither eliminated nor noticeably reduced up to 1938."[6]

Throughout this period, Slovak politics gradually stabilized around two poles: statewide parties of Czech origin that monopolized class-based politics and the large "autonomist bloc" dominated by the clerical-nationalist Hlinka Slovak People's Party. This party was the motivating force in the independent, Nazi-allied regime created after Germany's dismemberment of Czechoslovakia in March 1939. Though banned in 1945, the national cleavage remained paramount in Slovakia. More than 70 percent of the People's Party's prewar supporters shifted their allegiance to the Slovak Democratic Party, a broadly based "holding company" for nationally focused politics that won nearly two-thirds of the vote in Slovakia in 1946.[7]

For the communists, victorious in the Czech lands, the solution to the "Slovak question" following their *coup d'état* in February 1948 lay in "drawing together" (*zbliženie*) the two nations through economic equalization. By 1989 economic parity (measured in terms of output and national income) had, in fact, been achieved, with most development indicators such as urbanization and life expectancy similarly reaching Czech levels. However, integration in sociocultural terms proved no more successful than it had been during the interwar First Republic.[8] On the contrary, rapid industrialization fed increasingly assertive nationalist demands that were channeled through the Communist Party's Slovak organization, which had been separate until shortly after the coup. The political opening in 1968 gave Slovak nationalism further space, leading to the only systemic reforms that survived the Prague Spring, the binational federalization of both the state and the party.[9]

The Prague Spring movement held very different political meanings for Czechs and Slovaks. For the former, democratization was to be based on the individual citizen, while for the latter, it essentially meant "one nation, one vote."[10] This conceptualization clearly attracted the support of Slovak workers. While the most important democratic reform won by the labor movement was a greater role in enterprise management through the creation of elected works' councils, only 5 percent of them were in Slovakia due to what one observer described as Slovak workers' "preoccupation with the issue of federalization."[11]

Indeed, throughout the post-1968 period, the new industrial working class, barely one generation removed from village life, was harnessed to national aspirations by officially sanctioned renderings of Slovak identity. A myth of Slovaks as a nation of farmers and builders had originally been promoted in the mid–nineteenth century by the codifier of the Slovak language, Ludovít Stur, and subsequently dismantled by several generations of Slovak writers. By the 1970s it had returned as a major literary theme. As the socialist-realist author and critic Vladimir Minac wrote in 1985, "The Slovaks are a nation of constructors, builders, not only in the metaphorical, but also the literal sense of the term."[12] Workers' identification with Slovak nationalism was, of course, also anchored in the very real material gains they enjoyed under socialism and a wider identification with the regime than was the case for Czech workers.[13]

THE NEW TRADE UNIONS

KOZ was founded in March 1990 alongside its Czech counterpart, the Czech and Moravian Confederation of Trade Unions (ČMKOS), within the new Czechoslovak Confederation of Trade Unions (ČSKOS). These unions were direct heirs to the communist-era Revolutionary Trade Union Movement (ROH), whose transformation within four months of the Velvet Revolution forged an institutional template that has shaped trade union strategy ever since. The process thus merits close examination, particularly insofar as it embodied significant continuity with the pre-1989 past.

The establishment of separate Czech and Slovak trade union chambers was the end point of the succession process. At the outset, ROH's tight control over its twenty-two unions was abandoned with the abolition of its regional councils.[14] Although professional and industrial branch organizations were maintained, the elimination of the provincial levers of central control gave considerably greater autonomy to "primary" enterprise-based organizations, which formed the backbone of workers' spontaneous resistance to the regime during the statewide general strike on November 27, 1989.[15]

On this basis, ROH's successor central trade union bodies on the republic and federal levels were rapidly reconstituted from the bottom up. Representatives of the Czech Association of Strike Committees (SSV) met in Kladno in early December 1989 to extend these bodies' mandates and to adopt a program, which was ratified the following month at a statewide conference in Brno with the participation of the Slovak-based Forum of Workers' Coordinating Committees (FKVP). Newly elected leaders of local union organizations held a series of conventions over the next two months that transformed old branch unions or established new ones prior to an all-union congress in Prague, where ROH was officially abolished and ČSKOS established as its legal successor.[16]

Developments in Slovakia, however, moved more slowly at the outset of the revolution and subsequently followed the Czechs' lead. FKVP's influence within enterprises was initially weaker than that of the Czech SSV and was concentrated mainly in heavy industrial regions outside of Bratislava. It thus played a smaller role in coordinating Slovak participation in the general strike, and it expanded its authority and activities only after developing closer ties with the Czech movement following the Kladno meeting. While the Slovaks established a successor confederation, the Independent Slovak Trade Unions (NSO), prior to ČMKOS's founding, this was due to FKVP's faster reconciliation with ROH functionaries.[17] Within a matter of weeks, however, SSV brought the Czech ROH's more revanchist leaders to heel on the need for internal democratization and trade union independence. NSO, convening on March 1, 1990, to ratify its statutes, then deferred to the Prague congress in the interest of maintaining a unified labor movement—albeit one that was simultaneously committed to a provision of the NSO statutes calling for republic-level representation.[18] Formally constituted as ČSKOS's Slovak chamber on April 9–10, KOZ was immediately joined by forty-two professional and industrial branch unions, established either on a federal basis with Czech and Slovak executives or as separate Slovak organizations.[19]

While the union elections conducted prior to the Prague congress produced leadership turnover reaching 60–80 percent, around 60 percent of the ROH bureaucratic apparatus survived. This reflected a dearth of qualified replacements and the political compromise reached between the strike committees and ROH's Central Trade Union Council.[20] The council had opposed the general strike, but then it attempted to usurp rank-and-file leadership by renaming itself the "ROH Action Committee," calling for dialogue with the communist leadership "in the interests of quickening the pace of *perestroika*." In response, the strike committees, especially on the Czech side, "declared war."[21] Within the first month of the revolution, they won a ban on political parties in the workplace, thus severing ROH's official link with the Communist Party. But even SSV made no effort to expel or disenfranchise the ROH Action Committee. Assured of winning leadership positions at the Prague congress, the strike committees' inclusiveness was expedient to a smooth transfer to the new confederation of assets worth an estimated $300 million—including two republic-based publishing houses and real estate holdings amounting to 0.05 percent of Czechoslovakia's building stock.[22]

STRONG UNIONS, WEAK LABOR

KOZ's organizational cohesion remained intact following the demise of the Czechoslovak federation and the dissolution of ČSKOS into its constituent chambers. At independence in 1993, KOZ's membership stood at 1.5 million, indicating union density amounting to 57.6 percent of the active labor force,[23] and there have been only minor exceptions to KOZ's representational dominance ever since. These include the Confederation of Art and Culture, established throughout the former federation in February 1990 (but closely allied with KOZ in formulating labor strategy), and the Independent Christian Trade Unions, whose ten thousand members are overwhelmingly concentrated in the private Catholic school system. Several small, independent unions have also emerged, representing employees within occupational sectors that enjoy inherently strong bargaining power (primarily public-transportation workers such as train and municipal-bus drivers).[24]

Yet notwithstanding the general strike's *coup de grâce* to communism's legitimating myth of proletarian loyalty, labor radicalism never found a foothold among workers. On the contrary, the trade unions remained from the outset of their transformation politically subordinate to the more broadly based revolutionary mass movements, the Civic Forum in the Czech lands and Public against Violence (VPN) in Slovakia. As a representative of a VPN coordinating committee in a Bratislava chemical plant told the ROH official journal, organized labor's new leaders must "explain to people the purpose of independent trade unions in a democratically organized society." However, this could succeed only "in cooperation with VPN, which will understandably oversee the democratic development of the trade union movement until it stabilizes and takes hold in the operation of enterprises."[25]

Given their discredited status as an instrument of central planning for ensuring compliance with production quotas and the inward-looking focus of their transformation, the unions' subsidiary role was probably unavoidable. Indeed, their newly elected officials' main preoccupation was to *extend* depoliticization into a lasting principle of independence and legitimacy.[26] Moreover, the unconsolidated character of the party system has since maintained KOZ's resolutely nonpolitical credo as the cornerstone of its internal unity.[27] This has not prevented several union leaders from being elected to Parliament, either as independent "union" candidates running on party lists or, in accordance with a KOZ recommendation issued prior to the 1994 election, as party members acting on a non-union-affiliated basis. However, in both cases, labor leaders typically "forgot their union past" once in office, orienting themselves fully to their respective parties' programs.[28]

One early indicator of labor's political impotence was ČSKOS's docile approach to the central issue determining its own fate: the dissolution of the federal state. After all, notwithstanding its organizational mirroring of federalized nationality, ČSKOS was arguably the most nationally integrated of all post-1989 Czechoslovak social institutions, incorporating on a statewide basis the largest industrial branch unions, including metal workers, miners, and communications employees. Its structure, according to its first president, "ensured unified action on the whole territory of the federal state," and its leaders in both republics clearly favored maintaining that state.[29] Yet despite preparing an ominous report on the possible economic consequences of a breakup (and despite the support of popular majorities in both republics for some form of common state), ČSKOS ultimately took no public position on Czechoslovakia's demise. On the contrary, as one commentator observed, "the most vocal concern in the trade union movement at the time of the breakup of the Czechoslovak federation was that they should not take any stand at all."[30]

Maintaining a united front by upholding official nonpartisanship did, however, lead to greater effectiveness on issues directly concerning workers. ČSKOS focused on two areas over the course of 1990 and 1991. The first was initiating tripartite negotiations through the Council for Economic and Social Accord (RHSD), established at the federal and republic levels in October 1990. The second was to ensure, partly via participation in RHSD, that labor and employment law complied with standards promoted by the International Labor Organization (ILO).

To be sure, the ILO blueprint—which includes encouragement of tripartism itself—was attractive insofar as it provided the trade union leadership with a ready-made purpose and agenda. However, it also helped to ensure official guarantees of job security stronger than those afforded within the Anglo-American paradigm of "at will" employment as well as workplace health and safety provisions that reserved for trade unions a significant enforcement role. Similarly, the new law on collective bargaining supported the right to strike in practical terms by banning replacement workers during the course of a full or partial work stoppage—a prohibition that extended to employer lockouts as well.[31]

While this seemingly strong legal basis for labor militancy remained intact following independence, unions have rarely made use of it. This is hardly because Slovak workers have few unresolved grievances. To take only the most glaring and universal example, living standards declined steeply due to steep currency devaluation, price liberalization, and wage control imple-mented at the beginning of 1991. By 2000, average real household incomes had *still* not recovered to their 1990 levels. By the end of 1997, however, there had been only thirty-four total strikes, with twenty-one concentrated in 1991 alone. Strike frequency then dropped precipitously, to five the following year, one each in 1993 and 1994, and none whatsoever during 1995 and 1996 before climbing to six in 1997.[32] "Warning strikes" and announcements of "strike preparedness" have been more frequent, and KOZ has typically accompanied demonstrations against government policies with threats of wider action. However, in neither case have such pronouncements led to sus-tained mobilization.

One explanation for this dialectic of organizational and formal institutional strength on the one hand and low levels of labor militancy on the other might be trade unions' structurally weak bargaining position owing to the dramatic rise in unemployment. With Slovak enterprises more vulnerable to the col-lapse of the communist foreign-trade system, unemployment in early 1992 surged to more than four times the rate in the Czech Republic.[33] According to this logic, the persistence of high unemployment throughout the 1990s, combined with its long-term character (over one year) for more than 50 per-cent of those affected, sharply reduced workers' propensity to strike.

High unemployment probably has had a dampening effect on labor mili-tancy. However, the overall unemployment rate masks deep regional dispari-ties, ranging from under 4 percent in the capital, Bratislava, to nearly 30 percent in Rimavska streda and other depressed agricultural districts. High rates also prevail in the heavy engineering sector concentrated in monoindus-trial areas of central Slovakia.[34] This implies that, other things being equal—in particular, uniformly low labor mobility due to the underdevelop-ment of the housing market—trade unions' bargaining power should vary throughout the country. However, strike frequency has not correlated with the relative tightness of local labor markets. Moreover, unemployment as an explanation of labor quiescence cannot account for the modest but still sig-nificant rise in strike activity in 1997, when unemployment remained a very high 12.5 percent.

To be sure, much of the new legislative framework regulating industrial relations—most of which was simply transposed from the communist-era employment code—was riddled with ambiguous language that could encour-age fear and deference among employees. For example, the labor law main-tained the old code's provisions on financial penalties that could conceivably be imposed on employees even for relatively minor lapses, thus encouraging employers to regard poor work performance as a compensatory harm rather than a routine cost. The individualized nature of such disciplining, moreover, obviously creates a high barrier to collective forms of workplace resistance to managerial autocracy. Conversely, workers' formally strong right to strike can be powerfully undermined by employer-friendly interpretations of a provision that makes participants collectively rather than individually liable for "any damage due to an event occurring in the course of a strike." Similarly, the prohibition on hiring replacement workers could be read narrowly as referring only to recruitment at the workplace—thereby leaving open the possibility that employers may circumvent the ban by moving production elsewhere. In any case, given the ban's validity only during "the course of a strike," workers' willingness to participate might well hinge on their confidence in their union's ability to extract contractual assurances against discharging ex-strikers.[35]

KOZ has, in fact, repeatedly complained about lax enforcement of labor and employment law, widespread failure to uphold collective agreements, and impediments to the right to strike (particularly the requirement that lists of strikers be submitted to employers), all of which have prompted a long-standing demand for labor courts.[36] Yet the character and target of these grievances suggest the extent to which the trade unions have remained dependent almost exclusively on state action rather than rank-and-file mobilization to defend their members' interests. Above all, KOZ retains a strategic commitment to tripartism as the main institutional arena for pressing demands against the government and for collective bargaining with employers. The rise in strike activity in 1997, in fact, coincided with KOZ's withdrawal from tripartite negotiations, strongly suggesting that formal neocorporatism has served as a powerful mechanism of demobilization.

BARGAINING FROM THE TOP

A central theme in the literature on neocorporatism is the political trade-off this mode of interest representation imposes on the social actors it embraces. In exchange for official recognition and privileged, parademocratic access to the centers of the state's decision-making powers, an organized interest group accepts limitations on the scope and content of its demands and on the tactics by which it pursues them. However, as Claus Offe has argued, the impact of neocorporatist depoliticization is asymmetrical with respect to different types of organized interests. By inducing working-class organizations to moderate their demands and behave more "responsibly," neocorporatism restrains union power far more than is the case for employers' associations, whose power does not reside in organization.[37]

Yet the political antecedents of tripartism in the postcommunist context were very different from those found in Western Europe, where neocorporatist institutions, however detrimental to working-class autonomy they might ultimately be, arose out of existing conflicts. In contrast, the creation of a politically neutered system of labor relations in Czechoslovakia was entirely preemptive. As one observer succinctly put it, "In the beginning, we were all employees."[38] Prior to privatization and the emergence of autonomous employers' representatives, tripartism was largely a matter of negotiations between the trade unions and the state, with ministry officials representing enterprises. Indeed, "the majority of trade unions practically assisted in the establishment of the employer organizations because they wanted to find partners for collective bargaining."[39]

Why government officials committed to economic reform would welcome such arrangements is fairly clear. "Social dialogue" provides an opportunity to co-opt a potentially disruptive organized interest group whose resistance to market-generated inequalities might undermine political stability and overwhelm scarce social welfare resources. In the immediate postcommunist context, moreover, Civic Forum and Public against Violence manifested not only a pragmatic interest in maintaining social peace during the market transition, but also a strong normative commitment to social justice and a "civilizational" attraction to Western European practices. Each of these motives can be discerned in their decision—simultaneously with the federal government's adoption of the neoliberal Scenario for Economic Reform in September 1990—to accede to the trade unions' demand for the establishment of the RHSD.[40]

The same motives have been articulated by the trade unions—indeed, repeated in every annual general agreement concluded within the tripartite RHSD.[41] Tripartism was, in fact, an institutional vehicle ideally suited to the trade unions' firm yet qualified backing for economic reform. According to its manifesto issued after its third congress, in 1996, "KOZ has always supported the transition to a market economy, but a market economy neglecting the needs of the people who create value does not correspond to our ideas." Similarly, KOZ expressed its continued readiness to support "unpopular measures" required by marketization, although "they must be socially balanced," so that "every group would offer a just contribution."[42]

According to Offe, neocorporatist bargaining can crystallize into stable institutional structures due to "specific national traditions and forms of organization of the labor movement and/or to a high level of political repression and/or to a condition of uninterrupted economic prosperity."[43] The second two explanations can be excluded in the case of Slovakia. Pressure for institutionalizing the RHSD has come from the trade unions themselves, and none of them claims that its ten-year existence has meant sustained affluence for workers. On the other hand, the organization of the Slovak labor movement—namely, its dominance by a single, unified, nonpolitical trade union confederation—is a better causal candidate, although insufficient. After all, the Czech labor movement has been organized on the same basis since 1990, yet the RHSD there fell into abeyance in 1994.

Two national particularities of Slovak neocorporatism are worth noting in accounting for the different outcomes. First, unlike in the Czech Republic, the government never reduced the scope of the RHSD's jurisdiction by excluding economic policy issues from tripartite negotiations.[44] Second, while the Czech RHSD's demise was hastened by the government's determination to leave collective bargaining entirely in the hands of the unions and new private employers, the Slovak government remained committed to using the RHSD as a means of facilitating the conclusion of collective agreements.[45]

The formal status conferred upon the trade unions embodies a symbolic expression of the producerist ethos that has been a pervasive feature of Slovak nation building. Yet this has translated very poorly into an ability to influence public policy and workplace outcomes to the benefit of labor. For example, KOZ expends considerable resources on developing standpoints and arguments concerning a broad range of economic and social policy, often obtaining indicative promises of administrative, legislative, or executive action. Yet time and again, the government has simply failed to comply with many of the most important provisions on which agreement was reached.[46]

The disjuncture between the trade unions' high symbolic status and workers' low effective power is less obvious in collective bargaining with employers, yet ultimately all the more revealing of why tripartism has remained an attractive strategy for KOZ. Collective bargaining over wages and working conditions lies at the very heart of what unions do, and in terms of the number of agreements signed and the proportion of the labor force covered, KOZ has done its job very admirably. According to the Ministry of Labor and Social Affairs, the number of branch-level collective agreements rose from twenty-two in 1991 to fifty-six by 1997.[47] Indeed, one estimate suggests that the labor-force coverage of collective agreements is 70–80 percent, which is high not only for postcommunist economies but also in comparison with Western European rates.[48]

The Slovak state has contributed to this aspect of KOZ's formal power in two significant ways. First, the annual general agreements negotiated within the RHSD establish the overall framework for branch-level collective bargaining, while the Ministry of Labor and Social Affairs provides mediation, followed by binding arbitration, in cases where no collective agreement has been concluded. Second, the government has been very active in using its authority to extend the reach of branch-level collective agreements by enforcing their terms on workers and employers not represented in negotiations.

The state's facilitation of broad coverage for collective agreements, however, has come at a price. First, there has been a steady reduction of their content to little more than a recapitulation of existing labor law.[49] Second, trade unions are essentially prevented from ensuring compliance. Labor quiescence has largely been rooted in this trade-off. As the number of collective agreements has risen, so has the frequency of compliance disputes—from eight cases in 1991 to forty-six in 1998.[50] Yet all of them ended with inconsequential mediation, not resolution, because the law on collective bargaining sanctions strikes only as a means of gaining a collective agreement, not as a tool for compelling an employer to fulfill its terms. Since 1991, KOZ has pushed for a separate law that would address this—and other obstacles and ambiguities mentioned earlier concerning the right to strike—but its efforts have been conducted exclusively through bureaucratic channels. Trade unions have struck over unresolved compliance disputes only twice—and only when the RHSD had ceased to function.

THE LAPSE IN THE LOGIC

As early as January 1993, KOZ concluded that "while the RHSD fulfills the requirements of tripartism from a formal standpoint, in practice its significance is limited, and it fulfills its purpose only to a marginal degree."[51] This was followed by regular complaints that the government often submitted legislative proposals to the RHSD for discussion when it was too late for the unions to respond adequately, if at all. Nevertheless, KOZ continued signing the annual general agreements until July 1997, when it suspended its participation in tripartite negotiations and officially withdrew from the RHSD, leading it to adopt for the first time a politically assertive role.

By this point, KOZ had accumulated a long list of broken government promises. In its assessment of the government's fulfillment of its program prior to the 1998 election, KOZ emphasized the Meciar administration's failure to amend the labor code, to expand trade union rights and introduce enterprise codetermination, to "liberalize" collective bargaining by allowing wage negotiations in the public sector, and to expand employee participation in privatization. KOZ's critique similarly protested the government's refusal to abide by agreements reached within the RHSD, particularly a revision of the tax code that would index the rate schedule to inflation. With the tax burden on workers increasing steadily as nominal wage gains pushed them into higher brackets, KOZ had an especially strong case—and one that the government had pledged to support since 1995.[52]

However, had KOZ's refusal to continue tripartite negotiations been prompted merely by the government's nonfulfillment of successive general agreements, it would have withdrawn much earlier. Rather, KOZ's change of course was due to what underpinned the Meciar government's unwillingness to honor its commitments: a profound alteration of the political opportunity structure owing to the encroachment of a charismatic authoritarian regime favoring clientilist forms of interest intermediation. This not only further undermined the credibility of structured "social dialogue" as a means of expressing, representing, and satisfying workers' demands—it also posed an increasingly direct threat to the quasi-official status that constituted KOZ's most important organizational resource.

The threat originated from two quarters. First, as the employers' association steadily evolved into a base of HZDS support comprising beneficiaries of the Meciar administration's privatization program,[53] the government established its own trade unions. The most notable example was Metallurg, which split from the largest KOZ trade union, the metalworkers, in exchange for a 10 percent stake in a giant steel producer that had been sold to Meciar's transport minister in 1996. The steel company, VSZ, is a highly visible symbol of Slovak industrialization. It had accounted for 15–20 percent of export earnings and 10–15 percent of GDP in preceding years, while the metalworkers union so prominent at VSZ has produced each of KOZ's presidents. The creation of Metallurg catalyzed KOZ to suspend its participation in the tripartite, though the union soon pointed to numerous other examples of "yellow" unions. As one KOZ official put it, "If they were going to pick us apart, why should we continue as if nothing is happening?"[54]

The second, and final, blow came the following year, when the government reimposed wage controls without prior consultation in the RHSD. ČSKOS had opposed their introduction throughout Czechoslovakia in 1991, and KOZ continued the fight until controls were lifted in 1994. The government argued that controls were needed because real wage growth was outstripping productivity gains and thus generating inflationary pressure. For KOZ, however, the argument's underlying assumption that the proper role for trade unions is to assist the government in meeting its economic targets would, if accepted, thoroughly undermine its legitimacy as an independent labor confederation. Indeed, wage controls deprive unions of all power, even symbolic, over one of the most important issues subject to collective bargaining.

CONCLUSION: A NEW TRIPARTISM?

While the spread of clientilism throughout the economy, particularly after 1994, ultimately forced KOZ to abandon the RHSD, it did so only to save it. In adopting a partisan political role, KOZ never repudiated its underlying strategic commitment to neocorporatism. On the contrary, its measured defense of democracy and the autonomy of civil society were instrumental to enabling a return to apolitical "social dialogue" in the aftermath of the 1998 election.

There is thus an obvious element of truth in the claim that, as "the only major political structure to survive the 1989 revolution more or less intact," the trade unions settled for an implicit social contract in which they "accepted a politically passive role in order to ensure their organizational survival."[55] However, given the decline of "social partnership" in the Czech Republic and its endurance in Slovakia, it is necessary to look beyond the strategic constraints imposed by institutional continuity with the past and examine how more deeply rooted features of economic and political development enabled neocorporatist survival in Slovakia. I would argue that the combination of weak *pre*communist working-class autonomy, plus the RHSD's formal embodiment of communist-era symbolic esteem for workers, accounts for KOZ's enduring commitment to tripartite bargaining in succeeding years.

The 1999 Law on Economic and Social Partnership continues this pattern of high cultural recognition for trade unions and low effective power to satisfy labor's social demands. Although its adoption was preceded by the fulfillment of a key substantive KOZ demand to eliminate wage controls, the law merely codifies the reconstituted RHSD's organizational setup and procedural rules. It does not require the government to submit legislation to the Parliament in line with the outcome of negotiations (as indeed it should not on democratic grounds, given that neither KOZ nor the employers' association is a popularly elected body). This necessarily means that agreements reached through "social dialogue" remain subject to the will and ability of the government to implement them.

The likelihood that KOZ will ultimately come up empty-handed is already apparent with respect to the 2000 General Agreement, the first to be concluded since 1996. The agreement obliges the government to reduce unemployment by 3 percent by the end of the year while ensuring real wage growth. Since then, however, it has become evident that neither commitment will, or can, be met. Unemployment climbed to nearly 20 percent by the middle of the year, and real wages fell by around 6 percent as the government was forced over the course of 1999 to impose severe austerity measures owing to the disastrous fiscal and current-account legacies of the Meciar era. The clientelist legacy extends to the privatized enterprise sector as well, where huge tax and payment arrears necessitated a new bankruptcy law that will threaten precisely those firms where unions have traditionally been strongest.

The prospect of further job losses as insolvent enterprises are liquidated underscores the corrosive long-term consequences of KOZ's strategy. By placing their hopes in neocorporatism and on a tacit dependence on the state to realize members' interests, the trade unions have essentially ignored organizing new workplaces and have presided over a steady decline in membership. By 1998, KOZ's membership had fallen to 830,000, slightly more than half its level in 1993.[56]

More threatening to the long-term future of Slovak trade unionism is KOZ's almost complete neglect of recruitment activity. The union's mindset is well illustrated by its approach to the effects of foreign investment on union membership. While management depends on higher wages to dampen any desire for trade unions, KOZ says not to worry, because "foreign-owned companies, after all, must also respect our labor law." What organizing activities does KOZ conduct? Only one initiative stands out, and it is, once again, very much in line with the culturalist argument advanced here. KOZ has "asked the education ministry to consider adopting a unit on trade unions in the curriculum for secondary schools."[57] With a policy like this, however, trade unionism in Slovakia risks ending up being confined to the history curriculum alone.

GLOSSARY OF COMMON
ABBREVIATIONS

ČMKOS—Czech and Moravian Confederation of Trade Unions, the reformed trade union federation of the Czech Republic after 1990

ČSKOS—Czechoslovak Confederation of Trade Unions, the reformed trade union federation of Czechoslovakia from 1990 till the dissolution of the country at the end of the 1992

FKVP—Forum of Workers' Coordinating Committees, a Slovak initiative of late 1989 that began the reform of the existing trade unions

HZDS—Movement for a Democratic Slovakia, nationalist-authoritarian party led by former prime minister Vladimir Meciar

KOZ—Slovak Confederation of Trade Unions, founded in March 1990 as the new trade union federation of Slovakia

NSO—Independent Slovak Trade Unions, an intermediary Slovak union organization between the fall of the old regime and the establishment of KOZ

RHSD—Council for Economic and Social Accord, the tripartite body first established in Slovakia and the Czech Republic in October 1990

ROH—Revolutionary Trade Union Movement, the official communist-era trade union federation, until 1990

SSV—Czech Association of Strike Committees, a Czech initiative of late 1989 that began the reform of the existing trade unions

VPN—Public against Violence, the broad-based Slovak political movement that led the rebellion against communist rule

NOTES

1. Meciar also was removed as Slovak prime minister in early 1991, but this was accomplished by a vote of the Slovak National Council's presidium, that is, not of the full Parliament, leading him to establish HZDS.

2. On the changes in HZDS's electoral base between 1992 and 1994, see Vladimir Krivy, "Parlamentné volby 1994: privržencov politických stran, profil regionov," in *Slovensko: volby 1994. Pričiny-dosledky-perspektivy*, Soňa Szomolanyi and Grigorij Meseznikov, eds. (Bratislava: SLON, 1994), 123–25. On the effect of Meciar's personality on the party system and his government's subsequent rule, see Carol Skalnik Leff, "Dysfunctional Democratization? Institutional Conflict in Post-Communist Slovakia," in *Problems of Post-Communism*, September–October 1996, 36–50; and M. Steven Fish, "The End of Meciarism," *East European Constitutional Review* 8:1–2, winter–spring 1999, 47–55. Slovakia was the only postcommunist accession candidate excluded solely on political grounds from the start of EU membership negotiations in 1997.

3. Martin Butora, Grigorij Meseznikov, and Zora Butorova, eds., *Kto? Preco? Ako? Slovenske volby '98* (Bratislava: Institut pre verejne otazky, 1999); and the chapter in that book by Darina Malová, "Od vahania k premyslenej strategie: Konfederacia odborovych zvazov SR vo volbach 1998," 141–49.

4. Anna Pollert, "Labor and Trade Unions in the Czech Republic 1989–2000," in this book.

5. Victor S. Mamatey and Radomir Luza, eds., *A History of the Czechoslovak Republic 1918–1948* (Princeton: Princeton University Press, 1973), 7–8, 15; Carol Skalnik Leff, *National Conflict in Czechoslovakia: The Making and Remaking of a State, 1918–1987* (Princeton: Princeton University Press, 1988), ch. 1.

6. Alice Teichova, *The Czechoslovak Economy 1918–1980* (London: Routledge, 1988), 8–9, 36. See also Vlastislav Lacina, *Formovaní československe ekonomiky 1918–1923* (Prague: Academia, 1990), ch. 6.

7. Leff, *National Conflict in Czechoslovakia*, 95.

8. On *zbliž, enie*, see Leff, *National Conflict in Czechoslovakia*, 140–47.

9. Leff, *National Conflict in Czechoslovakia*, ch. 8; and H. Gordon Skilling, *Czechoslovakia's Interrupted Revolution* (Princeton: Princeton University Press, 1976), ch. 15.

10. Leff, *National Conflict in Czechoslovakia*, 126.

11. Vladimir Fišera, ed., *Workers' Councils in Czechoslovakia, Documents and Essays, 1968–69* (London: Allison & Busby, 1978), 13.

12. Robert B. Pynsent, *Questions of Identity: Czech and Slovak Ideas of Nationality and Personality* (Budapest: Central European University Press, 1994), 153–54.

13. For public opinion data from the post-1968 period pointing out the different perceptions of socialism among Czech and Slovak workers, see Miroslav Vaněk, *Verejne mineni*

o socialismu pred 17. Listopadem 1989 (Prague: Ustav pro soudobe dejiny AV CR, 1994), 46.

14. For the communist period, see Joseph Porket, "Czechoslovak Trade Unions under Soviet-Type Socialism," in *Trade Unions in Communist States,* Alex Pravda and Blair A. Ruble, eds. (Boston: Allen & Unwin, 1986), 87–88.

15. Igor Pleskot, "Czech and Slovak Trade Union Movement in the Period of Transformation to a Civil Democratic Society, 1989–1993," paper prepared for the Convention of the Bohemian and Moravian Confederation of Trade Unions, April 1994, p. 2; Peter Rutland, "Workers' Responses to the Market Transition: The Czech Case," unpublished manuscript (Wesleyan University, 1994), 14–15. For a good summary of the general strike and of broader working-class activism in support of the revolution, see Bernard Wheaton and Zdenek Kavan, *The Velvet Revolution: Czechoslovakia, 1988–1991* (Boulder: Westview, 1992), chs. 4–5. A wealth of documentary material attesting to widespread participation in the general strike among enterprise-level union organizations is collected in *Deset prazskych dnu. 10. – 27. listopadu 1989* (Prague: Academia, 1990).

16. Pleskot, "Czech and Slovak Trade Union Movement," 2–5.

17. "Komunike z rokovania fra koordinacnych vyborov pracujucich na Slovensku," in *Odborar* 1, 1990, 1.

18. "Docasne stanovy nezavislych slovenskych odborov," in *Odborar* 3, 1990, 2–4; "Uznesenie vseodboroveho a vsezvazoveho zjazdu na Slovensku, konaneho dna 1. Marca 1990 v Bratislave," in *Odborar* 5, 1990, 2.

19. Pleskot, "Czech and Slovak Trade Union Movement," 2–5, 22; interview with Jozef Kollar, KOZ vice president for union policy, Bratislava, April 23, 1999; *KOZ 1990–1995. Bulletin vydany pri prílezitosti 5. vyrocia vzniku KOZ SR* (Bratislava: Konfederacia odborovych zvazov, 1995), 3–5.

20. The lower figure for turnover of elected union leadership and the figure for continuity of bureaucratic personnel is found in Martin Myant, "Czech and Slovak Trade Unions," *Journal of Communist Studies* 9:4, 1993. The higher figure for leadership turnover is provided by Rutland, "Workers' Responses to the Market Transition," 14. Myant's figures draw on an earlier assessment by the ČSKOS. See Igor Pleskot, "17. Listopad," in *Sondy odborovych svazu* 47:4, 1992.

21. Pleskot, "Czech and Slovak Trade Union Movement," 2–5.

22. Wheaton and Kavan, *The Velvet Revolution*, 100; Rutland, "Workers' Responses to the Market Transition"; Myant, "Czech and Slovak Trade Unions," 61, 82fn3.

23. Statisticky urad Slovenskej republiky, "Ziadost o poskytnutie udajov o clenstve," February 23, 1999. Mimeo obtained from KOZ headquarters.

24. Kollar interview; Anna Machalikova, "Tripartism in the Slovak Republic," unpublished manuscript (Bratislava: Sekretariat Rady hospodarskej a socialnej dohody, 1999), 4.

25. "S plnou zodpovednostou," in *Odborar* 3, 1990, 8. In their introduction to the interview, the editors generalized the point: "In the current period it is particularly necessary to welcome every good idea, appreciate its value, and provide sufficient space for its realization. Virtually all of these ideas are coming to the trade union organizations precisely from representatives of the VPN coordinating committees."

26. As the strike committees saw it, "Independent unions require of political party members that they behave as unionists and not as representatives of individual political

parties." "Dvanast principov nezavislosti, samostatnosti a jednoty novych odborov," in *Odborar* 2, 1990, overleaf. See also Myant, "Czech and Slovak Trade Unions," 62.

27. Darina Malova and Monika Cambaliková, *Co vieme a co nevieme o representacii zaujmov na Slovensku* (Bratislava: Friedrich Ebert Stiftung, 1998), 16. Three new parties entered the Parliament following the first free election in 1990, and one new party has entered both the Parliament and the government in all three elections since, while one "established" party has disappeared in each—most recently the ZRS in 1998.

28. Pavol Barinych, "Odbory-volby-politika," in *Nove slovo* 3, 1998, 6–7.

29. Pleskot, "Czech and Slovak Trade Union Movement," 23–24.

30. Myant, "Czech and Slovak Trade Unions," 80.

31. Mark McLaughlin Hager, "Constructing a New Liberal Capitalism: Czechoslovakian Labor Law in Transition," in *The American University Journal of International Law and Policy* 7:3, spring 1992, 503–28.

32. Machalikova, "Tripartism in the Slovak Republic," 23–24.

33. By this point, Slovak unemployment had reached 14 percent, while the Czech rate was slightly over 3 percent. See John Ilam, Jan Švejnar, and Katherine Terrell, "The Emergence of Unemployment in the Czech and Slovak Republics," in *Comparative Economic Studies* 35:4, 1993, 121–34.

34. OECD, *Regional Problems and Policies in the Czech Republic and the Slovak Republic* (Paris: Organization for Economic Cooperation and Development, 1996), 37–74.

35. Hager, "Constructing a New Liberal Capitalism: Czechoslovakian Labor Law in Transition."

36. See, for example, *Dostojna zivotna uroven—nase pravo. Dokumenty III. Zjazdu KOZ SR* (Bratislava: Konfederacia odborovych zvazov, 1996), 42–43.

37. Claus Offe, "The Attribution of Public Status to Interest Groups: Observations on the West German Case," in *Organizing Interests in Western Europe: Pluralism, Corporatism, and the Transformation of Politics,* Suzanne Berger, ed. (Cambridge: Cambridge University Press, 1981). See also Philippe Schmitter, "Still the Century of Corporatism?" in *Trends toward Corporatist Intermediation*, Gerhard Lehmbruch and Phillipe Schmitter, eds. (London: Sage, 1979).

38. Monika Cambaliková, "Tripartita na Slovensku—prazdna struktura?" in *Nove slovo* 2, 1999, 11.

39. Pleskot, "Czech and Slovak Trade Union Movement," 19.

40. See Rutland, "Worker's Responses to the Market Transition"; Myant, "Czech and Slovak Trade Unions"; Mitchell Orenstein, "The Czech Tripartite Council and Its Contribution to Social Peace," in *Parliaments and Organised Interests: The Second Steps*, Attila Agh and Gabriella Ilonszki, eds. (Budapest: Hungarian Centre for Democracy Studies, 1996); Monika Cambaliková, "Slovenskí socialni partneri v transformacnych a integracnych procesoch," in *Sociológia*, 30:6, 1998. For VPN's support of a "socially just market economy," see its 1990 election program, *Sance pre Slovensko* (Bratislava: Verejnost proti násiliu, 1990), 3.

41. For the boilerplate formulation, see, for example, *Generalna dohoda na rok 1994*, art. 10: "In fulfilling the obligations of this agreement, the parties to it recognize their co-responsibility, and the necessity of social dialogue, in the interest of maintaining social peace." See also "Tripartizmus v Europe a u nas," in *Informacny buletin*, no. 1 (Bratislava: Konfederacia odborovych zvazov, 1994).

42. *Dostojna zivotna uroven—nase pravo. Dokumenty III. Zjazdu KOZ SR*, 40–41.

43. Offe, "The Attribution of Public Status to Interest Groups," 152.

44. Cambaliková, "Slovenski socialni partneri v transformacnych a integracnych procesoch," 627.

45. On the Czech government's position, see Orenstein, "The Czech Tripartite Council and Its Contribution to Social Peace," 183–84.

46. For example, the copy of the 1994 General Agreement obtainable at the RHSD's secretariat contains seven provisions concerning economic, social, and wage policies accompanied by the marginal notation "unfulfilled." The secretariat's director, who made the notations, pointed out that the government failed to comply with another three of the twenty-two provisions for which it bore responsibility. Almost all were carried over to succeeding years' general agreements and similarly went unfulfilled. Author's interview with Anna Machalikova, Bratislava, April 21, 1999. See also Cambaliková, "Tripartita na Slovensku—prazdna struktura?" in *Nove slovo* 2, 1999, 11.

47. Ludovit Cziria, "Development of Industrial Relations and Collective Bargaining in Slovakia," unpublished manuscript (Bratislava: Research Institute of Labor, Social Affairs and Family, 1999), 10.

48. World Bank, *Slovak Republic: A Strategy for Growth and European Integration* (Washington, D.C.: International Bank for Reconstruction and Development, 1998), 89.

49. Cambaliková, "Tripartita na Slovensku—prazdna struktura?"

50. Cziria, "Development of Industrial Relations and Collective Bargaining in Slovakia," 13–14. Cziria notes that "most usually the trade union side" initiated the mediation.

51. Quoted in Malova and Cambaliková, *Co vieme a nevieme o representácii zaujmov na Slovensku*, 23.

52. Konfederacia odborovych zvazov SR, "Ako plnila tretia vlada V. Meciara svoje Programove vzhlasenie," in *Praca*, September 11, 1998.

53. On the deep implication of the employers' association in crony privatization and its expressions of support for the government against opposition activists, see Malova and Cambaliková, *Co vieme a nevieme o representacii zaujmov na Slovensku*, 20.

54. Kollar interview. See also Konfederacia odborovych zvazov SR, "Ako plnila tretia vlada V. Meciara svoje Programove vzhlasenie."

55. Rutland, "Worker's Responses to the Market Transition," 13.

56. Statisticky urad Slovenskej republiky, "Ziadost o poskytnutie udajov o clenstve."

57. Kollar interview.

Chapter Four

The Weakness of Symbolic Strength: Labor and Union Identity in Poland, 1989–2000

David Ost

Unionism in Poland is marked by the paradox of symbolically strong unions at the national level and poor outcomes in the workplace. Poland is, of course, the country whose name almost seems synonymous with strong unionism. The collapse of communism began with the emergence of the region's first independent trade union, Solidarity, and since 1989 that union has several times produced the country's political leadership. In 1989, Solidarity created the first noncommunist government in Eastern Europe, and a year later union president Lech Wałęsa was elected president of Poland. After his defeat in 1995, only a couple of years elapsed before the union seemed to regain political power. When Solidarity Electoral Action (AWS) won parliamentary elections in Poland in 1997, it seemed the trade unions had won too. Of course, AWS was not *just* a trade union organization. Over twenty different self-proclaimed right-wing groups and parties counted themselves as its official founders. Yet AWS was clearly led by a trade union. Marian Krzaklewski, the head of the Solidarity trade union, was the undisputed leader of AWS. Its other members were unable to enter Parliament without union support, and they knew it. After AWS won the elections, Krzaklewski chose the prime minister without even consulting other AWS deputies. With all this coming after the earlier experience of Solidarity founder Wałęsa elected president of Poland, it is no surprise that commentators began to speak about all-powerful trade unions. In the words of one observer, Poland had become a "unionocracy."[1]

But what exactly is union strength? To argue convincingly that unions are strong, one must show that they are able and committed to improve the position of their constituents. Polish unions, however, have won little except the regular co-optation of their leaders. Since 1989, Polish unions have watched over a dramatic decline in labor conditions and a profound dismantling of worker influence. The litany of setbacks is well known, particularly for the first postcommunist years:

- a 30 percent decline in real wages from 1989 to 1991
- the abolition of workers' self-management boards
- a general decline in union influence
- double-digit unemployment rates, reaching up to 25 percent in some regions
- the loss of hundreds of thousands of once-secure jobs
- the creation of new jobs often lacking basic health and safety conditions and frequently outside the legal economy altogether

One might have expected workers to consolidate behind unions at a time like this, particularly given the legacy of Polish labor since 1980. Yet union membership dropped as it did throughout the region. Asked who best represents their interests, workers regularly respond "no one." Even when the economy began growing again in 1995, unions did not recover their strength. Membership in Solidarity, for example, declined from about 2 million in 1995 to 1.2 million by the end of the century. (At its heyday in 1981, Solidarity membership stood at 9.5 million.) In the fast-growing private sphere, the tendency is toward no unions at all. Political leaders may have tried to ride trade union organizations to political power, reflecting unions' dominant position in civil society in the 1980s, but they have not done much to defend members' interests once there.

The aim of this chapter is to examine and account for the decline of unions in Poland since 1989. While structural changes and global economic pressures certainly constitute an important part of the explanation, my focus here will be on ideological factors—in particular, the pro-market sensibilities of unions themselves. While unions are easy to form in Poland, and there are plenty of them, I will speak here only about those that count: Solidarity, OPZZ (the National Confederation of Trade Unions, the former quasi-official union confederation created after Solidarity was outlawed in 1981), and Solidarity-'80 (the militant, nationalist split from Solidarity that gained some prominence beginning in 1992). Mainly, however, I talk about Solidarity, for despite its close connection to political power in the decade since 1989 and a smaller membership than OPZZ, it remains the main force of union mobilization. OPZZ remains too hobbled by its past, saddled with a conservative local leadership of mostly older men with low-level managerial positions that makes it inadequate as an organ of labor protest. The growth of Solidarity-'80, meanwhile, has been restrained by a militancy out of touch with the popular mood. The story of Polish labor weakness and quiescence is largely the story of Solidarity.

PERIODIZING THE POSTCOMMUNIST DECADE

Except for a short period between 1992 and 1993, Solidarity has been intimately involved in governmental activity: first supporting it, then opposing it, then ostensibly running it. We can periodize the first postcommunist decade as follows:

- the union attempt to impose market reform (1989–1992)
- an interlude of budding class militancy (1992–1993)
- the turn to direct political engagement (1994–2001, with 1997 as a moment of political victory)

While the entire decade was marked by a great deal of activity by Solidarity, as befits an organization with its unmatched symbolic resources,[2] the reality is that except for the moment between 1992 and 1993, the union leadership has not sought to mobilize workers to win class benefits for labor. Instead, it has cashed in on Solidarity's renown to push either an ideological agenda or its own political ambitions. Though ever present in the decade of transformation, unions have done little to improve the interests of workers as workers. The paradoxical reality is, thus, a weak and quiescent labor movement in postcommunist Poland, despite its public prominence.

Let us look at the evolution of this labor movement, beginning with the breakthrough year of 1989. Unlike other countries in Eastern Europe, Poland experienced 1989 not as a time when independent unions were finally possible but as the moment when they no longer seemed necessary. This, in any case, is how Solidarity interpreted the moment. It had focused so much on the need for political transformation that, at the moment of victory, the union's economic aims seemed not only secondary but troublesome.

Having imbibed a stylized ideology—according to which, my enemy's enemy is my friend—Solidarity heralded as the savior of 1989 nothing other than the capitalist bogeyman of the past. In this view, the main danger to that new savior was the union's own members. At Solidarity's first National Commission meeting after the communist government fell, Lech Wałęsa explicitly appealed against the rebuilding of a strong Solidarity: "We will not catch up to Europe if we build a strong union."[3] In the weeks ahead he argued the point repeatedly: We oppose a strong union because a strong union would oppose reform. "We cannot have a strong trade union," he announced, "until we have a strong economy."[4]

Wałęsa's position was not without its critics, but we see the seeds of union crisis even in that criticism. Władysław Frasyniuk, the popular union leader from Wrocław, argued *for* a "strong union" but only because he thought that was necessary to persuade people to accept market reform.[5] Similarly, Warsaw union leader Zbigniew Bujak contended that only a "strong union" could ward off attacks from antireformers unwilling to impose the "tough economic decisions" lying ahead.[6] Both Bujak and Frasyniuk had resisted entering Parliament precisely because they believed in the need for a trade union. As their remarks made clear, however, they imagined a trade union only as an institution pushing the reform agenda on anyone who resisted it, whether workers, managers, or bureaucrats.

Instead of building a strong union, Solidarity set out to build a weak one, meaning a union that would follow the government as it pursued a painful economic reform.

The new Solidarity emerged as a much smaller one than in the past. This was due to three factors: a changing political environment, a changing intellectual consensus, and an unwillingness of unionists to recruit.

The new political environment itself refers to three developments. First, there is the obvious point that with democratization a matter of fact, Solidarity membership no longer contributed to larger political goals. Second, it refers to the abolition of universal union membership, which began already under the old regime. When the government in 1983 risked reviving trade unions in the aftermath of the first Solidarity experience, it broke with the traditional communist practice of encouraging (that is, requiring) 100 percent employee membership. Many workers refrained from union membership then, and saw no need to rejoin when Solidarity was relegalized. (There was considerable rank-and-file distrust of unions in general, as some suspected that Solidarity would now be simply the new "official" trade union.) Finally, this new political environment meant that workers no longer saw the need to break with OPZZ. Without the burden of universal membership, OPZZ never functioned according to the standard "transmission belt" model of communist unionism. It even occasionally organized protests against governmental policies, a practice that accelerated after Solidarity and the party began their roundtable negotiations in 1989. OPZZ therefore did not experience the kind of crushing existential blow that befell other communist-party unions at the time. Because there had been no compulsion to join, members felt little immediate need to flee. Because the structures remained intact, OPZZ held onto most of its resources, such as vacation homes and mutual aid funds. Unlike in 1980, workers in 1989 did not need to join Solidarity to express their desire for systemic reform (it had already occurred) or to follow those who controlled all the resources (the old unions retained theirs). The symbolic and resource mobilization factors that drove Solidarity's spectacular numbers in 1980 no longer applied at the end of the decade.

The changing intellectual consensus led to a smaller Solidarity because it meant that intellectuals and higher-educated employees were no longer anxious to join trade unions. They too had other opportunities. Those who in the past had joined Solidarity to use it as a battering ram against the constraints of the old system now had other ways to get ahead. Some joined the government, some went into business, and political activists joined the civic committees that were formed to contest the first elections.[7]

Besides not needing to join the union anymore, liberal intellectuals no longer wanted to. As the greatest converts to market ideology, vigorous proponents of "joining the West," they saw unions not only as no longer necessary for fighting communism but as inappropriate to capitalism. Their flagship journal, *Gazeta Wyborcza*, the daily newspaper formally associated with Solidarity until mid-1990, regularly presented unions as institutions of the past capable only of jeopardizing reform.[8] We see here the widespread influence of Hayekian ideas on the opposition over the previous decade, the pervasiveness of a purist free-market ideology that had little to do with the realities of the Europe they hoped to join.[9] Those intellectuals who still saw some usefulness for unions tended to see them as useful for blue-collar workers only, certainly not for people like themselves. And so, Solidarity revived without the educated members of the past. Factory locals were still usually *run* by professionals, who correctly saw these posts as stepping stones to higher positions.[10] But the Solidarity rank and file was now almost exclusively blue-collar.

Of course, it no longer organized all blue-collar workers. As noted above, many stayed with OPZZ. Many more, however, were nonunionized, either because they stayed unaligned in the 1980s or because they were working in the new private enterprises that grew wildly after 1989. This was a difficult group to organize, including many workers in small shops or the new service sector not traditionally associated with unionism. The point, however, is that no unions sought to organize them. This stemmed partly from a general belief, part of the new hegemonic pro-market ideology, that the private sector did not need trade unions. Survey evidence shows conclusively that Polish union leaders believe employee institutions, such as unions or works' councils, are needed in state-owned firms but not private ones.[11] Yet the more important reason for the unions' unwillingness to organize the unorganized—and this concerns the unaligned in traditional state firms as well—is an ingrained belief that it is unseemly, "unmanly," and smacks too much of communism to solicit new members. "If they want to join, they'll join," a regional Solidarity leader in Rzeszów told me in 1993. "Asking people to join—that's something the old system did, not us."[12] Continuing the struggle against communism, the unions helped to undermine themselves.

With a leadership afraid of a strong union movement, the new Solidarity emerged as a union committed to bringing about the new government's overall plan of systemic reform. Intellectuals were not the only ones who had embraced a market economy. Union activists did too. They understood it to mean no more queues, the end of the *nomenklatura* system, and good pay for hard work. They also understood it as a more just system. Justice always entails a countersystemic principle. If in capitalist societies this usually means balancing capital's dominance with a dose of state interventionism, in socialist societies it entails more emphasis on market mechanisms. As Ivan Szelenyi put it, "while under capitalism the market creates the basic inequalities, and the administrative allocation of welfare modifies and moderates them slightly, under socialism the major inequalities are created by administrative allocation, and the market can be used to reduce inequalities."[13] Lower-level Solidarity activists saw marketization as synonymous with reform and democracy, and they understood tough economic times as the price to be paid for future prosperity.[14]

So the much-feared "social explosion" of the rank and file never happened. Besides the quelling effect of the pro-market, union-skeptical views discussed above,[15] union activists were kept in line by organizational pressures and by postcommunist specificities that made some forms of militancy compatible with subservience to new market rules.

Organizational pressure refers to the leadership's insistence on towing the line. Such pressure was unavailable in 1980, when the nature of the conflict against the state meant that no one would be excluded from Solidarity. Democracy, however, facilitates greater organizational discipline since excluded opponents are free to set up alternative organizations, inhibitions against the exercise of discipline are reduced. The official Solidarity leadership began excluding opponents before 1989, when Wałęsa kept his three militant 1981 rivals for the union presidency out of all new union bodies and kept Western material aid out of their hands. This practice of exclusion continued after 1989 as well. The strategy worked. Union militants left Solidarity and created their own organizations (most notably, "Solidarity-'80"). The message for those who remained was that union allegiance meant loyalty to the leadership's moderate line.

Finally, labor unrest was contained by the postcommunist peculiarity that makes acceptance of market reform not incompatible with certain forms of militancy. Support for neoliberalism in a postcommunist context, after all, does not entail the kind of deference to management that it does in a capitalist context. Rather, managers were seen as the problem to be overcome, and Solidarity saw itself as the force to overcome them. In this way, Solidarity activists could continue to be "militant" even while fighting for a program that would reduce union influence. Thanks to anticommunism, unionists who in a capitalist context might have mobilized against marketization mobilized instead against managers in the *name* of marketization. Solidarity was, in fact, actively involved in the enterprises in 1990. It forced the resignation of old managers and the election of new ones committed to privatization. It also prepared its own plans for privatization in case the new managers stalled.[16] Unions may have been quiescent in terms of defending labor interests, but they were not passive. They just used their energies to promote reform rather than obstruct it. When core militant workers protested, Solidarity turned against them in a flash. The only significant strike of 1990 occurred in the railways. The workers had a good case. They were protesting a peculiar provision that penalized them precisely for having been moderate in the past.[17] Nevertheless, national Solidarity denounced the strikers and got them to return to work without having won anything. Social protest was minimal, therefore, because workers' representatives continually tried to prevent it.

Lech Wałęsa said shock therapy would cause a downturn for three months, and then things would get better. When they didn't, labor discontent emerged, and Solidarity had to do something about it. Its strategy was to channel that discontent away from the new capitalist system and onto the old communist one. In this new view, articulated by Wałęsa in his campaign for the Polish presidency (a campaign itself intended to minimize anger against the new system), the problem was not capitalism but that there was not enough of it. "Real" capitalism was being blocked by enemies who must be uprooted. Chief among the enemies were the old communists, against whom Wałęsa promised a radical lustration law. However, "egghead intellectuals" were also targeted—and even, in a hint of a nationalist-populist evolution of the movement, "Jews."[18] By diverting anger at the economic system toward personalized enemies, Solidarity maintained labor support for market reform, but at the price of promulgating a dangerous, vindictive political culture. When Wałęsa was himself caught in a lustration crisis in 1992,[19] the working-class anger that Wałęsa had diverted against "communists" now rebounded against him. With the economy still deep in recession, Solidarity could no longer use anticommunism to maintain labor discipline.

This became clear in the summer of 1992. Between July and August, workers went on strike in the auto, steel, copper, coal, and aircraft manufacturing industries. Wages were the key issue—higher wages in auto and steel, simply *getting* wages in the tottering aircraft industry. Despite rank-and-file anger with Wałęsa over the lustration issue, Solidarity still saw itself as the "protective parasol" for market reform, and it immediately opposed the strikes as "contrary to labor's interests." Three years after 1989, however, these arguments had worn thin. Though some of these strikes were initiated by local Solidarity activists, the non-Solidarity unions (chiefly Solidarity-'80) soon emerged strong. They did not prevail. Opposition from Solidarity, pressure from the government, and small concessions by management led to a collapse of the strike wave by mid-September. However, the forceful expression of discontent shook Solidarity, leading to a new stage of action.

No longer plausibly able to divert that anger, and unable to ignore it, Solidarity finally made that anger its own. For a short time, Solidarity became a militant organization championing workers' economic interests rather than lecturing these workers on the need for restraint. The union's survival as a dominant social force hinged on this transition. In December 1992, it was Solidarity that organized a massive strike in the coal mines, bringing out some 180,000 miners throughout the country, making it the largest single coal strike in European history. The union ultimately settled without winning much for the miners, suggesting that its aim was more to demonstrate leadership in the workforce rather than to win gains for its members.[20] In early 1993, Solidarity then brought hospital workers and teachers out on strike, precisely those sectors that had traditionally refrained from striking in the past. But in the every-sector-for-itself environment of the postcommunist era, reluctance to protest had led to their dramatic relative decline vis-à-vis other professions, and many blamed Solidarity for allowing it to happen. In compensation, Solidarity now organized a massive strike wave on their behalf, coming into direct conflict with the government and not turning back. When the government, still run by Solidarity-allied politicians, said pay hikes would break the budget, Solidarity parliamentarians fought to revise the budget. When the budget was passed anyway, and the government refused to change it, Solidarity deputies tendered a vote of no confidence, and the government fell by one vote.

The parasol, it seemed, had finally folded. Solidarity had pushed an economic fight to the point of ousting a government of pure Solidarity pedigree. Perhaps if the Solidarity-affiliated parties had won the new elections, the union would have continued its new practice of acting like a proper union. However, the 1993 elections brought the Alliance of the Democratic Left (SLD), led by former communists, to power, and Solidarity entered into its third phase.

This phase has seen a decisive turn to direct political engagement and further movement away from economic trade-unionism. It began with Solidarity turning from hostility to government policy to hostility to the government per se. With its old enemy in power, Solidarity now denounced every government initiative regardless of content, even those that were clearly pro-labor. The new government raised public-sector pay, increased retirement pensions, granted employees more free shares of their privatized firms, cracked down on employer violations of labor law, and energetically convened a tripartite commission headed by a respected former Solidarity underground activist that the SLD specially invited for the job. Still, Solidarity found ways to denounce the government. Virtually everything Solidarity had asked the liberals to do, and then ousted for not doing, the SLD now did, and Solidarity never forgave them.

The SLD government's relatively pro-union position stemmed from its quest for legitimacy and its own considerable union base. Solidarity may not have had a single party representing it, but OPZZ did. More than one-fourth of SLD deputies were OPZZ unionists. Aware that it needed to reach out to Solidarity to gain broader social legitimacy, the government made a number of gestures. Immediately upon coming to power, the new labor minister offered to travel to Gdańsk to meet with the Solidarity leadership. However, the union spurned this like it did most SLD offers.

Solidarity was guided not just by ideological enmity but by simple electoral logic. The political fragmentation of the right, combined with an electoral law promoting large parties, meant that only one rightist party had broken the 5 percent threshold for entry into Parliament in 1993. Almost one-third of the electorate had its vote wasted. Solidarity saw itself as the only force able to change this. As a self-professed right-wing organization—a label it proudly adopted both because of its Catholic predilections and because its enemy had defined itself as "the left"—and the only one with local organizational structures and name recognition, Solidarity was in a far better position to oust the SLD than any of the new parties that had arisen. So Solidarity turned from its budding class agenda back into the anticommunist movement it once was.

If a pro-union party had succeeded in organizing workers, the union might have been able to embrace a more limited union role. The liberals who ran Solidarity in 1989 had the best chance of creating such a party. They had engineered the spectacular electoral victory of June 1989 with enormous working-class support and were well placed to continue to get their votes, provided they proffered a program that spoke to labor's needs and offered (even symbolically) to include them. However, those leaders, who went on to form the Democratic Union and then the Freedom Union, saw their historical role as representing the interests of a nascent bourgeoisie instead. Labor for them was the group doomed to suffer for the foreseeable future, and the liberals' gentlemanly cult of "honesty" compelled them to tell workers this "truth" and to legislate it into being. Far from trying to organize labor discontent and direct it toward liberal democratic ends, by encouraging participation or getting workers involved in party work, the liberals simply ignored workers. When I asked a Democratic Union leader in a small, declining industrial city in 1993 what the party was doing to win the votes of townspeople whose livelihoods were threatened, he replied simply, "Nothing." The "reality," he continued, was that "we have nothing to offer them; their lives are only going to get worse."[21] In this way, workers were left without a party to call their own. And Solidarity was pushed onto the political road.

The union's first response to the SLD victory was to promote conflict. It sought to turn every local conflict into a war aimed at ousting the government. When there were no local workplace conflicts, the union initiated political ones. Identity issues more and more replaced economic ones. Solidarity denounced the government for proposing an "atheistic" constitution and seeking to liberalize abortion. (The fight against a woman's right to choose all but consumed the Solidarity leadership in 1996.) It called for a tough anticommunist lustration law and for greater church involvement in public life. Virtually the only economic issue it campaigned for was a "universal privatization" scheme giving employees a one-shot windfall at their share of privatized state assets. Even this had a clear pro-market pedigree: Workers were to be empowered as potential investors or consumers, not as workers. On workplace issues or organizing the unorganized, Solidarity remained silent.

In 1995 the union put most of its energies into defeating SLD candidate Aleksandr Kwaśniewski for president. When Kwaśniewski won anyway, it turned its attention to building its own political party to recapture power from "the communists." In 1997, Solidarity attracted a couple of dozen small, right-wing parties that had failed to pass the 5 percent threshold and formed the Solidarity Electoral Action (AWS) coalition. Emphasizing nationalist, religious, and anticommunist issues rather than union ones—but deploying Solidarity locals as their campaign committees—AWS won parliamentary elections and took control in a coalition government with the third-place Freedom Union.

The late 1990s saw cries of "unionocracy" by political pundits, but far from proffering policy beneficial to unions, the AWS government initiated measures weakening union power, particularly in health and education, and passed legislation detailing conditions for the virtual liquidation of the mining sector. Union officials were indeed influential in government, but their policy emphasized "Christian values" and lustration, not union power or improvements for labor.

Formally speaking, the Solidarity trade union remained separate from AWS. However, the union for the most part refrained from challenging the political authorities. When the AWS government introduced painful reforms in health and education, only the non-Solidarity unions responded with protests. In the growing private sector, Solidarity continued to discourage union organization, arguing that nothing should be done to hinder the introduction of new capital, especially foreign capital.[22]

In 1999 four prominent Polish industrial sociologists published a volume on trade unions titled *Collapse of the Bastion?* The signs of demise were evident everywhere. Even as the economy grew, membership declined. Part of the problem, as just noted, was the creation of a union-free private sector. Even the "Unionocracy" article admitted that union "influence in new private firms . . . is practically nil."[23] Scholarly research is clearer on the matter. In *Collapse of the Bastion?* Juliusz Gardawski shows that there are barely any unions in new private firms and that they "are undergoing steady erosion" in firms preparing for privatization (the so-called "commercialized" firms). In firms founded after 1989, only 17 percent had trade unions.[24] Only in state firms were unions holding their own. In other words, unions survive chiefly in obsolescent firms, auguring poorly for the future.

Members are leaving, and new ones aren't joining. All unions have had a problem recruiting young workers. A Solidarity official trying to form a youth section in Gdańsk, the heartland of the union, had to give up "because there were not enough people willing to take part."[25] Although Solidarity-'80 has managed to arouse some interest among younger workers, most union members are over forty years of age.[26]

TRIPARTISM

Contrary to the immediate post-1989 period elsewhere in Eastern Europe, no one even proposed tripartism in Poland. The coming to power of Solidarity meant that its activists went into positions of state power, and they saw no need to formally negotiate with unions whose interests they considered themselves to be representing. If unions had demanded a formal tripartite body, they certainly could have gotten one. However, Wałęsa committed Solidarity to supporting government policy, and OPZZ, anxious to demonstrate new moderate credentials, followed suit. Nor did any demands come from Parliament. Between 1989 and 1991 parliamentary opposition was entirely in the hands of the former communists, who neither wanted to boost a union movement that Solidarity was about to control nor do anything (such as seeming overly sympathetic to trade unions) that might challenge their new pro-market image. On the front page of the *Solidarity Weekly*, a leading union activist urged workers in the new era to "learn that their wages and jobs depend on productivity; that their salaries are a function of the talents and capabilities of the managers . . . and that the general state of our factories depends on the level of the cadre governing the firm."[27] Governing elites often see tripartism as a way of preserving social peace, but in this situation no one proposed tripartism because no one needed to. The unions made it clear that they were going to discipline themselves.[28]

Unions had access to political decision makers. Bonds of friendship and informal obligations allowed Solidarity unionists to come to Warsaw and demand—and receive—visits with top government officials. Most of them came to discuss the situation of their particular firm, such as why it should get additional subsidies, why it should be allowed to raise wages without being taxed, or why it should be privatized in a particular way. (Union officials often worked together with management on these issues, leading some critics to see them merely as management's tool.)[29]

Anxious to demonstrate a new democratic style, officials met with OPZZ too, when the latter demanded it.[30] Contacts, therefore, were maintained by informal, ad hoc, bilateral negotiations. Unions had a right to comment on legislation affecting them, but no institutional forms ensured this would happen. When it did, the unions were often unprepared to take advantage because their experts had gone over to the other side—including about 95 percent of Warsaw Solidarity experts. One journalist tells the story of a late-1989 meeting of the Solidarity Presidium to work out the union's position on an indexation bill before Parliament. The union was unable to decide anything because "all its experts on this question had in fact joined the Ministry of Labor."[31] Other unions also had the right to comment, but government officials did not take them seriously—OPZZ because of its old-regime ties and Solidarity-'80 because of its renegade status. Talking with unions meant talking with Solidarity, and the latter not pursuing this meant there were few organized consultations at all.

Only after the strike wave of 1992 did the government see the need for regular, institutionalized contact with trade unions. Labor Minister Jacek Kuroń proposed a "pact on state enterprises" that included the creation of a tripartite commission. It began its work in January 1994. The first experiences were not promising. Solidarity refused to coordinate any positions with OPZZ, the newly elected government did not have a program for which it sought societal approval, and continuing wage controls meant that the employers' organization—which in any case represented only a tiny portion of employers—had no power to discuss what was most important to workers. Solidarity had supported the establishment of the commission earlier in the year, but after the elections, it turned its focus to toppling the government, not making deals with it. Tripartite meetings dragged on inconclusively until a public-sector deal was negotiated in early 1995. For the next two years, tripartism and an economy that finally started to grow served to limit labor unrest. This is evident in the dramatic drop in the number of strikes—from 429 strikes with 211,000 participants in 1994 to 42 strikes and 18,000 strikers a year later.[32] In 1997, with parliamentary elections pending, Solidarity refused to sign any more deals. When AWS won those elections, far from continuing with tripartism, union leaders reverted instead to their pre-1993 (and very Bolshevik) position that because the government represented union interests, it did not need formalized contacts with union representatives. Tripartism limped on, barely, until the new government's lack of interest precipitated OPZZ to walk out in 1999. According to one union negotiator, AWS ministers would come to tripartite meetings saying they would not negotiate government proposals but only take questions.[33] By the end of 1999, tripartism had fallen into such desuetude that an embarrassed government minister called for a special meeting to revive it. The government needed this, it seemed, more to mollify the EU and ILO than to work with the trade unions.

CONCLUSION

There are two major objections to the claim about union weakness in Poland. The first points to the presence of unionists in government ever since 1989 and argues (or assumes) that unions exert influence through these personal connections. The second focuses on the large number of labor protests and contends that labor has won concessions in enterprises and in public policy by its persistent presence in civil society.

The first objection has been a familiar refrain. Although it proved false in the first years after 1989—Solidarity's power clearly did not prevent the government from introducing radical market reform—it resurfaced again during the AWS administration. In 1999, Transport Minister Eugeniusz Morawski resigned because, he said, trade unions had too much control over the rail industry. "I cannot accept a situation where unions control the national railways," Morawski said upon announcing his resignation.[34] Suddenly the alleged power of trade unions became the topic of the day. The influential weekly *Polityka* ran a cover story titled "Unionocracy" without even a question mark. Its first line: "Poland is governed by trade unions."[35]

The problem here is a false identification of unionists' power and union power. Controversy over the transport minister's resignation, for example, exclusively concerned the number of unionists (some "with only a secondary education," the press emphasized) who had taken key leadership positions in the rail industry.[36] That unionists get jobs in companies and ministries does not mean that they act on behalf of labor, but only that some individuals have used political connections to get management jobs. Solidarity has been a stepping stone into business and government ever since the Round Table accords of 1989. It has also been chiefly responsible for maintaining labor's acceptance of painful economic reform. Unionists as individuals may get clout thanks to national connections, but when they are unable to stop a steady deterioration of union influence and labor conditions, and when they do not even seek to organize the private sector, it is difficult to talk of union strength.

In his influential piece in *Polityka*, Mariusz Janicki also pointed to organizational aspects of union power. Unions are easy to form, go on strike whenever they feel like it without regard for the law, and treat any challenge as an intolerable sign of disrespect for the movement that brought down communism. "Unions," he concludes, "constitute virtually a separate state."[37] Rather than seeing such organizational privileges as a sign of strength, however, I would suggest that we see them as a historical peculiarity of the Polish corporate governance structure.[38] My point is not that unions don't have a special position in Poland, but that they have not used this position to promote labor's economic interests and have frequently even used it *against* those interests. It is true that unions are easy to create. Ten employees signing a union registration form is all that is needed. Old legislation still on the books gives unions the right to have full-time union officials paid for by the company, depending on the number of members. It mandates that companies consult unions on layoffs, and it gives unions the right to question layoffs. However, these rules signify nothing other than that institutions called trade unions have long been involved in Polish enterprise management. Union participation in corporate governance is partly a legacy of the past, when unions were a key part of the enterprise because it was the place where social benefits were administered, and unions did much of the administering. This is also due to the particularities of postcommunist capitalist transition. In the first years after 1989, managers usually supported unions in their protests against Warsaw—or even initiated such protests—because this was a way to help enterprises get capital. In the competition for funds or favors, such as debt forgiveness, Solidarity unions had clout where managers still did not. Having clout does not mean they used it on behalf of their employees.

In one factory where I did research in 1993 and 1994, company officials talked with unionists all the time. Then they went and did what they wanted to in the first place. "We bargained with unionists over wage policy," the personnel manager, himself a Solidarity member, told me in 1994. "And when they wouldn't sign the deal we presented them with, we implemented the deal ourselves."[39] In the end, unions have helped get things done for the factory, not for workers per se. They remain part of the enterprise structure, not an autonomous source of employee strength.

The *Polityka* piece also pointed to the prominence of labor protest, a theme stressed in recent scholarly work by Ekiert and Kubik and by Maryjane Osa.[40] The question, however, is not whether there is protest but what the protests are actually about. The common assumption is that protest entails strength and defiance. Much of the time, however, Solidarity has led protests not to lead workers but to *contain* them. I visited many manufacturing firms where Solidarity leaders explained that, yes, they "led" a strike at their plant, but they did so only because their members were demanding that someone do something (for example, about nonpayment of wages), and the union leaders wanted to make sure that the membership stayed loyal to them. What appears in newspapers and in the public imagination as Solidarity-sponsored protests may only refer to a union seeking to *demobilize* discontent.

One might also ask whether frequent rallies and protests are a sign not of strength but of weakness. Power, after all, is best exercised out of the public eye. Business interests are hardly less likely to be met just because they don't stage rallies in front of the Sejm. Miners have staged more strikes and protests than any other group in Poland, but the mines are being closed all the same—perhaps more slowly than if there hadn't been any protests, but then all that can be said is that miners have been able to negotiate the terms of their own demise.

Unions have not disappeared in Poland. Historical legacies and the weakness of the party system keep them in the center of public attention. The bottom line, however, is that unions have not used their enormous resources to fight economically on behalf of labor or even to create the kind of solid class identity that might help labor when postcommunist primitive accumulation comes to an end. Their chief accomplishment has been to smooth the transformation into a liberal market economy by diverting labor anger onto "safe" targets. Successive cohorts of unionists have ridden this anger into power for themselves—but not into any lasting, long-term power for trade unions as organizations defending the interests of labor.

NOTES

1. Mariusz Janicki, "Związkokracja," in *Polityka*, December 12, 1998, 3.
2. By symbolic resources, I mean the assets an organization can attract by virtue of

its historical associations and name recognition. Chief among such assets is the free and unlimited publicity for what the leaders of such an organization do in its name. This is an undertheorized topic in social movement theory, where it is more common to talk about how symbols are mobilized by movements (Sidney Tarrow, *Power in Movement* [Cambridge: Cambridge University Press, 1998], ch.7) than on how postmovement institutions cash in on the symbols of the past.

3. Cited by Paweł Ławiński, "Ile Wytrzymacie?" in *Tygodnik Solidarność* 18, September 29, 1989, 2.

4. Interview with *Gazeta Wyborcza*, cited in *Tygodnik Solidarność*, October 20, 1989, 23.

5. Ławiński, "Ile Wytrzymacie?"

6. Zbigniew Bujak, "Chciałbym zachować niezależną pozycję," in *Gazeta Wyborcza* 2, May 9, 1989, 5.

7. On the civic committees, see Tomek Grabowski, "The Party That Never Was: The Rise and Fall of the Solidarity Citizens' Committees in Poland," in *East European Politics and Societies* 10:2, spring 1996, 214–54.

8. See, for example, the coverage of a miners strike in January 1990 that was filled with derision for the strikers' comportment and was an attempt to portray them as unruly and unreasonable characters with whom "modern" citizens have nothing in common. We are told by the author, who not long ago had written encomiums to unions in the underground press, that the strikers behave generally as hooligans, trying to bring vodka into the plant and cursing their leaders (just the kind of story told by the communist authorities in the past), but we are not told about the conditions that led to the strike. Grzegorz Gorny, "Strajk gorników," in *Gazeta Wyborcza*, January 22, 1990.

9. Hayek's works were published extensively by the underground press and distributed through Solidarity channels. This excitement went beyond Poland; see Hilary Wainwright's description of coming to postcommunist Czechoslovakia and finding Hayek on every student's lips. (*Arguments for a New Left* [London: Verso, 1992]).

10. Solidarity leaders at the large Ursus Tractor Plant in Warsaw and the WSK aircraft manufacturing plant in Mielec, for example, quickly went on to become directors of their respective firms. Many other post-1989 professional union leaders became government administrators.

11. See David Ost and Marc Weinstein, "Unionists against Unions: Towards Hierarchical Management in Post-Communist Poland," in *East European Politics and Societies* 13:1, winter 1999, 1–32.

12. The AFL-CIO began a recruitment education program for Solidarity in 1993, teaching unions how to organize new members, but the program declined when the union turned its energies toward political organizing instead.

13. Ivan Szelenyi, *Urban Inequalities under State Socialism* (Oxford: Oxford University Press, 1983), 11.

14. Ost and Weinstein, "Unionists against Unions." See also survey results published by Juliusz Gardawski, *Robotnicy 1991* (Warsaw: Friedrich Ebert Foundation, 1992); Juliusz Gardawski and Tomasz Żukowski, *Robotnicy 1993* (Warsaw: Friedrich Ebert Foundation, 1994); and Juliusz Gardawski, *Poland's Industrial Workers on the Return to Democracy and Market Economy* (Warsaw: Friedrich Ebert Foundation, 1996).

15. The belief that hard work without union rights leads to good outcomes followed, in

part, from Poles' widespread experience as illegal laborers in the West, where they worked tough jobs without any benefits or protection for wages that, though a pittance in the "guest" country, turned to gold when brought back home. Because of a relatively liberal visa policy, Poland supplied more black-market labor to the West than any Eastern European country except Yugoslavia.

16. See Janusz Dąbrowski, Michał Federowicz, and Anthony Levitas, "Polish State Enterprises and the Property of Performance: Stabilization, Marketization, Privatization," in *Politics and Society* 19:4, December 1991, 403–38.

17. Rail workers had refrained from striking in 1989, when other core sectors won wage increases, largely due to a pervasive ethos proscribing strikes in sectors of generalized public use such as transport, health, and education. Other workers had struck *for* them in 1980, but not in the new, more individualist era of 1989. When the government passed a law indexing wage increases according to pay levels of late 1989, rail workers lost out because their failure to strike meant they had failed to win the wage increases other workers had. They struck to rectify this injustice, demanding average rail wages be set at 116 percent of the national average. See Kazimierz Kloc, "Przyczyny i Przebieg Strajku na PKP w maju 1990," in *Studia nad Ruchami Społecznymi*, vol. 5 (Warsaw: Institute of Sociology, Warsaw University, 1990), 159–201.

18. Mirosława Grabowska and Ireneusz Krzemiński, eds., *Bitwa o Belweder* (Warsaw: Myśl, 1991). On Jews, see Konstanty Gebert's chapter "Rola antysemitzmu."

19. Wałęsa was accused by the interior minister of being a former communist "collaborator."

20. See Wojciech Błaziak, "Górniczy Strajk Generalny na Śląsku," in *Górnicy Górnośląscy—ludzie zbędni, ludzie luźni?*, Marek Szczepański, ed. (Krakow: amp, 1994).

21. Personal interview with Democratic Union leader in Rzeszów, September 1993.

22. When General Motors opened a new greenfield site in Gliwice in November 1998, local Solidarity officials told me they saw no need to try to unionize the plant. The notion that private capital might work more effectively with unions than without apparently made more sense to Western European capitalists than to Eastern European unionists.

23. Mariusz Janicki, "Związkokracja," in *Polityka*, December 12, 1998.

24. Juliusz Gardawski, "Zasieg związków zawodowych w wybranych działach przemysłu i sekcjach usług publicznych," in *Rozpad Bastionu?*, Gardawski et al., eds. (Warsaw: Instytut Spraw Publicznych, 1999).

25. See "Juniorzy," in *Magazyn Solidarność* 10, October 1996, 5.

26. No precise figures are available, but union activists and industrial sociologists both agree that this is the case.

27. Wojciech Arkuszewski, "Od góry do dolu," in *Tygodnik Solidarność*, September 22, 1989.

28. See David Ost, "Illusory Corporatism in Eastern Europe: Neoliberal Tripartism and Postcommunist Class Identities," in *Politics and Society* 28:4, December 2000, 503–30.

29. "Unionists would come in for negotiations," said Jan Lityński, a Solidarity parliamentary leader in 1990, "and there'd always be some guy sitting in the back not saying anything. And it would always turn out to be the director!" Personal interview, Warsaw, October 1998.

30. OPZZ, of course, had better access to SLD officials, but the powerlessness of the latter in the first postcommunist years made pursuing such contacts hardly worthwhile.

31. Anna Bikont, "Zwyciężyło i coś pękło," in *Gazeta Wyborcza*, January 29, 1990, 5.

32. *Rocznik Statystyczny* 1995, 1998, and 2000. (Warsaw: GUS). Totals were as follows:

	No. of strikes	No. of strikers
1990	250	115,687
1991	305	221,547
1992	6,351	752,472
1993	7,443	383,222
1994	429	211,442
1995	42	18,114
1996	21	42,250
1997	35	14,210
1998	37	16,907
1999	920	27,149

33. Personal interview with Ewa Tomaszewska, Warsaw, June 1999.

34. Quoted in "Tak chciała S," in *Trybuna*, November 25, 1998, 1.

35. Mariusz Janicki, "Związkokracja," in *Polityka*, December 12, 1998.

36. Two Solidarity union leaders entered the company's managerial board (*zarząd*), and six local officials became regional directors. These officials appointed their buddies to other positions. See Mieczysław Wodzicki, "Kadrowe trzesienie na torach," in *Trybuna*, November 24, 1998.

37. Janicki, "Związkokracja," 3.

38. Michał Federowicz, "Pojęcie 'corporate governance' w odniesieniu do przemian ustrojowych," paper presented at Polish sociological conference on "Socjologia gospodarcza *sensu largo*," Łódź, February 1999. The term refers to the way enterprise management guarantees smooth decision making and capital flow in reality, as opposed to legality.

39. Personal interview in Mielec, May 1994.

40. Grzegorz Ekiert and Jan Kubik, "Contentious Politics in New Democracies: East Germany, Hungary, Poland, and Slovakia, 1989–1993," in *World Politics* 50, July 1998, 547–81; and Grzegorz Ekiert and Jan Kubik, *Rebellious Civil Society: Popular Protest and Democratic Consolidation in Poland* (Ann Arbor: University of Michigan Press, 1999). Maryjane Osa, "Contention and Democracy: Labor Protest in Poland, 1989–1993," in *Communist and Postcommunist Studies* 31:1, 1998, 29–42.

Chapter Five

Winning the Battles, Losing the War: Contradictions of Romanian Labor in the Postcommunist Transformation

David A. Kideckel

The conditions of organized labor in Romania today are highly ambiguous. Despite a compromised history, structural impediments, and a problematic image, labor can relish some recent successes and hope for a future of even greater promise. Romanian unions still represent about two-thirds of 6.5 million potential nonagricultural workers. Among unions of the former socialist nations of East Central Europe, Romanian unions seem to have the greatest degree of political power. This is reinforced by constant militancy, from localized walkouts to nationwide general strikes to threatened invasions of cities and towns. Union leaders also play a large role in national politics. They have the ear of presidents and prime ministers, make pronouncements about Romanian social and foreign policy, and are even influential in national economic decision making and International Monetary Fund (IMF) negotiations. One former union president, Victor Ciorbea, even served as prime minister from late 1996 to early 1999. Finally, the National Labor Agreement (*Contracte Colective de Munca*) originally drawn up in 1992 under labor's pressure, was revised in 1999 with some expanded protections and extended coverage for workers.[1]

Yet despite this long list of accomplishments (the so-called "battles"), I argue that labor's power has been ineffective in the overall war where it counts most: preserving or expanding jobs, improving working conditions, and preserving and extending labor's purchasing power.[2] In fact, the tactical successes of Romanian labor actually camouflage a number of labor's strategic weaknesses and even magnify those weaknesses by fueling popular misperceptions and critiques of labor practices.

97

Labor's strategic weakness first derives from competition within the union movement, bred by its postsocialist history, structure, and organization. The same political relationship of unions and parties that seems to give unions such power[3] intensifies this competition. Furthermore, opportunities to achieve labor's strategic goals are weakened, if not nullified altogether, by the overall state of the Romanian economy. In an environment of hyperinflation, job loss, and black-market labor, Romania's politicized unions end up seeking to change the political conditions of local and national life through constant militancy. Local strikes end up as merely stopgap actions to preserve workplaces and living standards, even as the overall political economy trends away from union goals. Thus, the frustration of Romania's workers and unions at their steady decline is palpable and erupts in frequent strikes, both legal and illegal. In response to this unending militancy, Romania's population, government, employers, and even labor itself increasingly deride its practices and institutions, further weakening labor's power.

To consider the ambiguities of Romanian labor today, I first examine the heightened emotions about labor (both positive and negative) spurred by socialist-state practices that shape the context for labor's tactical success and strategic stumbles. Second, I consider the tensions and obstacles to labor's effectiveness by analysis of its history, structures, and relationships with society and government. Third, I discuss the actual social context of Romanian labor and show how increasing unemployment, black-market labor, and the deterioration of working conditions further degrade labor's power. Finally, I conclude with a discussion of the problematic identity of Romanian workers, but I also offer a somewhat salutary prognosis for labor's future. This in particular depends on changes in labor policy and practice. Only then can labor directly help arrest the postsocialist decline and extend its influence in a changing Romania.

LABOR'S PARADOX BRIEFLY OBSERVED

Events of 1999 amply illustrate labor's visible power and marginal results. The year began with protests and a threatened march on Bucharest by Jiu Valley miners. These threats ended with the miners gassed and strafed in the Jiu defile, their leader—Miron Cosma—arrested, and the agreement between the government and miners for job protection and job growth largely ignored. At the end of March, protests against state economic policies brought four hundred thousand union members into major city streets,[4] but again with little result. Subsequently, a nationwide general strike planned for May was postponed at the last minute, partly the result of fallout from the Kosovo war but more because of disagreements between the union confederations. Finally, violent wildcat protests in November at the Braşov truck factory, Roman S.A., brought further scorn on the labor movement, though a last-minute agreement kept job levels stable (at the expense of salary increases, however, and only until plant operations are restructured).[5]

The miners' actions highlight the questionable efficacy of labor's power. Miner anger was stoked by fears of job security as, in the last two years, eighteen thousand of the forty-two thousand workers in Jiu Valley left their jobs, enticed by large severance pay.[6] The protest began in response to rumors that more mines were to close than government officials had previously indicated. The miners were also demonstrating against the guilty verdict for Miron Cosma for "undermining state authority" during the 1991 march on Bucharest, when they toppled the government of Prime Minister Petre Roman.[7] As the miners neared the town of Rîmnicu Vîlcea, then–Prime Minister Radu Vasile met with Cosma and assuaged the protest by offering some stopgap measures. Though rumors first said the government capitulated in the secret agreement and that reform was threatened,[8] in fact, labor was the big loser. The government showed its mettle and commitment to reform by arresting and imprisoning Cosma.[9] Miner jobs were further eroded, and many of labor's allies withdrew their support due to the violent protests. Even the Romanian Party of Social Democracy (PDSR)—base of Ion Iliescu, benefactor and alleged sponsor of previous miner action—said that a labor-inspired revolt threatened Romania.

These events are only the latest in Romania's intense labor unrest, which essentially began coincidentally to the fall of Ceauşescu in 1989. Because of unending strikes, the government passed Law 15 in 1991 to dampen labor unrest by mediating labor disagreements, severely limiting the types of legal strikes, and punishing illegal strikers.[10] Still, in the last five years there have been an endless number of strikes, many of which are now illegal. Strikes have affected virtually every sector of the Romanian economy. These include striking truckers, subway and railway workers, farmers, power-plant employees, auto and tractor assembly workers, medical personnel, teachers, and of course, the ubiquitous miners. Even university and grade school students have taken to the picket line to express their displeasure at the conditions in which they live and learn.

Despite the degree of activism, there appears to be an inverse relationship between the number of strikes and the improvement in workers' conditions. Labor's anger grows from frustration at unsteady privatization, declining standards of living,[11] and increased class differentiation in the context of economic and political corruption. To counter these processes, unions call for labor law changes, transparent reform, and full privatization, but they simul-

taneously seek protection from reform's worst consequences like unemployment and inflation. However, labor and government are caught in a catch-22
where labor attacks government for its failures, labor action encourages further national political and economic instability, the crisis deepens, and further
labor action is provoked.[12] Most problematically, neither labor nor government seems able to break this vicious circle.

ROMANIAN LABOR IN SOCIALISM AND
REVOLUTION: THE CONTEXT
OF PARADOX

The contradictory position of labor in Romanian society grows first from
experiences in socialism. This encourages both labor's sense of prominence
and society's jaundiced eye. During socialism, state-centralized control over,
and material degradation of, labor[13] was combined with profuse, almost gush-
ing, symbolic support of workers. Workers were portrayed as the source of
all value and cultural and scientific achievement.[14] They were heroic and stal-
wart, and they exhibited a high degree of collective (that is, socialist) consciousness.[15] Socialist ideology even indirectly supported labor militancy
through tales of anticapitalist battles and celebrations of important events like
the 1929 Lupeni (Jiu Valley) miners' strike. Here, according to socialist histo-
riography, twenty-two heroic striking workers were shot dead by a squad of
soldiers on explicit orders of a (right-of-center) Peasant Party prefect.[16]

Memories of this socialist "cult of labor" (*cultul muncii*) encourage workers' expectations and others' derisive responses. Workers are nostalgic for the
security of the socialist years and consider themselves beleaguered heroes in
the fight for a reasonable standard of living. However, Romanian society now
rejects socialist boilerplates, and as expressed in national print and broadcast
media, it sees labor's demands as self-indulgent. The plethora of strikes
merely represents resistance to labor intensification in the new capitalist
economy. Employers, officials, and even some working people suggest that
the failure of economic reform is partly due to poor labor productivity,
related to the coddling of workers during socialism, when job security gave
little reason to intensify work effort.[17]

Aside from workers' nostalgia, contemporary Romanian unions bear little
resemblance to the socialist organization that predates them. The Romanian
union movement today is highly pluralistic, but during socialism, all Romanian nonagricultural workers were encapsulated within the General Union of
Romanian Syndicates (UGSR).[18] Like socialist unions generally, the UGSR
acted as a "transmission belt" for resources like housing and access to subsi-
dized restaurants and health spas.[19] However, as a state-controlled corporate

structure, the UGSR smothered dissent by denying troublesome workers housing and other benefits. The UGSR was even complicit in the Ceauşescu regime's extreme pro-natalism that restricted women workers from many occupations and forced regular gynecological exams at workplace clinics, among other abuses.[20]

Labor today seeks historical distance from the UGSR and instead seeks legitimacy by claiming a role in the fall of the socialist regime. Though labor was mostly cowed and docile throughout the socialist years, current union leaders point to two events a decade apart to justify their revolutionary credentials. In 1977, thirty-five thousand Jiu Valley miners took to the streets to protest increases in the retirement age and decreases in pension benefits, forcing Ceauşescu to meet with them personally and accede to their demands.[21] Similarly, in November 1987 a strike for better working conditions at the Red Flag truck factory in Braşov quickly grew into a violent attack on the Braşov County People's Council offices. However, neither of these movements was sustained, and it took the actions of Timişoara preachers, students, and housewives to finally move the revolution off square one.

Though labor was left behind in the revolution per se, it was exceedingly active right afterward, but it left an ambiguous legacy. Immediately after Ceauşescu's fall, workers unilaterally dissolved local UGSR branches and established over two thousand new independent unions.[22] Militant workers threatened and dismissed suspect factory administrators at will. As one local union president in Cluj told me, "There was so much chaos, the directors would stop at the plant gates before entering every morning to make sure all was safe." In the midst of the chaos, labor's appetite for militancy and political involvement was whetted by its success in forcing national adoption of the forty-hour workweek and in increasing workers' salaries across the board. However, militancy also contributed to tense labor-management relations, falling production, and stuttering reform. It thus linked government, management, and unions in a cycle of mutual fear and mistrust. Certainly, there are exceptions to this. Some production organizations are strengthened and workers' jobs preserved by clear-sighted labor-management cooperation. However, even these relationships often succumb to declining markets, outmoded technology, and the political or economic corruption and fiscally predatory state system of the Romanian present.

ROMANIAN LABOR TODAY: WEAKNESS IN STRENGTH, DISORGANIZED ORGANIZATION

Romanian labor today confronts numerous obstacles impeding its goals. Some are imposed on labor from outside its ranks, but others are internally generated. The structure of the union movement itself has been one of labor's greatest obstacles. Union formation immediately after 1989 encouraged the nascent organizations to compete over the UGSR patrimony, an ethos that remains today. Laws governing formation of labor organizations further obstruct interunion cooperation. Unions also had to develop leadership, organizational capacities, and legal knowledge quickly and almost from scratch. Those unable to work on a sharp learning curve stumbled organizationally and in serving members' interests. However, perhaps the biggest obstacle to union goals is Romanian political and economic corruption. This destroys firms internally by emptying them of resources and externally by excessive taxation, inflated business costs, and the co-opting of some union leaders.

The present shape of the Romanian labor movement emerged in the days after the revolution, when three major labor confederations came to dominate Romanian organized labor.[23] The initially dominant group was the National Confederation of Free Romanian Trade Unions (*Confederaţia Naţionala a Sindecatelor Liberi din România*, or CNSLR), whose position was supported by the National Salvation Front, the group forming the first postsocialist Romanian government.[24] Through the CNSLR, the NSF sought a return to economic calm out of postrevolutionary disorder. Informally, then, CNSLR seemed like an official union as it replaced the UGSR, took over most of its assets, and established a close, cooperative (and some would say, corrupt) relation with the NSF.

As heir to the UGSR patrimony but operating in politically uncertain and economically threatening times, the CNSLR sought to consolidate its power by direct involvement in national politics, walking right and left at the same time. Thus, the confederation's constitution denied former communist union officials roles in the organization, and its first president, Victor Ciorbea, was a former judge, public prosecutor, mayor of Bucharest, and (right-of-center) Peasant Party fixture. Simultaneously, CNSLR officials maintained a close relationship with the dominant but suspect NSF. The CNSLR represented, among other groups, chemical workers, oil workers, telecommunications workers, wood-industry workers, state power-company workers, and other service-sector organizations.

CNSLR politics, in part, encouraged challengers to its domination of the union movement. Thus, CSI-Fraţia (the Confederation of Independent Trade Unions, the Brotherhood) was also formed in January 1990, motivated either by its leaders' desire to gain part of the UGSR holdings or by its opposition to CNSLR's tainted politics.[25] Representing various machine and transportation assembly workers and truck and taxi drivers, CSI-Fraţia grew quickly by attacking the NSF and CNSLR, calling for labor peace and union and factory democracy, and making good use of foreign assistance, such as that from the

U.S. Teamsters Union. Despite potshots between CNSLR and CSI-Fraţia, early 1990 was the heyday for Romanian trade unionism. General revulsion at socialist policies assured government and popular support of labor's program, including the forty-hour week, indexed wages, and better working conditions. However, due to those early successes and attempts by political leaders to curry union favor, labor soon gained an unrealistic sense of power. Its leaders thus shifted their attention from labor issues per se to the character and organization of the national government.

With spring and summer, the 1990 revolutionary optimism waned as inflation and unemployment grew and economic stagnation spread. Strikes became more frequent and were concerned with bread-and-butter issues like job security and salaries. In this increasingly confrontational labor environment, many workers began to feel ill served by both CNSLR and CSI-Fraţia. Thus, seven union federations based in metallurgy, steel, electronics, coal mining, and petrochemicals united in June 1990 to form the third major labor confederation, the National Union Confederation (CNS) or Cartel Alfa. Shortly afterward, the National Trade Union Bloc (BNS) was formed by subway workers and teamsters who also thought CNSLR and CSI-Fraţia were too compromised.

As the union confederations took shape, those vying for national political power sought to co-opt union leaders for their purposes. This took such forms as Ion Iliescu's calling on the Jiu Valley miners to invade Bucharest in January 1990 to disrupt the government of Petre Roman, or Victor Ciorbea being actively courted by the developing Democratic Convention. Thus,

> The unions were the last effort of workers to participate in political power in one way or the other. . . . In the factories the unions tried to control the technical and economic decisions of the leadership. However, at the national level the labor confederations tried to impose political, social, and economic modifications. Not one of these attempts succeeded. However, at the beginning at least, the pressure exercised by the working class through mediation of the unions was sufficiently large to make those seeking power bow to them.[26]

The unions' entry into politics was of uncertain advantage, as it produced disunity in their ranks and declining credibility with the Romanian population. Still, the potential political spoils were sufficiently large to encourage CNSLR and CSI-Fraţia to merge in June 1993, with Ciorbea as president and CSI-Fraţia president Miron Mitrea as vice president. However, Ciorbea was close to the political opposition, the Democratic Convention of Romania (CDR), and Mitrea was allied with the ruling Social Democratic party (PDSR) of president Ion Iliescu (and is currently PDSR deputy chairman). Infighting between the two men soon split their coalition. In the dispute, Ciorbea was supported by only four hundred thousand of the confederation's 2.2 million members. Defeated, they left to found the Democratic Trade Union Confederation of Romania (CSDR).[27]

To be fair, the political infighting was not solely the unions' doing. The Trade Union Act, Law 54/1991, stipulates a complicated and competitive process of union formation and dissolution—and so encourages interunion competition and rupture.[28] The law specifies that fifteen individuals are necessary to form a union, only two unions in the same sector or profession are needed to form a federation, and two federations can found a confederation.[29] Because affiliation with a confederation is necessary for a union to benefit from the National Collective Labor Contract, the law generated the creation of many miniunions, federations, and confederations at all levels of society— local, regional, and national. Though many were formed for sound purposes with sound leaders, others were goaded by charismatic or demagogic leaders seeking union spoils. Even more than the absolute number of labor unions, as Larry Bush suggests,

> There is no logical division of unions based on professions, trade, or industry among the various confederations and federations. Workers in the same industries, and sometimes the same factories, are represented by several different unions, each of which is affiliated with a different federation.[30]

Though there are degrees of overlap, the main confederations are still somewhat based in industrial sectors with different ownership principles and production profiles, differences that produce different interests and orientations.[31] CNSLR-Fraţia is strong in state-controlled autonomous companies (*regia autonoma*) like utilities and petroleum. CSDR, its spin-off, is concentrated in the service wing of the state sector, (e.g., education and health care). Consequently, CNSLR and CSDR seek to maintain state budget interventions for their state-sector members. Cartel Alfa, however, is based more in "commercial societies," privatizing state firms with an "old economy" profile (e.g., heavy industry, mining, and so on). BNS also is based in privatizing state firms in the manufacturing and assembly sector, like automobiles and shipbuilding. Thus, the latter two groups are in favor of more rapid and thorough privatization, industrial restructuring, and legal reform. Cartel Alfa was the chief supporter of the 1997 general strike and the aborted spring 1999 strike.[32] However, with Kosovo in the background, promised increases in state budget subsidies, and rumors of payoffs to union leaders, the other confederations backed out at the last moment.

Fiscal matters also heighten interunion tensions. The unions handle large sums of money and often have access to other resources, like the union culture halls and special shops that CNSLR inherited from the UGSR. Addition-

Table 5.1 Major Romanian Labor Confederations

Union	Date Founded	Constituent Organizations	No. Workers Represented	Political Affiliation	Leader
CNSLR-Fraţia	12-26-89 June 1990 Merged, 6-93	Commercial, Petroleum, Telecom	2.1 million	PSDR (Iliescu)	P. Todoran (also pres. of Syndicate Central)
Cartel Alfa	June 1990	Metal workers, Miners	1.1 million	Unaffiliated	B. Hossu, D. Racolta (U Metal)
BNS	1991	Subway workers, Drivers, Auto workers, Shipwrights	750,000	PD (Roman)	D. Costin
CSDR	Split from CNSLR in July 1994	Food industry, Education	400,000	Ciorbea	

Source: Compiled by author.

Note: Along with the four confederations included in this table, a fifth confederation, Meridian, has also received formal recognition as a signatory to the 1999 Collective National Labor Contract. However, given that it represents only about four thousand workers and is thus smaller than some local enterprise unions, its recognition is considered a legal fluke by the union officials with whom I spoke.

ally, many unions, federations, and confederations maintain stores for workers or have special relationships with other commercial outlets. Rumors suggest that such stores and/or relationships often fatten the coffers of the unions and their leaders. Whether this is so, they point out a serious area of tension and disagreement within and between diverse labor organizations.

Regular and predictable access to member dues is even more significant for confederation coffers than commercial deals are.[33] National statutes peg union dues at 1 percent of a worker's wages, but how much is transmitted from the local to the federations and confederations depends on a range of factors, from personal to ideological. More militant Cartel Alfa, with its charismatic leaders, is generally supported by its constituent organizations. However, the accounts of CNSLR have recently dwindled. In response to questions about this, a CNSLR officer suggested that

This [nonpayment of dues] is a reaction to the situation under Communism when all dues went from workers to the center. People now want to see where their money is going and what it is used for. We would prefer that the center receives the dues and then send it back to locals like in America. We tried to explain this to the locals, but the hardest thing to change in people is their mentality. That is a titanic task.

Thus, the lack of a predictable financial base for the central organizations implicates a union's ability to organize, to inform members and society about union activities and perspectives, and to support members during job actions. Uncertain finances thus severely weaken union prospects and leave the confederations perpetually short of cash for their nationwide activities. This situation, then, contributes to pressures on union leaders for recruitment and retention of members and constituent organizations. This is occasionally fueled by personal animus or individual ambitions. Thus, for example, in the Fâgâraş Nitramonia factory, a separate union affiliated with the League of Jiu Valley Miners split off from the main Chemical Workers union (Cartel Alfa). Others say that the two leaders of this separate union were eager to have a larger say in factory affairs and have a forum for themselves.

ROMANIAN POLITICAL ECONOMY AND THE ACTUAL CONDITIONS OF ROMANIAN LABOR

Of all the impediments to organized labor in postsocialist Romania, none are so problematic as the actual pressures created by the Romanian political economy. These include conditions generated by the country's economic crisis:

1. increasing unemployment
2. enterprise restructuring or outright failure
3. unprecedented expansion of black-market labor
4. rapidly declining living standards
5. employer and government disrespect for labor laws
6. growth of the nonunion workforce

Furthermore, these pressures occur within, and are intensified by, the context of a Romanian institutional culture that encourages extremes of narrow, self-interested decision making and behavior like rapacious state taxation, political egoism, and/or economic profiteering in businesses and in unions. One corrupt practice often cited is how state enterprises of great potential, and with them their workplaces, are made to wither and die. Their demise is effected by a managerial strategy to siphon resources to parasitical firms (*firme capuşe*, literally "tick firms") controlled by relatives and/or clients. As the host firm dies, those involved in unproductive work grow rich at the expense of working people. These conditions and others—like the great salaries and extravagant expense accounts of politicians and state technocratic managers—show how ultimately ineffective unionism has been in influencing appropriate political and economic change. As labor's frustrations mount, dissent and apathy within union locals spills out into local wildcat strikes,[34] demands for wholesale political change, and tremendous pressure on local union leaders.

Unemployment

Massive unemployment, actual and threatened, especially confounds Romanian labor, severely pressuring labor relations and workplace conditions.[35] The actual number of unemployed in Romania is an uncertain statistic. About 12 percent of the Romanian workforce receive unemployment benefits, up from 9 percent as recently as 1998, and is slated to rise to 16 percent by the end of 2000.[36] However, this number hides those who have stopped looking for work altogether and workers from some state enterprises periodically furloughed but retained at 75 percent of their wages (*şomer tehnic*). Statistics also paint an aggregate portrait, though unemployment is regionally variable. In some zones with mixed economies, like Bucharest or the region around Timişoara in the southwest, unemployment is less of a concern. In rural areas like Moldavia or zones dependent on a single industrial sector, like chemicals in the Făgăraş region or hard coal mining in the Jiu Valley, unemployment is high and dominates social and economic relationships and discourse. Earle and Oprescu further distinguish "favored" and "disfavored" state sectors.[37] The former—often CNSLR-Frăţia industries like CONEL, the power monopoly—preserve their often redundant labor forces while the latter, like mining and chemicals, must heavily pare theirs. Such state-sponsored "sectoral whipsawing" especially drives a wedge between union confederations.

Union attempts at job preservation are particularly weakened by recent state programs to entice workers to leave their jobs by offering them large severance packets with regular unemployment. This process of "disponbilization" (*disponibilizarea)* was instituted by various government decrees (*ordonanţe*) beginning in 1997. Severance packets differ based on seniority and on the particular industry. For miners, Ordinance 22/1997 established that those who worked more than fifteen years would receive a severance package worth up to an additional twenty monthly salaries, a sum averaging about 44 million lei, or more than three thousand dollars in 1997 exchange rates.[38] For other workers, severance packages totaled less than one year's salary.

Worker response to the government's offers exceeded expectations, despite attempts by union leaders to dissuade them from "disponibilizing." Visions of quick riches and unrealistic expectations of quickly finding another job prompted many to leave their workplaces. In some zones like Fâgâraş, where young workers immigrate as guest workers to Italy, unions had a particularly difficult challenge in preserving jobs. Similarly, in the Jiu Valley and other mining districts, with the large severance packages and rumors of wholesale mine closings, about 50 percent more workers filed applications than was foreseen.[39] However, with their severance pay spent and unemployment benefits exhausted, workers blame government, their enterprises, and above all their unions and union leaders, adding yet another chapter in the sad tale of tactical victory and strategic loss.

Job loss has many problematic implications for organized Romanian labor. First, it pits active workers against the unemployed, who demonize the unions that are compelled to protect their members. Law 54/1991 on union organization specifies that only active workers can be union members. Thus, the moment an individual leaves his job, he loses all union rights and assistance. Union leaders recognize the potential power of a movement unifying the active and unemployed, but they are stumped to overcome this problem. Meanwhile, the unemployed have few organizations of their own, and even those are severely underfunded.

The demography of Romanian unemployment also adds to tensions between active and unemployed workers. For example, women and youth are more often unemployed than middle-aged men, the bastion of the union movement. Men's position is also supported by an ideology that more often gives preference to the male role in the household despite the extensive economic participation of women throughout Romanian history, especially during socialism. Women constitute about 44 percent of Romania's workforce, but they make up nearly 50 percent of the unemployed, are twice as likely to be unemployed as men, and more often are long-term unemployed.[40] Furthermore, economic stagnation has resulted in hiring freezes in many factories, thus limiting the number of new workers (that is, the young). Though unions do not generally purposefully differentiate between men on one hand and women and youth on the other,[41] this demographic imbalance contributes to a sense in society of the union movement being unrepresentative, whether true or not.

Most significantly, unemployment affects the daily identities and lives of workers in their factories and homes, and it feeds back on relations between unions and their worker constituencies. In interviews in Fâgâraş chemical plants, Jiu Valley mines, and Cluj heavy machinery factories, "stress" is the word that people use to describe their physical and emotional states. There is the stress of increased workloads due to layoffs. There is the stress of class anger emerging from tales of government corruption. There is the stress in family life as standards of living plummet and new, cheaper living arrangements must be found. There is the stress that comes from working an extra job and putting up with indignities to keep it. All these produce worker demands on unions that they are unable to resolve.

Growth of the Nonunion Workforce

The increased number of private-sector and black-market workers undercuts the growth of the union movement. Most of these workers fear joining a union lest they lose their job, while some disparage union membership outright. Large firms based exclusively on foreign capital or joint ventures are often most respectful of unionization, but many smaller enterprises, especially those controlled by Romanian capital, intensively discourage unions among their workers.[42] The expansion of this sector depresses workers' wages and negates hard-won contractual relationships negotiated at the national level. As a spin-off, even managers of state-controlled enterprises seek to prevent or weaken unions in their enterprises by threatening union leaders and workers and by organizing antiunion campaigns.

The fantastic expansion of the labor black market (*la negru*) especially negates labor's agenda. The number of black-market workers has increased steadily in recent years, though the union confederations have only recently made this one of their most pressing issues in negotiations with government and employers.[43] There are many contributing factors to the growth of black-market work. These days of primitive capitalism encourage a certain unscrupulousness among some Romanian business owners, who seek profit by any means possible. More than this, many employers say that because of heavy state employment costs, they are almost forced to hire workers "*la negru.*" Though there are high fines if apprehended, this is not likely.[44] State labor-law enforcement suffers from a lack of field observers and perhaps disinterest.[45] Though the unions counter that "serious business owners" avoid hiring illegal labor, the national political economy makes their complaint futile. Black-market work is even spurred by union members, that is, formally employed workers seeking additional income, though they face fines and a loss of pension if caught.

The growth in the labor black market has a number of unfortunate consequences for labor generally and for organized labor in particular. It also provides a clear indication of the unions' losing war. Black-market work depresses all workers' wages and encourages great abuses of labor. Black-market workers never know how long they will work. Many are promised long stints, but often they are let go after a few months. Black-market workers are also frequently forced to perform other work, including personal services, than that for which they were hired. Some women, for example, are accosted by their bosses for sexual favors and threatened with firing if they resist. According to an International Labor Organization report, workplace sexual assault and harassment has become epidemic in Romania. [46]

Unscrupulous employers often pay black-market workers less than agreed upon, as these workers have no recourse for redress. Since many black-market workers are also legally employed elsewhere, they absorb many potential jobs for the unemployed and remove many potential members from union rolls. However, those who accept dual employment ultimately harm themselves. Because of the growth of black-market work, even workers with formal labor contracts suffer illegal labor practices. Wage kickbacks are demanded of them when hired. In Fâgâraş, 300 DM (approximately $146) was the common figure. Sometimes, workers are even expected to partially pay state-mandated employer payments.

Unions, Union Leaders, and Labor Sentiments at the Local Level

The weakness of labor is reflected in the lot of many committed local union leaders. Their offices are understaffed and poorly endowed. They work almost nonstop and receive minimal assistance from the national confederation. Their commitments to the union movement are tempted everyday as they see vast, rapid fortunes made by others, mainly illegally. They are occasionally even offered the chance to do so themselves. Those who avail themselves of these opportunities bring charges of corruption upon the whole union movement, alienating members and further eroding labor's long-term position in Romanian society. The position of union leader is also precarious, locally and at the federation and confederation level. Locally, as discussed below, union leaders are frequently trapped in contradictions between management and union members and are at a loss to mediate this relationship. At more comprehensive levels, Law 54/1991 stipulates that local union leaders elected to federation or confederation positions are considered to have left their workplace. If a leader loses a federation or confederation election, he faces the likelihood of unemployment.

One of the greatest difficulties for Romanian union leaders today is the need to walk a fine line between frustrated workers and often-uncertain management. The relationship between union leaders and rank-and-file members is often a personal one. Though some rank-and-file members occasionally do not know the name of the confederation to which their union belongs—nor sometimes the name of their own union—they all know the union president. One of the most extreme personal relationships was between Miron Cosma and the Jiu Valley miners. Many miners today speak of how Cosma provided them with personal benefits and gifts to their children, and he supported their health needs by demanding beds in tuberculosis sanatoria and taking workers on mass outings to the countryside.

However, Cosma was not alone. In fact, leader-member relationships seemed personal in almost every enterprise where I conducted interviews. Workers appeal directly to union presidents for extra financial help, medical aid, or other kinds of interventions. Presidents seem to know the specifics of every member supplicant. However, satisfying member requests is increasingly difficult today for the pinched unions, which only frustrates members further. Union members expect results from their leaders, often more than the leader can deliver. As one union president told me, "I spent days negotiating an increase in wages, and the main response that people had was 'is that the best you can do (*numai atîtâ*)!' " Beyond complaints and requests, members waver between poles of apathy and militancy. The declining participation of members is one of the most frequently heard gripes of union leaders.

In their relationship with management, union leaders range from fairly compliant CNSLR-Fraţia leaders of *regie autonom* to highly militant leaders of privatizing manufacturing and machine-tool industries. Most union leaders, even militant ones, still strongly support compromise between management and labor that, they say, is needed to keep their enterprise afloat and maintain member workplaces. Still, such an orientation to compromise is often interpreted by rank-and-file members as knuckling under to management demands. In the locals of the League of Jiu Valley Miners, the union leadership (with one or two exceptions) increasingly supports management's position on the restructuring of the industry. The miners, however, see this as capitulation, and as a result they have tended to reject participation in the union. Rumors of corruption among union leaders also alienate members. Prodded by a concern for their members' perception, even though sympathetic to management, many union leaders participate in wildcat strikes organized by workers but illegal by terms of Law 15/1991. Though supporting these strikes places the leader in legal jeopardy, as one local president said, "If you are not willing to stand up for the workers, they will not believe in you."

Labor's Response

Frustration at failed reform thus explains the constant political engagement of the Romanian labor movement at the national level and the ready militancy of local unions. As one journalist recently put it:

> In essence, the government have found themselves in a "Catch-22" situation. They are facing increasing demands from the Romanian population but are also dealing

with severe economic restrictions which prevent them from offering any immediate financial appeasement. Consequently, the Romanian population (read: labor) is becoming more and more frustrated with their own economic position, and they are venting these frustrations on the government. [47]

Nationally, the demand for changes of government gives the illusion of labor's power, but it actually only shows labor's lack of alternatives. In response to Romania's economic crisis, the confederations generally adopt the same basic positions: reform has failed due to corruption, greed, and collusion among the political and business classes. Labor cannot address these problems because the legislative deck is stacked against them. Hence, the only solution is national political action.

At the national level, labor's common positions are visible in the demands over which the confederations threatened the spring 1999 general strike.[48] These included

1. adopting legislation defining the responsibilities of public officials and controlling their behavior
2. creating a legislative body to recommend reorganization of labor relations, including a) creating a labor tribunal, b) modifying the law on collective labor conflicts (Law 15/1991), c) modifying planned legislation on public pensions and introducing legislation to punish those utilizing black-market labor
3. modifying the state budget to allow salary indexation, to create a larger social fund, to apply the law regarding food subsidies for disadvantaged groups, to liberalize collective bargaining, and to increase funds for education, research, and culture
4. modifying the functions and activities of the State Privatization Fund (FPS) through a) more precisely delimiting its activities in the privatization process, b) publishing a list of its members, c) devising the rapid privatization and termination of the FPS
5. modifying state fiscal policy
6. revising the system of taxes and contracts for electrical and thermal energy, gas, water, gasoline, transportation, and communications with an eye toward decreasing prices for these products and services
7. urgently elaborating and implementing a development strategy for the national economy for every sector of activity, to be determined by all social partners (that is, workers, unemployed, pensioners, and patrons) to enable a program of social measures
8. resolving the financial blockage of local economic units with a restructuring of debt for a five-year period, with a grace period of six to twelve months

This long, complex agenda is truly remarkable for its comprehensiveness. However, that same comprehensiveness is part of the problem. Fully five of eight agenda items (1, 2 [excluding "c"], 4, 5, and 7) are issues of national political importance as opposed to bread-and-butter labor issues. Also, the disparate agenda gives the different confederations ample raw material for disagreements in policy that emerge in the political process. Thus, CNSLR-Fraţia and (to a lesser extent) CSDR are self-styled Social Democratic organizations, while Cartel Alfa considers itself Christian Democratic. The former, fearing inroads against their largely autonomous workforce, support go-slow reform and fear the privatization demands of the IMF and World Bank. Meanwhile Cartel Alfa pushes for rapid privatization, and legal reform, and it generally agrees with international institutions' policies toward Romania.[49] Furthermore, the disunity and inconsistency of labor exacerbates the uncertainty of Romania's weak governments and intensifies labor's poor public image.

LABOR, CULTURE, SOCIETY, AND IDENTITY

In the introduction to the conference for which this chapter was written, Stephen Crowley and David Ost suggest that uncertainties in postsocialist labor are likely to contribute to uncertain identities of workers and their representative organizations.[50] In Romania this is certainly the case. Though workers generally, and unionized workers in particular, are still imbued with strong though waning senses of their social roots and common interests, the frustrations of failed reform actively call these into question. The structural confusion of the union movement, union participation in electoral politics, the differentiation of the workforce into factions—favored and disfavored, active and unemployed, legal and illegal—and society's hyperbolized accusations of labor's role in Romania's economic downturn all keep labor off balance and diffuse its focus to issues over which it has little control.

Labor's agenda is especially challenged by the generally poor opinion of the union movement throughout Romanian society, itself influenced by the discordance between labor's mission and its actual activities. Labor's image is further tarnished by its former favored position in socialism and its allegedly anachronistic status in the new commercial, service-oriented economy. It is criticized for its demands for greater worker benefits and its failure to secure those same benefits. Labor is dismissed due to the lavish and corrupt lives of some leaders compared with the meager lives of workers. Images of older workers in hard hat (*casca*) and shop tunic (*şalopetâ*) are especially discordant with contemporary Romanian aspirations. Workers have thus largely disappeared from print and broadcast media, except when they are severely criticized for their actions that cause economic blockages and other problems. Mass media advertise financial instruments and upscale, high-tech items. "Help wanted" ads are rife with listings for speakers of foreign languages (preferably English), the computer literate, and the commercially adept.

As labor declines, then, its position and image are diminished with Romania's successive governments, with the multinational and international lenders and investors on whom the country is increasingly dependent, and in the perceptions of the general population. Despite labor's support of necessary and meaningful reform, workers in Romanian society are thought to be a main obstacle to reform, with unions ranked near the bottom in national opinion polls. In a late 1997 poll, for example, only banks and bankers scored lower.[51] Similarly, in a poll conducted for the Soros Foundation in June 1997, only 21 percent expressed confidence in the unions, the lowest score for all institutions, including banks.[52] The opinion of unions has declined even further since the protests of October 1997, the threatened general strikes of 1998 and 1999, and the *mineriada* of January 1999.

Thus, despite the general recognition of workers' plight, there is remarkable antipathy to those who answer economic decline through organized action. Workers have become "others" in Romanian social and political discourse. As politics has changed from an ethnic-based to class-based system,[53] Romanian workers, the paragons of the socialist state, are reviled, distanced, and readily blamed—often by themselves—for both the battles won and the losing war effort.

PROGNOSIS FOR LABOR: A PROACTIVE AGENDA

The picture painted above is a decidedly glum one. Nonetheless, there are some bright spots in labor's future and increasing possibilities for labor's goals to be legitimized and implemented. Romania's fervent desire and steady efforts to enter the European Union are especially hopeful in this regard. One goal of the EU enlargement process is to improve the relative situation of workers in the candidate states to prevent emigration of Eastern European workers and relieve pressure on workers' wages in the EU core itself. In the EU's own language, candidate states must evidence "the existence of a functioning market economy as well as the capacity to cope with competitive pressures and market forces within the union."[54] While this, of course, does not guarantee respect for labor and its issues, it nonetheless requires labor's concerns be taken into consideration.

As a response to such international pressures, there has been the salutary development of an effective tripartism in Romania that combines labor, management, and government in a permanent body to thrash out labor-related issues. Though labor is concerned that the tripartite commission be given real power and not be merely an advisory entity, tripartism has been effective most recently in assisting in the adoption of the new collective labor contract. Analogously, the Romanian labor movement has been increasingly involved in other international bodies such as the International Labor Organization (ILO) and the International Confederation of Free Trade Unions (ICFTU).

Still, despite the general improvement in the quality of union structures and management, labor's practices have yet to bear fruit. The militancy bred by frustration is understandable, at times laudable, but it is frequently counterproductive. Romania needs labor peace for investment, for productivity, and for the citizenry's own sense of stability and predictability in social life. Labor needs labor peace to rebuild support in society generally and to rethink its organizational and political strategies. The ultimate success of the country will lie in the willingness to compromise that all parties bring to subsequent labor negotiations—a willingness to sacrifice certain claims in favor of the common good, to take incremental steps in achieving labor goals, and to participate in a system of checks and balances so that mutual trust between labor, government, and employers can take root.

Thus, in place of lists of nonnegotiable demands or demands so comprehensive that basic bread-and-butter issues are lost in the detail, labor must set out its program clearly and indicate specific measures and ordered steps necessary to achieve each goal. For example, all parties can show a common interest by developing a list of objectives and steps to attack black-market work and related labor abuse, which sits at the heart of so many of labor's other issues. Similar attention can be given to specific mechanisms for enforcing the new national labor contract.

Beyond this, labor's challenge is to get its own house in order to improve its position within Romanian society, its bargaining power with government and employers, and its own internal organization. This first means a thorough review of union relations with Romania's political parties and a forswearing of formal participation in the political process in favor of intensifying labor's strong advisory role in the national economy. For labor to carry the day against widespread corruption, unions and their leaders must themselves be squeaky clean. Attention must be turned to methods to better streamline and systematize labor union organization and serve the needs of union members through such institutions as credit associations. Additionally, the role of, and

support for, the agenda of women, youth, disadvantaged minorities, and the
unemployed also must be highlighted by current labor unions, even if current
legislation prevents formalizing such relationships.

In closing, the challenges for Romanian labor in the immediate future are
great. They are magnified by an array of cultural pressures emanating from
the powerful relationships and practices that define emerging capitalism in
Romania. Rising to them is crucial due to economic decline and the health
and demographic challenges workers experience. Still, though labor's frustration at the inertia of economic change and the corruption of the political
classes is palpable and legitimate, Romanian workers have to break the failed
cycle of protest and decline through unity, principled and positive action, and
creative engagement. Only in this way can the victory in local battles ultimately translate into a winning war effort in national political economy.

NOTES

1. *Adevarul*, January 23, 1992, 3–5, translated by National Technical Information Service, Springfield, Va.; "Contracte Colective de Munca," in *Monitorul Oficial al România.
Parlamentul României—Camera Deputatilor*, July 18, 1999.

2. Ilie Stefan, "Putere de cumparare a populatiei se deterioreaza pe zi ce trece," in
Adevarul, June 30, 1997, 5.

3. Vladimir Rodina, "Romania: Unions Running out of Steam," in *The Warsaw Post*,
June 26, 1994, cited in Lexis-Nexis European News Service.

4. Eliade Balan, "Atentie la seismograf!," in *Romania Libera On-line*, March 26,
1999.

5. Simona Popica and Carmelia Csiki, "Stegarii au renuntat la revendicarile salari-
ale," in *Monitorul de Brasov*, November 12, 1999, 1, 3.

6. "Romania: Government Frees Prices, Unions Close Ranks," in *International
Labour Review* 132:3, 285–86; "Majoritatea silentioasa demonstrand pentru reforma,
Democratie, normalitate si ordine de drept," in *Romania Libera On-line*, January 23,
1999; "Striking Romanian Miners Clash with Police on March," in *The New York Times*,
January 20, 1999, A11; Ion Gâf-Deac, "The Strategy of Restructuring the Mining Industry
in Romania," in *The Mining Industry on the Threshold of the XXI Century: Proceedings
of the 16th World Mining Congress* (Sofia, Bulgaria: World Mining Congress), 90–99;
David A. Kideckel, Bianca E. Botea, Raluca Nahorniac, and Vasile Soflâu, "Discourses
of Despair: A Critical Ethnography of Labor and Crisis in Two Romanian Regions," in
*La ricerca antropologica in Romania. Prospettive storiche ed etnografiche, SMAC, Studi
e Materiali di Antropologia Culturale, nuova serie*, vol. 3, C. Papa, G. Pizza, and F. M.
Zerilli, eds. (Naples, Italy: Edizioni Scientifiche Italiane, forthcoming); Maria Larionescu,
Sorin Radulescu, and Cosima Rughinis, *Cu Ochii Minerului: Reforma Mineritul în România*, (Bucharest: Editura Gnosis, 1997).

7. John Lloyd, "The Last Bandit King: The Plight of Romania's Miners and Their
Arrested Leader, Miron Cozma," *Financial Times* (London), February 20, 1999, 1. The

miners first marched on Bucharest in January 1990 and again in June 1990 at the behest of then–acting president Ion Iliescu. In January they threatened the opposition building against the FSN and Iliescu. In June they broke up a tent encampment of protesters in Bucharest's University Square. Dorel Abraham, "Post-revolutionary Social Phenomena in Romania: 'The University Square' and the Violent Collective Behavior of June 13 to 15," in *Romanian Journal of Sociology* 1:1–2, 121–30; Sam Beck, "Toward a Civil Society: The Struggle over University Square in Bucharest, Romania, June, 1990," in *Socialism and Democracy* 13:135–54; Gabriela Gheorghe and Adelina Huminic, "Istoria mineriadelor din anii 1990–1991," in *Sfera Politicii On-line*, Number 67, 1999.

8. Adina Croitoru, "Reforma in minerit a fost negociata," in *Romania Libera*, January 20, 1999; Joe Cook, "Miners' Victory Sets Back Reform Hopes in Romania," in *Financial Times* (London) January 23, 1999, 3; Ron Synovitz, "The East: Labor Leader Says Unreformed Unions Fail Workers," in *RFE/RL Newsline*, December 2, 1997.

9. Mircea Dinescu, "Incordarea Puterilor în Stat," in *Academia Catavencu* 6:1–2, February 16, 1999.

10. Gheorghe Brehoi and A. Popescu, *Conflictul Colectiv de Munca si Greva* (Bucharest: Forum, 1992); Larry Bush, "Collective Labor Disputes in Post-Ceauşescu Romania," in *Cornell International Law Journal* 26:2, 373–85; Edzard Ockenga, "Trade Unions in Romania," in *Transfer: European Review of Labour and Research* 3:2, 313–28; "Law on the Settlement of Collective Labor Conflicts," in *Parliament of Romania* (Springfield, Va.: National Technical Information Service, 1991).

11. "Marile Centrale Sindicale—Nemultumite de Procentul de Indexare a Salariilor," in *Cartel Alfa*, http://www.robust-east.net/greva/ind2.html, 1997.

12. Dan Perjovschi, "Mineri buni, mineri rai," in *Revista* 22:3, 1–3, January 19–25, 1999.

13. Among other provisions in effect at the end of the Ceauşescu regime, Romanian factory work teams not only had production quotas to meet but also had restrictions on the use of energy and raw materials in meeting these quotas. Failure to limit energy and raw materials usage resulted in holdbacks of salary.

14. See, for example, Oscar Hoffman, Simona Raseev, and Dinu Tenovici, *Clasa Muncitoare din România în Conditiile Revolutiei Tehnico-Stiintifice* (Bucharest: Editura Academiei, 1984); David A. Kideckel, *The Solitude of Collectivism: Romanian Villagers to the Revolution and Beyond* (Ithaca, N.Y.: Cornell University Press, 1993), 189.

15. Valeriu Bârgau, "Oamenii Subpamîntului," in *Planeta Carbunului*, Gligor Hasa, ed. (Bucharest: Editura Eminescu, 1984), 115–70; E. J. Hobsbawm, "Man and Woman: Images on the Left," in *Workers: Worlds of Labor*, E. J. Hobsbawm, ed. (New York: Pantheon, 1984), 49–65; Mircea Pospai, *Amintiri din Valea Luminii: Viata si Activitatea Minerilor din Oltenia* (Craiova, Romania: Scrisul Românesc, 1978).

16. Ion Oprea, *Istoria Românilor* (Bucharest: Editura Didactica si Pedagogica, 1970), 486. See also Nicolae Tic, *Rosu pe Alb* (Craiova, Romania, 1977). The contemporary period has produced a wide range of works challenging the socialist interpretation of these events. For example, a booklet published by the National Peasant Party—Christian Democrat (PNTCD), suggests the Lupeni strike was an attack by striking workers on nonstrikers and a conflict between local government and the Ministry of Labor. See Victor Isac, *Problema Muncitoreasca în Viziune Nationala* (Bucharest: PNTCD Cenaclul "Gândirea Româneasca," 1994), 11–12. In contrast, a recent work published on the seventieth anni-

versary of the Lupeni strike avers the miners were killed in the confusion of a government attack on them. See Ioan Velica, *Lupeni '29: Blestemul Carbunului* (Self-published manuscript).

17. The adage "They pretend to pay us, so we pretend to work" was also operative in Romanian factories. In Romanian this is rendered as *"Ei sa fac ca ne platesc. Noi ne facem ca muncim."*

18. Similarly, in agriculture, peasants were organized in cooperative farms and represented by their national organization, the National Union of Agricultural Production Cooperatives (UNCAP).

19. Beyond these functions, the unions were barely visible in Romanian workplaces. Their general irrelevance is suggested by the lack of a mention of the local labor union in a 320-page monograph on the history of a major socialist chemical factory. See Traian Herseni et al., *Combinatul Chimic Fâgâraş: 50 de ani de existenta.* (Sibiu: Intreprindera Poligrafica, 1974).

20. Gail Kligman, *The Politics of Duplicity: Controlling Reproduction in Ceauşescu's Romania* (Berkeley: University of California Press, 1998).

21. The miners were repaid as, over the next years, the Ceauşescu regime organized the mass migration of workers from other regions into the Jiu Valley mines, thereby weakening the miners' political unity and transforming the mining industry and region in the process. See Kideckel et al., "Discourses of Despair."

22. Mihai Sturdza, "The Labor Movement," in *Report on Eastern Europe*, July 27, 1990, 36.

23. A comprehensive summary of the history of Romanian organized labor from 1990 to 1992 is found in Bush, "Collective Labor Disputes."

24. The NSF emerged immediately in the first days of the anti-Ceauşescu revolution, allegedly as an ad hoc group. However, Romanians soon thought it to be a cabal of former Communist officials with a few other individuals thrown in for window dressing. Ion Iliescu and Petre Roman were its leading members, and Romanians thought they used the NSF structure for the preservation of their own power.

25. Bush, "Collective Labor Disputes," 385–86.

26. Vladimir Pasti, *România în Tranzitie: Caderea în Viitor* (Bucharest: Editura Nemira, 1995), 256–58. According to Florian, Pasti considers union actions to be one factor behind the failure of democracy in Romania. Florian, in contrast, suggests union actions are entirely democratic. See Radu Florian, "Probleme Critice ale Tranzitiei Societatii Românesti," in *Societate & Cultura* 34:3, 3–9 and 35:4, 3–10.

27. To a great extent, the CNSLR-Fraţia/Ciorbea-Mitrea alliance was clearly an unnatural one, combining both right-wing and left-wing elements.

28. "Law on the Settlement of Collective Labor Conflicts."

29. Ockenga, "Trade Unions in Romania," 317–18.

30. Bush, "Collective Labor Disputes," 387.

31. Stephen Crowley, *Hot Coal, Cold Steel: Russian and Ukrainian Workers from the End of the Soviet Union to the Post-Communist Transformations* (Ann Arbor: University of Michigan Press, 1997).

32. "General Strike on October 14, Bucharest, Romania," in *Cartel Alfa*, http://www.robust-east.net/union/oct.html, 1997. Last accessed August 8, 2000.

33. *Report: The Activity of the Daily Board of U METAL Trade Union Federation, March 1998-March 1999* (Bucharest: U Metal, 1999).

34. Ion Iordachel, "Relatii între salariu, bugetele de familie," and "si conflictele colective de munca," in *Munca si Progres Social* 13–14:1–2, 1993, 29–33.

35. David A. Kideckel, "Left Behind: Labor, Poverty, and Subalternity in Contemporary Romania," paper delivered at annual meeting of the American Anthropological Association, Washington, D.C., November 1997; David A. Kideckel, "On the Margins: State-Space and Subject Formation in Romania," paper delivered at annual meeting of the American Anthropological Association, Philadelphia, December 1998.

36. Christine Allison and Dena Ringold, "Labor Markets in Transition in Central and Eastern Europe, 1989–1995," in *World Bank Technical Paper No. 352* (Washington, D.C.: The World Bank, 1996), 58; J. S. Earle and C. Pauna, "The Incidence and Duration of Unemployment in Romania," in *European Economic Review* 40:3–5, 1996.

37. J. S. Earle and G. Oprescu, "Romania," in *Unemployment, Restructuring, and the Labor Market in Eastern Europe and Russia*, S. Commander and F. Coricelli, eds. (Washington, D.C.: The World Bank, 1995), 234.

38. *Ordonanta privind unele masuri de protectie ce se acorda personalului din industria miniera si din activitatile de prospectiuni si explorari geologice* (Bucharest: Monitorul Oficial al României, 1997).

39. Lamaraso Group, *Social Assessment of Mining Sector Restructuring in Romania: Monitoring Social Impacts and Mitigating Adverse Impacts* (Bucharest: The World Bank, 1998), 5.

40. Comisia Nationala Pentru Statistica, *Anuarul Statistic al României 1996*, (Bucharest: Comisia Nationala Pentru Statistica, 1996), 152; Earle and Pauna, "The Incidence and Duration of Unemployment," 831; Walter M. Bacon Jr. and Louis G. Pol, "The Economic Status of Women in Romania," in *Women in the Age of Economic Transformation: Gender Impact of Reforms in Post-Socialist and Developing Countries*, Nahid Aslanbeigui, Steven Pressman, and Gale Summerfield, eds. (London and New York: Routledge, 1994), 55–56; "Women Make Up Nearly 50 Per Cent of Unemployed in Romania," in *BBC Summary of World Broadcasts*, Part 2 Central Europe, October 8, 1998.

41. The actual position of women and youth in existing labor unions is an idiosyncratic one and depends much on the type of industry, the local leadership, the history of women in local unions, and a range of other factors.

42. Dorel Racolta, "The East-Central European Trade Union Movement Since 1989," speech at Hunter College, City University of New York, May 2, 2000.

43. Laura Birtalan, "Munca la negru atinge dimensiuni fara precedent," in *Adevarul*, July 26, 1999, 8.

44. Mihaela Codin and Mirele Zecheriu, *Starea de Somaj si Comportamentul Somerilor*, (Bucharest: Institute for Research on the Quality of Life of the Romanian Academy, 1992).

45. State regulations on hiring, remuneration, and social benefits of labor are extensive. Employers typically pay an additional 40 percent of a worker's salary for various benefits, about 38 percent on profits, and annual interest rates of 65 percent to 85 percent on business loans. This compels many to avoid such costs by hiring at least a portion of their workers illegally.

46. Andrew Bolger, "Management Violence at Work," *Financial Times* (London), July 20, 1998, 13.

47. Catherine Lovatt, "Restless in Romania: Civil Unrest Causes Problems for the

Government," in *Central Europe Review* 1:22, November 1999. http://www.cereview.org/ 99/22/lovatt22.html. Last accessed August 8, 2000.

48. *Memorandum în legatura cu negocierile privind lista de revendicari commune pe temen scurt convenite la întâlnirea Primului-ministru Radu Vasile cu confederatiile sindicale Cartel Alfa, BNS, CNSLR-Fraţia, si CSDR la data de 21 aprilie 1999* (Bucharest: Comisia de Monitorizare, 1999).

49. Certainly not all the recommendations of the IMF sit well, even with Cartel Alfa. Most recently, the IMF's recommendation for Romania to close the COMTIM pork production complex in Timişoara while financing a similar complex essentially "down the road," in Kecskemeti, Hungary, was used to illustrate the unfair treatment of Romania in international circles. Nonetheless, as Bogdan Hossu, president of Cartel Alfa indicates, "If people loan you money, they have a right to expect things for that money."

50. Stephen Crowley and David Ost, "Class Dismissed: Labor Quiescence in Post-Communist Transformations," unpublished manuscript, 1999, 2.

51. Georgeta Muntean, *Atitudini Politice, Civice, si Morale ale Populatiei României Fata de Procesul de Tranzitiei: Faza Unic* (Bucharest: Research Group Romania Ltd., 1997), 21.

52. *National Public Opinion Poll* (Bucharest: Center for Urban and Regional Sociology, 1997), 29–30.

53. See also Kazimierz Slomczynski and Goldie Shabad, "Systemic Transformation and the Salience of Class Structure in East Central Europe," in *East European Politics and Societies* 11:1, 1997, 155–89; Vladimir Tismaneanu, "The Quasi-Revolution and Its Discontents: Emerging Political Pluralism in Post-Ceauşescu Romania," in *East European Politics and Societies* 7:2, 1993, 309–48.

54. *European Union 2000 Enlargement*. http://www.europa.eu.int/comm/enlargement/ intro/criteria.htm. Last accessed March 7, 2000.

Chapter Six

Bulgarian Trade Unions in Transition: The Taming of the Hedgehog

Grigor Gradev

What is the most independent state in the world?
Mongolia. Nothing depends on it.

(Joke popular prior to 1989)

"Independence," like "private," will remain among the key words that describe the transition from the world of "socialism" to democracy and a market economy after 1989. It has been used as a spell, a magic circle placed around civic organizations, businesses, or political structures to protect them from the demons of the past.

Trade unions were not excluded from this process, and the freedom to make their own policies immediately confronted them with severe challenges. More often than not, trade unions were caught in a catch-22 situation. The road to the promised land of Western lifestyles and security passed through a deep and turbulent sea of economic and social transformation.

If governments had to operate in an almost constant state of limited sovereignty due to international constraints, then how much space was open for trade union policies? In other words, what strategies make unions strong during deep transformation—focusing on current needs and endangering the future, or promoting reforms while compromising survival in the hope of securing a better future? Also, who receives this better future?

It is hardly possible to embrace either option completely even in a single case. Within a highly dynamic process of change, strength in one situation may turn into a major problem in the next—for society, for union members, or for the organization itself. This is especially true for Bulgaria, where transformation has amounted to a recurring cycle of crisis and stabilization. In these circumstances, trade unions need to be sensitive to shifting grounds of power, and they need to respond flexibly and make strategic choices while preserving the integrity and identity of the organization. It is thus indicative that the symbol of the Confederation of Independent Trade Unions in the initial period of its existence was the hedgehog.

It is not difficult to argue that, despite the row of successes in particular policy areas or individual cases, trade unions face a continuing loss of power. The key channels for political influence, tripartism, and the social dialogue system, have been degraded by the government and persistently emptied of their main content as institutions of representative democracy. Such pressures have also eroded the prospects for an effective civil society.

These negative trends, however, should be assessed cautiously, and neither the dangers nor the positive opportunities should be underestimated. The new economic and industrial relations systems are not far beyond their initial stages of development, and the constellation of interests in these fields is markedly unstable. As the European Commission stated it in its 1998 report on Bulgaria, the social dimension is still in its embryonic stage, and the really big work still lies ahead.

This chapter is aimed at providing an analytical overview of the transformation of trade union power in the period of transition. It is organized into five parts:

- the impact of unions on the initial transition
- the evolution of successor and newly independent trade unions
- the nature of these unions' political alliances
- the shifts in the locus of power of enterprises undergoing restructuring
- the attempt to create meaningful social dialogue between unions, employers, and the state[1]

1986–1989: THE SELF-MANAGEMENT EXPERIMENT

Following decades of accumulating tension, with mounting difficulties in the economy, the rise of Solidarity in Poland in the 1980s threw a big rock into the swamp of socialist labor relations in Bulgaria. The authorities quickly embarked on intensive economic reforms, including redesigning the enterprise and "democratizing" the workplace.

The search for solutions started in the 1980s and soon included the self-management of the enterprise as a channel for higher motivation, productivity, and efficiency. The pillars of the project were the formation of the work brigade and the basic collective—all employees of the enterprise. The forums for representation—the brigade assembly, the General Assembly of the employees (or representatives), and seats on the Economic Council of the enterprise—formed the main power structures of self-management inside the organization. At the corresponding levels, they elected brigade leaders and managing directors by voting, but nominations had to be approved and supported by an authorized Communist Party body.

Trade unions were at the core of the experiment and kept it running for a couple of years. Yet in the conditions of central planning and a shortage economy, the idea became politically risky. The elections for directors revealed the hidden power of the collectives. In some cases people had to vote several times but still rejected the party-approved nominations. In many others they stood by their choices against party preferences. Although exceptions, these were clear signals to the political elite.

Due to the obvious failure of the project and to avoid further dangers, self-management was soon replaced with a new model of economic management. However, the "transmission belt" concept of unionism was irreparably torn and so cleared a space for real trade union action. It was in the period of transition when these efforts bore fruit.

Socialism with a market touch was introduced in 1988, when Decree 56 was adopted by the Council of Ministers, heralding the virtual end of self-management. The new model for economic development attempted to make the rigid structures and processes of central planning more flexible and dynamic. It also sought to open some space for private initiative. It allowed state enterprises to make certain decisions at their own discretion—80 percent of production was defined by the plan and 20 percent by the enterprise, for which they had to find their own resources and markets.

With this, the fulcrum of labor relations shifted from the labor collective to the managing director. The change meant that a tacit step in the direction of classic labor-management roles had been taken. It increased the contradictions between the potential of a participatory labor code on the one hand and a de facto push for a classical management prerogative on the other. The clearest indications were a couple of small conflicts that ended with strikes, the first in decades. Trade unions were in support of the actions, and they were not suppressed, even receiving official (party) media attention. Obviously, the shadow of Solidarity and Gorbachev's perestroika kept the authorities extremely cautious.

With the deepening of the economic crisis, trade unions found themselves more often treated as scapegoats, and their limited area of activities became limited still further. In 1988 the government took back parts of the unions' traditional social functions—such as social security, rest, and recreation—without even consulting the leadership of the unions. In a leading article in the Communist Party daily, trade union "interference" in management was claimed to be a major reason for the poor performance of enterprises. These events, perhaps limited in themselves, pointed to serious problems that were now emerging in the open.

The growing crisis was confirmed by the attitudes of trade union members in surveys conducted by the Research Institute for Trade Union Studies. On the eve of the tenth congress of the Central Council of Bulgarian Trade Unions in 1988, only 4 percent of the surveyed employees believed that production problems should be included on the agenda of the union congress (as was traditional in the communist period). In a survey taken in autumn of 1989, a majority agreed with the statement "trade unions exist outside and independently of the needs and interests of the people" and two-thirds of those surveyed stated that they never turned to the unions for assistance when in need. Activists themselves considered their union jobs as "distributors of vacation vouchers." Still, only 10 percent stated they would leave the organizations if membership became voluntary. The need for a change, the need for other unions with "genuine" trade union policies, was more than obvious.

In February 1989 a group of intellectuals launched a new, alternative, and independent trade union. It was called Podkrepa (Support). Initially, they were engaged mostly in the defense of human and ethnic rights and were directly involved in the explosive conflict between the government and the Turkish minority. For that, the leaders were soon arrested, and the organization resumed activity after they were freed in the autumn of 1989.

These developments in the 1980s foresaw the collapse of the system of industrial relations immediately after November 1989. Even before the real change of the political system, the pillars of employment security, the monopoly on trade union representation, and Communist Party control over "organized" labor had already disappeared. The establishment of a new industrial relations system, compatible with a market economy and political democracy, would have to start virtually from scratch and be based predominantly on assumptions and experiences from abroad. However, numerous structural and habitual dependencies—in the areas of legal norms, economic institutions, and patterns of organizational behavior (especially those stemming from the reforms of the 1980s)—remained in place and created certain expectations.

THE POLITICAL CONTEXT OF TRANSITION

The drive toward the independence of trade unions has been guided by the need to draw a strong line of demarcation between union submission to the Communist Party and a new, real trade unionism.

The first specific feature of the transformation process was the simultaneous building of new political and economic systems, a process dominated by political concerns. The need for the liberalization of the economy and society, for restructuring and privatization, dictated a central role for the state. This role was strengthened further by the reform model pushed by international financial institutions. This model was negotiated at a supranational level and entailed the implementation in top-down fashion of blueprints coming from outside the country. All this required guarantees that only the state could provide.

The second feature was the transition's "resource gap"—the lack of capital to enable massive restructuring and privatization at a tolerable social cost. Special significance was given to foreign investment and participatory forms such as voucher privatization or management-employee buyouts. The transition gave rise to a new phenomenon, which might be called "network capital"—an alliance of business and political groups that gradually began to take over privatization and restructuring.[2]

In this way, the core of the transition process—decentralization and the withdrawal of the state, especially from economic life—was dependent on the state itself. The political implications of this included the following:

- Governments repeatedly attempted to centralize resources, narrow the decision-making process to a small group at the top, and effectively exclude other public interests from access. Thus, the management of reforms, including especially the fate and operation of state-owned enterprises, was left to ministry administrators, creating fertile ground for "network capital."
- Each political party's terms in government became a crucial chance for securing its control over the economy, society, and the personal future of party leaders.
- The imperative nature of the agreements with international financial institutions provided a convenient cover for governments to shift responsibility away from themselves and promote narrow political or group interests within reform policies.
- The bipolarity of the political system along ideological extremes, which generates pressure on political actors to identify with either the "left" or the "right" (or "red" or "blue") squeezed out centrist policies, whether social-democratic or liberal. The resultant high level of polarization of society and politicization of economic and social reforms has constantly hindered the emerging civil society.

The main result has been the inherent instability of the political process. Bulgaria changed eight governments in the first ten years of transition. The political support enjoyed by each government has followed a common trajectory over time, despite differences of political orientation. With each term of office, the incoming government enjoyed a high degree of legitimacy across social and economic groups, and then within a year experienced a growing isolation from political, social, and business interests and relied instead on outside sources of legitimacy, above all the International Monetary Fund (IMF).

In the turbulent beginning to the transition, the rhetorical shield of trade union "independence" proved an extremely useful tool in forging a new identity for trade unionism and differentiating industrial relations as a separate field of action within the reforms. The process started immediately after the shifts at the top of the Communist Party on November 10, 1989, and moved in several directions.

Two weeks later, the old Central Council of Bulgarian Trade Unions came out with a declaration of independence from the Communist Party. The act heralded the official collapse of the socialist labor relations system. However, it came too late. Within the next couple of months, the union intensively disintegrated in terms of institutional structures and membership.

A wave of labor unrest flooded the country—more than five hundred conflicts until March 1990, of which about only 10 percent were initiated by Podkrepa and about 5 percent by the once-official union. For the newly created Podkrepa, the situation offered unique chances for quick organizational development, and they were used quite successfully as the organization grew every day. The new union provided the core of the emerging democratic opposition, the Union of Democratic Forces (UDF), commonly referred to as the "blue" side of the political spectrum as opposed to the "red," the former Communist Party. The UDF was a broad popular coalition at the beginning, though with time it evolved in the direction of Christian Democracy.

The sweeping changes resulted in the total restructuring of organized labor. Spontaneous industrial actions and self-organization through strike committees replaced old trade union structures, and strike committees selected new leaders on the spot.

The last key step was the resignation of the entire leadership of the old Central Council of Bulgarian Trade Unions. The new provisional team combined its policy of transformation with pressure from below. At an extraordinary congress a new organization was set up, the Confederation of Independent Trade Unions in Bulgaria (KNSB), whose policies focused on reforms, social dialogue, and collective bargaining. Yet the problem with restructuring the midlevel bureaucracy, especially in certain federations and branch unions, took years to solve.

The major result of such changes was a plurality of options for people to move from the old to the new type of union, which avoided the dilemma of having to choose to be in or out of unions altogether. Such a range of choices was important because the new trade union Podkrepa was highly active on the political scene, emulating Polish Solidarity and becoming a founding member of the United Democratic Forces. Still, society as a whole was more reluctant to move so quickly, and the Socialist Party (as the Communist Party was renamed) won the first democratic elections, in June 1990. Thus, the accumulated tension in the trade union field splashed horizontally among diverse organizations, and overall union density did not suffer a sharp decline.

The freedom to undertake action at the grassroots level and to enter an organization of one's own choosing resulted in a quick redirection of union dynamics from the bottom up, and it led to the creation of organizations on a variety of organizational principles. Some of the old industry federations split or disintegrated, opening a space for new ones along with industrial or branch unions, craft unions, professional organizations, and even autonomous single-enterprise unions. This organizational dynamism can best be seen in the high number of member organizations of KNSB, which reached seventy-eight in the first years of the transition, as the statute allowed enterprise unions to affiliate directly with the confederation. Member organizations in the new confederation were almost totally independent from the central union leadership, even at times of common national actions. Over the years, such arrangements have posed serious challenges to the effectiveness of the confederation, and they have strongly limited the flexibility and speed of its response.

While paradoxical at first glance, the newly created Podkrepa adopted much more unified and strict organizational principles that were based on industrial federations combined with strong and active territorial (regional) structures, as Solidarity had done in Poland. Using the advantage of starting from scratch, and with an aura as an important force for democratic change, the organization set its own criteria for accepting individual members, such as barring people linked in any way with the Communist Party or the old trade unions. With time, however, these limitations hindered the organization, impeded its growth, and were abandoned. Nevertheless, the union was left with a membership with substantial homogeneity in their political orientation—pro-UDF, easy to mobilize, and effective in action.

TRADE UNIONS AND
POLITICAL PARTIES

The role of Podkrepa in the broad UDF coalition did not mean these two groups were in full agreement. Podkrepa provided the social base for the

UDF in the initial period, and the union did so out of political motivations. The trade union contributed decisively to the UDF victory in the 1991 elections, which brought the first democratic government to power. At that point, Podkrepa left the coalition and continued its independent policy. The union sought to assess the particular policies and steps of the government on their own merits and react accordingly.

The separation of Podkrepa from the UDF completed the transformation of trade unions into a truly independent labor movement that was a potential barrier to the aspirations of political parties in Bulgaria. The two major trade union confederations maintained an independent policy and working relations with all parties (with the major exception of Podkrepa and the Socialist Party). This made internal union decision making more complicated because it transferred party rivalries to inside the trade unions.

KNSB's membership has been a political mosaic, though it has strong clusters of pro-Socialist Party members. The decisive moments for the confederation came with the decision to join the national strike against the Socialist Party government in November 1990 and at the extraordinary congress in February 1992, when the independence of the union was firmly established. The confederation was preserved as the biggest union in the country, and it successfully wiped out attempts to paint it as a crypto-communist institution. The confederation, however, retained an image of indecisiveness, being difficult to mobilize and slow to act.

Podkrepa's politics became more complicated. After the 1991 elections, it formed a substantial group of about seventy members of Parliament (MPs), who were often referred to as the "Podkrepa lobby." The most important achievement of the lobby was probably the inclusion of KNSB in the law calling for the confiscation of the property of totalitarian organizations. However, the lobby was not of much help when the government suspended the social dialogue mechanism and adopted openly antiunion policies. In fact, within several months the lobby disappeared, and the MPs continued in political or business careers.

The experience of the 1990s clearly points to two outcomes in party-union relations. Any attempts to create party-oriented trade unions ended with failure, even when they participated in the social dialogue mechanism. In a survey by the Institute for Social and Trade Union Research at the beginning of 1999, about two-thirds of KNSB members unconditionally insisted on keeping political parties at a distance, stating they would cancel their membership if this orientation were changed. All attempts to openly use trade unions for political purposes, including in election campaigns, ended with failure for the political parties and led to tensions inside the unions.

Special attention has to be paid to the Bulgarian "winter of discontent" of

1996–1997, when all actors of political and civil society joined forces to replace the governing Socialist Party, which had brought the country to the brink of economic and social collapse. The campaign was started by KNSB in December 1996, but the results were marginal without support from Podkrepa or the political opposition. Then in January a united offensive was launched with support from citizens and the political opposition. At a key moment, both trade unions and a newly created union-civic organization, Promyana, joined together, and strikes broke out in key enterprises and branches of industry. This pressure, combined with other political factors, compelled the Socialist Party to withdraw from power.

After ten years of party-union interactions, it has become increasingly clear that the big political problem of trade unions is the tacit hostile attitude of the political elite, whether "red" or "blue," toward representative democracy. In fact, the influence of civil society has withered away over the years. Thus, trade unions had little opportunity to work with reliable political partners. For example, in the wake of the "winter of discontent" trade unions signed a "Social Charter" and an "Action Plan" with the newly elected UDF government. Neither was fulfilled, and the social dialogue was used instead to marginalize the trade unions.

Such deficiencies sharply increase the importance of trade unions—the only other source of political power besides the opposition parties. With the proclaimed evenhanded approach of unions toward all parties, there seem to be two options for trade unions. First, they can use their industrial power to protest excessive reforms. For this they need a motivated membership. Second, while continuing to proclaim independence, they can accept tacitly the policies of the governing party in the hope of fostering their organization, but this is at the risk of losing long-term political influence. For these reasons, trade unions seem increasingly unable to influence the political process at a time when the legal and institutional base of the new economy is being created. Thus, there is a paradox: Political independence, so helpful at the start of the transition, may become a trap for trade unions in the later stages of the development of democracy and a market economy.

Together with these political developments, two levels of industrial relations—the local and the national or confederation level—have provided the major arenas for action. We will examine each in turn.

LOCUS OF POWER ONE:
THE SHIFTING ENTERPRISE

The enterprise was the center of local political and social activities in the period of socialism. This is why the transformation of the enterprise turned out to be the most difficult part of the reform process, as evidenced by the delay in the privatization of state-owned companies. With the need for economic restructuring, trade unions faced the dilemma of the survival of employees vs. the survival of the enterprise, which inevitably exerts pressure not only on union members but also on the balance of forces at the workplace. The good news for unions was that the legal framework of privatization stipulated that the trade union organization, collective agreements, and mechanisms for partnership would be transferred to the privatized firm. So the "day after" has most often been business as usual.

The transformation of the core of the socialist economy, the enterprise, entailed two distinct actions. The first was the dismantling of central planning (or marketization), and the second was privatization. However, unlike the usual approach in the West, restructuring did not necessarily precede privatization, and most often it had to be accomplished by the new owners.

Dismantling the System

The initial period of change was the time of the hedgehog, when the balance of forces inside the enterprise typically shifted in favor of trade unions. With the removal of Communist Party control, the field was cleared for a new type of enterprise management and a new labor relations.

The collapse of central planning pressed the enterprise for concrete solutions. Initially, this "creeping" enterprise autonomy breathed fresh air into the mechanisms of self-management, which were still in place and mandated by the Labor Code. Along with the existing general assemblies—meant to be a voice in overall decision making—there were powerful instruments for trade union influence, like the obligatory consent of the union for any redundancies and the right to demand the resignation of the director on accusations of antiunion behavior.

Labor's advantages, however, did not always lead to conflict with management. Reactions ranged from replacing old party-appointed directors with competent professionals to coalitions of management and unions seeking to split off the enterprise from the higher-level associations imposed by the state. Thus, the first steps in economic restructuring started in a quite spontaneous manner, and they were essentially defensive because the associations aimed at centralizing enterprise profits (especially in hard currency) and distributing accumulated debts back to the enterprise.

Ironically, the centralized structure of the economy further strengthened labor's advantages. The internal linkages and dependencies readily transferred tensions upward, and conflict in one branch or key enterprise easily turned into a political problem for the government.

Probably the best illustration of this is the case of the electronics plant in Stara Zagora in the summer of 1990. The plant was one of the biggest in Eastern Europe, and it was an important link in the division of labor and integration within the COMECON countries. It was tightly connected to Bulgarian and Soviet civilian and military production. Mainframe computers (and other electronic equipment) produced at the plant were the key commodity traded between the two countries and was also a major source of hard currency for the Bulgarian state.

In August 1990 the employees from the unit that produced hard-disk devices, about 460 people—members of Podkrepa, both workers and managers—embarked on a strike action. Within a week the plant of several thousand employees practically came to a standstill. The long list of demands included an attack on the director, charges of financial mismanagement, demands for restructuring the plant, and the possibility for employees to privatize their units. The key demand concerned representation on the general assembly of the company, so that the body could be used to decide these and other issues.

The conflict continued for several weeks and generated internal tension with the workers from other units before it was settled. Before the strike, computers from Stara Zagora were exchanged for Russian oil, and the failure to keep the deadlines for delivery from Bulgaria could have endangered the oil supply of Bulgaria's only refinery. This would have expanded the conflict because members in the refinery were ready to stop work, and the lack of fuel would have seriously destabilized the Socialist Party government. The strike stopped short of that point, but the plant incurred heavy losses. It never fully recovered, and by 1999 there were less than one thousand employees (out of nearly six thousand originally).

The task of deposing the Socialist Party from power, which it had won at the polls in June 1990, was accomplished in November 1990 when Podkrepa called a national action demanding the resignation of the government. KNSB soon joined this action.

The "hedgehog period" marked some of the peaks of trade union power in the transformation period. Unions enjoyed considerable freedom to pursue autonomous strategies and create significant pressure from below. They forced political actors to take the union confederations into account and opened a space for the inclusion of labor policies within the reform process.

At the same time, it was to some extent a self-defeating exercise. The democratic political forces enjoyed the power of unions, especially that of Podkrepa, when they were in opposition, but those same political forces also realized union power could be used against any government. Hence, when the first UDF government came to power in 1991, it declared that trade unions had too much power and that they hindered reforms. That attitude has been consistently shared by most of the governments and political elite since then.

Privatization and Beyond

The privatization process was dominated by three factors: the lack of capital for a quick transfer of ownership, the simultaneous change in political and economic realms, and the social factor—the way the social costs of the transformation placed political pressure on ruling parties. The combination of these factors led to various dilemmas, the solutions to which were provided by a number of sources:

- Foreign direct investment, especially multinational corporations (MNCs), have terms and conditions of work that are much higher than the average for the country, provided one is not let go in the initial stage of personnel reduction. Trade unions found themselves facing a more complicated international context for which they were largely unprepared, especially the problem of shifting identities of employees under new personnel management policies.
- Participatory methods of privatization such as mass (voucher) privatization and management-employee buyouts were schemes that gave rise to a lot of unclear ownership and corporate governance, which led to growing tensions in the collective bargaining process. However, these schemes also provided a way to overcome insufficient capital and meet the requirements of the IMF for the establishment of a private sector and a tight budget. Assets and responsibility were also, at least formally, shifted away from the state. Thus, the possibility for applying direct pressure on the government through enterprise actions was significantly reduced.
- "Network capital" was the symbiosis of politicians, bureaucrats, and business groups for promoting their mutual interests in dominant positions in the emerging market economy. Such networks are aimed at maximizing profit and, even more so, at developing strategies for shaping reforms. State bureaucrats would use "network power" to keep seats on managing boards of state companies until there were favorable conditions to retain their positions in the eventual privatization.

The last of these, network arrangements, threatened the future of the enterprises, but they were not entirely against immediate trade union interests. Such management bodies could be more easily pressured because of the possible political implications for the state bureaucrats and their political patrons. At the same time, trade union pressure could be a useful argument for management in bargaining for state resources.

Networks often maintain supplies and sales through network channels. In successful cases this guarantees the continued operation of the company—and the jobs and incomes of the employees—at least for a period of time. Then the effect of decapitalization strikes. It took the attempts of three governments to remove the director of a steel mill near Sofia (which had about sixteen thousand workers and a factory integrated with hundreds of other enterprises) on accusations of networking. Each attempt was met with fierce resistance from trade unions in the plant, which made the respective governments quite cautious in their actions.

The enterprise director played the key role in privatization. Intersecting interests and lines of power exposed the director to pressures from trade unions, the ministry, or the network. The manager could secure substantial freedom if he or she were skillful enough to play one interest against the other. This fueled the drive of the government for recentralizing the economy, most clearly expressed in the periodic purges of directors since 1992 once each new government came to power. The fate of directors became one of the most common issues in labor conflicts, especially after 1995. Whatever demands are put forward in such conflicts, they tend to focus on the director, and the outcomes often depend on the match of interests between the government and the union.

The attitudes of trade unions toward privatization differed significantly from those of Western trade unions. Bulgarian trade unions strongly supported the idea from the very beginning, provided there would be effective protections from the inevitably high social costs. Their approach was based on the need to improve the performance and competitiveness of the companies to secure jobs and maintain living standards. As experience demonstrated, state-owned enterprises—starved for investment, at some points even for operation capital—found it difficult to survive.

Trade unions were also in the pincers of IMF requirements for a tight budget and a restrictive wage policy for state-owned companies. The budget for each year involved a mechanism for regulating growth in wages that would permit a "negotiated" pay raise at the workplace of typically about 1 percent. Should wages rise more than this amount, the enterprise would be charged a tax with a steeply rising scale that varied over the years. For instance, the penalty could be a 50 percent tax when wages increased more than 1 percent and could reach up to 700–800 percent for a wage increase of 4 percent or more. These restrictions serve as a powerful incentive for employees to accept privatization to gain the ability to freely bargain over wages.

Government policies have kept unions mainly on the periphery of decision making about the privatization process. Initially, union representatives sat on the Supervisory Board of the Agency for Privatization, but the union seats were later eliminated. Still, trade union organizations put a lot of effort into promoting privatization, helping people define their interests, and participating directly in the voucher rounds of acquiring shares of companies. KNSB created its own privatization fund, which later turned into a quite successful holding company, and Podkrepa was a major shareholder in another privatization fund. Throughout the years, national and local unions tried almost everything to facilitate the process by finding partners and convenient privatization schemes or obtaining credits for management-employee buyouts.

As noted above, a combination of factors delayed the real transfer of ownership and maintained an image of the economy that was unattractive to foreign interests. The inflation rate has been extremely high—consumer prices increased by a factor of 1,204 after 1990. With the restrictive incomes policy, wage growth was severely depressed, and in 1998 real wages were still 55.7 percent below their 1990 level. At times of total collapse, like February 1997, wages fell to twenty-eight dollars per month for industry and thirteen dollars for the public sector. The share of wages in total household incomes declined to 40.1 percent in 1998.[3] The real figure would be lower still if the impact of the informal economy were included. This sector is estimated to account for about 40 percent or more of GDP.[4] In 1996 more than 35 percent of those employed had a second job in the informal economy, and at least one in ten workers received additional payments "under the table."[5]

The persistent uncertainty that such change entails inevitably influences employees' attitudes toward trade unions. A January 1999 study by the Institute for Social and Trade Union Research of two thousand KNSB members revealed the problem of attitudes toward unions at the workplace. The result clearly confirmed that the membership decline in KNSB (the confederation is one-sixth of its size before the start of the transition) has been accompanied by a considerable increase in alienation from trade unions. This was most clearly expressed in union members's answers to a question concerning from whom they would seek assistance for problems on the job. Thirty-three percent of the members responded that they would try to manage the difficulties themselves, 53 percent would turn to the trade unions, an almost identical number (52.4 percent) would look to their immediate supervisor, and 43 percent would approach the director (more than one answer to the question was possible). Ten years after the start of transition, trade unions are viewed by their members as no more effective in resolving problems than their bosses.

The overall impact of the economic reform, especially privatization, has created strong pressures on trade unions and generated quite consistent trends toward the decentralization of industrial relations and the fragmentation of union structures at lower levels. The process has created fertile ground for the seeds of "company unionism" and visibly eroded the mobilization potential of unions for national actions.

LOCUS OF POWER TWO:
THE SOCIAL DIALOGUE PUZZLE

In the beginning of the transition, two strategic lines of reasoning drove trade union policies:

- that trade unions had to be active participants in the transformation process and not simply the passive recipients of policy decisions
- that they needed to create a system of industrial relations based on social dialogue[6] and free collective bargaining

To a considerable extent, the second strategy would have provided the power base for the first, and the achievements of the first strategy would have increased the efficiency of the second. In reality, the gradual weakening of the social dialogue institutions permitted the continuing marginalization of trade unions in the design and implementation of reform policies.

Tripartism and collective bargaining formed the basis on which the new Confederation of Independent Trade Unions (KSNB) was created and developed. In the initial period, Podkrepa relied more on direct conflict and strikes for dismantling the system. Later, it also joined the process of tripartism.

A high point for the social dialogue mechanism was the agreement for social peace in 1991, which allowed the start of economic reform and achieved the main targets of macroeconomic stabilization. Thus, the way for intensive restructuring and privatization was opened. However, the momentum was lost by the first UDF government, which redirected the policy not toward changing the economy but instead toward the restitution of property (mainly real estate) nationalized during the communist period. This delayed the key transformations and allowed networks to form and accumulate resources. The policy destabilized parliamentary support for the government, which together with heavy conflicts in key industries and neglect for social dialogue, led the government to resign in the autumn of 1992.

The new Labor Code of 1993 turned the initial shaky achievements of tripartism and collective bargaining into a well-structured system of industrial relations. It tried to diminish state interference in the relations between the social partners and provide more freedom for joint decision making. As noted previously, the periodic attempts of governments to recentralize decision making, coupled with the restrictions imposed by the IMF reform model, significantly eroded the scope of tripartite bargaining. In this sense, the configuration of the interaction has not been tripartite but quadripartite, with the main partner—the IMF—outside the system.[7]

The delay of economic reforms had an additional consequence. It made the nature of employers, their interests, and their organizations persistently unclear. It also contributed to the low efficiency of tripartite negotiations and to a certain discrediting of such democratic means of resolving differences.

The tripartite system was designed as a top-down operation, and in that it matched the general logic of the reforms. The parameters agreed to at the higher level of negotiations, starting with the national tripartite body, were obligatory for lower levels. There, the parties were free to negotiate better terms and conditions, provided that the enterprise could afford it or find a way to avoid the restrictions of the IMF.

The procedures for recognition as a nationally representative union follow similar logic. The state awards representative status to union organizations that meet the requirements of the Labor Code, based on quantitative membership criteria. Then the representative confederations transfer the status to the federations and lower-level unions, and they in turn transfer it to the workplace organizations. In the first couple of years after the 1993 law was enacted, only officially recognized organizations could engage in collective bargaining at the workplace, and only their leadership was protected against dismissals. These requirements became an instrument of control for union hierarchies over lower union levels. However, the effect should not be overestimated because the statutes of the organizations often defined loose obligations to higher levels. Moreover, amendments to the labor law since 1996 allow all organizations at the enterprise to enjoy equal rights and participate in collective bargaining.

The most vivid and drastic violations of the law were made by the last two governments, led respectively by the Socialist Party and UDF. In the first round of recognition in 1993, only KNSB and Podkrepa qualified for national representation. When the Socialist Party came to power, another union was recognized on the basis of an application that had been previously rejected. A couple of days before withdrawing from power, in an impulse of revenge, the government added three more previously rejected unions. After the "winter of discontent" (1996–1997), the new UDF government promised to clear the tripartite system of illegal entrants through a trade union census. Still, the government's first step was to install the pro-UDF Promyana to the tripartite negotiating table. Not surprisingly, with seven trade union representatives and four representatives from the employer side, the social dialogue process was effectively blocked. After strong trade union pressure, the promised census of members started in 1998; these confirmed the representative status of only KNSB and Podkrepa, and all party-based unions were excluded.

The tripartite system resulted in some positive outcomes, even under the difficult conditions of the transition.

- The Labor Code changed the basis of labor relations in the direction of democracy and market economy.
- The social partners developed a new culture of interaction, which stressed negotiated solutions and consensus, and they managed to avoid the establishment of adversarial relations in the first ten years of the transformation.

However, the above list exhausts the positive outcomes of tripartism. The failures seem to make a more substantial list:

- The political powers—Parliament and government—never accepted the social partners and especially trade unions as responsible agents of change, and they jealously protected their sovereignty from encroachment by the social partners.
- In terms of quality of life and work, tripartism did not deliver obvious and lasting gains to the social partners. Rather, as part of a negative-sum game, it served to distribute losses more equally.
- The tripartite mechanism was not able to solve significant labor conflicts or consolidate more cooperative approaches in industrial relations.

Trade union policies have mainly dealt with the need to react to government attempts to downplay and neglect the institutions of social dialogue. Unions have twice demonstratively left the tripartite bodies—in 1994 and almost throughout 1996. With sharp deviations up and down, on the whole the process has declined in importance.

Thus, usually the only winner has been the government, which could maintain its public image by reporting the success of the necessary restrictions to the IMF and receiving approval and encouragement in return. The policy of the Socialist Party government has been overtly antiunion, and with the collapse of the economy it paid the price. The new prime minister of UDF, a person of Thatcherist orientation, obviously drew some lessons from the fate of the first UDF government and has since applied a subtler marginalization of trade unions. The government did not confront trade unions openly, and it appointed the former vice president of KNSB as minister of labor and social policy. The government also provided union leaders and actions with visibility in the mass media, particularly on state-controlled television. Meanwhile, the government proceeded easily with policies defined by it alone.

The exclusion practices involve simple technical tricks like providing unions with the drafts of annual budgets, laws, or other documents (as required by law) two days or less before a meeting, where their opinions might be aired. At the same time, union experts in politically explosive fields, such as privatization or wage and social policy, are often included during the drafting stage and excluded during the final stage.

After 1997, under conditions of a currency board and accelerated reforms, the contradictory evolution of trade unions within the tripartite framework has become clear. First, the number of laws that work against the interest of trade unions has expanded to include legislation prepared with substantial trade union input or passed through the tripartite machinery in the drafting stages, only to be replaced with the initial government version when put before Parliament. Second, most industrial actions in the last two years, linked to intensive restructuring and privatization, more often than not have been organized without consulting or even informing higher-level trade union bodies. As such, they proceeded more in the form of civil society actions than strikes per se. At the bottom of that phenomenon lies the unhidden reluctance, particularly of the KNSB leadership, to engage in activities that would generate tension with the government and its policies. Third, not surprisingly, there has been a continuing decline in union membership.[8]

At the end of 1998, Podkrepa presented a protest memorandum, threatening to withdraw from the tripartite mechanism. The evaluations of both the prime minister and the social partners at the end of 1998 confirmed that the results of the social dialogue differed considerably from the expectations of the spring and summer of 1997. Still, KNSB accepted the results of the negotiations despite periodic criticisms, and Podkrepa is not confident enough to undertake a more decisive action without the support of the bigger organization. Thus, tripartite relations continued to develop as a peculiar permissive regime that the government could switch on and off, depending on the needs of the situation, especially the need to spread responsibility for its policies to others.

CONCLUSION

The developments in industrial relations and trade unions unquestionably speak of the growing weakness of trade unions in the transition period. Such a conclusion cannot be an unexpected outcome given the process of transformation, including the liberalization of the economy, and the deep restructuring and privatization of state assets. Similar processes in the West led to a deep erosion of union positions in the political process. Still, the results in Bulgaria cannot be defined in such unidimensional terms.

The "transition" has developed as a series of crises and stabilizations. In this sense, the transitional character of the processes, based on uncertainty, is far from eliminated, and the rearrangement of interests on a real market basis still lies ahead. In the political domain, the "red-blue" bipolar political model has come under mounting pressure and may change at any time.

Crisis situations have been fruitful periods for unions because they provide the possibility to demonstrate the power of consensual politics and social dialogue. The withering away of the Socialist Party's old-fashioned political profile as "red" will significantly weaken the charge that trade unions are acting in favor of the past when they disagree with other political forces.

The argument for union decline also needs to be judged cautiously. It is basically backed by quantitative changes, while in qualitative terms there is a completely new system of industrial relations in place, and the change itself is a source of positive dynamics. It can be facilitated by enlarging the European Union through the introduction of the well-established labor and social standards of the European social model. Finally, the unions need to identify the advantages of independence in the new market environment and use them for the benefit of their members and the wider society—and not only for their organizational advancement.

NOTES

1. Some of the sources consulted in the writing of this chapter include Pekka Aro and Paula Repo, *Trade Union Experiences in Collective Bargaining in Central Europe* (Geneva: ILO, 1997); Maurice Ernst, Michael Alexeev, and Paul Marer, *Transforming the Core: Restructuring Industrial Enterprises in Russia and Central Europe* (Boulder: Westview Press, 1996); Daniel Vaughan-Whitehead, ed., *Reforming Wage Policy in Central and Eastern Europe,* (Geneva: ILO, 1995); Stephen Hill, Roderic Martin, and Anna Vidinova, "Institutional Theory and Economic Transformation: Enterprise Employment Relations in Bulgaria," in *European Journal of Industrial Relations* 3:2, 1997, 229–51; International Labor Organization, *The Bulgarian Challenge: Reforming Labor Market and Social Policy* (Budapest: ILO-CEET, 1994); International Labor Organization, *Republic of Bulgaria: Poverty in Transition* (Geneva: ILO, 1998); International Labor Organization, *Republic of Bulgaria: For a New Incomes Policy and Strategy* (Geneva: ILO, 1998); Krastyo Petkov and John Thirkell, *Labor Relations in Eastern Europe: Organisational Design and Dynamics* (London: Routledge, 1991); Krastyo Petkov and Grigor Gradev, "Bulgaria" in *Labor Relations and Political Change in Eastern Europe: A Comparative Perspective*, John Thirkell, Richard Scase, and Sarah Vickerstaff, eds. (London: UCL Press, 1995); Kenneth Spenner, Olga Suhomlinova, Sten Thore, Kenneth Land, and Derek Jones, "Strong Legacies and Weak Markets: Bulgarian State-Owned Enterprises during Early

Transition," in *American Sociological Review* 1998; Guy Standing, "Globalization, Labor Flexibility and Insecurity: The Era of Market Regulation," in *European Journal of Industrial Relations* 3:1, 1997, 7–37; John Thirkell, Krastyo Petkov, and Sarah Vickerstaff, *The Transformation of Labor Relations: Restructuring and Privatization in Eastern Europe and Russia* (Oxford: OUP, 1998); John Thirkell, Boyko Atanasov, and Grigor Gradev, "Trade Unions, Political Parties and Governments in Bulgaria, 1989–1992," in *Parties, Trade Unions and Society in East-Central Europe,* Michael Waller and Martin Myant, eds. (Newbury House: Frank Cass, 1994).

2. The term "network capital" is suggested by Endre Sik, "Network Capital in Capitalist, Communist and Post-Communist Societies," working paper #212 (Notre Dame, Ind.: The Hellen Kellog Institute for International Studies, University of Notre Dame, February 1995).

3. Data from the Ministry of Labor and Social Policy.

4. World Bank estimates in International Labor Organization, *Republic of Bulgaria: Poverty in Transition* (Geneva: ILO, 1998), 5.

5. Y. Hristoskov, G.Shopov, and I. Beleva, "Non-Institutionalised Employment and Self-Employment," unpublished survey data, Sofia, 1996.

6. The ILO social dialogue is centered on tripartism promoting the participation of trade unions and employers in the formulation and, where appropriate, implementation of national policy on social and economic affairs affecting labor. See A. Trebilcock, *Towards Social Dialogue: Tripartite Cooperation in National Economic and Social Policy Making* (Geneva: ILO, 1994). Within the European Union, social dialogue forms the core of the so-called European social model with a much wider sociopolitical perspective—a combination of solidarity, consensus, long-term foresight, and economic efficiency. Naturally, it may involve a broader range of actors and forms—national economic and social councils, employee information and consultation systems, other interest and pressure groups, consumers, cooperatives, and so on. See W. Kowalsky, *Focus on European Social Policy: Countering Europessimism* (Brussels: ETUI, 2000).

7. K. Petkov, "Shadow Partner," paper presented at the pre-Congress meeting on Eastern Europe of the XVI World Congress of the International Confederation of Free Trade Unions, Brussels, June 1996.

8. In 1989, the membership of the Central Council of Bulgarian Trade Unions was over 4 million (based on the number of people employed in Bulgaria and compulsory trade union membership, *Statistical Yearbook 1989,* [Sofia: National Statistical Institute, 1990]). Following the 1999 census, KNSB membership was approximately 680,000, an almost sixfold decline. At the same time, Podkrepa had roughly 154,000 members, and there were thousands of union members in other unions who did not qualify for national representation.

Chapter Seven

The Cost of Nationalism: Croatian Labor, 1990–1999

Marina Kokanović

Are workers and trade unions in Croatia today strong or weak? The answer is contradictory: Organized workers in Croatia today are both. They are strong because they have simply survived and because the union movement has not disappeared due to the conditions of war or the collapse of the nation's economic, social, and welfare infrastructure. They have survived the deindustrialization of the country and pressure on, and even the murder of, trade union leaders. However, they are weak because trade unions (and other segments of civil society) do not have any real influence on the creation of social reality, labor and welfare legislation, tax policy—or, in a word, the living and working conditions of workers. Officially, trade unions are social partners, but in reality workers are just an object of authoritarian and unscrupulous rule.[1]

The problems workers face in Croatia stem in part from the lack of developed civil and democratic traditions. Social development in that direction was violently stopped by the war (which lasted from August 1991 to August 1995), the rise of nationalism and exclusivity, and the lack of tolerance. People in Croatia are only now learning (though very quickly as of late) that there are no "innate rights." Rights can only be gained through struggle, personal involvement, civil courage, resistance, and personal activity.

Trade unions are learning too—resistance and dissatisfaction with the existing situation is growing; they are asking for social dialogue, mutual decision making, and the establishment of democratic institutions through which the trade unions would have a real influence on the decisions of vital importance for workers. The strength of the trade unions is seriously limited by an extremely high unemployment rate (while the official rate is 19 percent, the actual rate is closer to 30 percent) and the mass poverty of the laboring population. Croatian society is not used to such huge social differences. The descent of large numbers of people below the subsistence minimum, which is taken for granted in Croatian society, destroys the potential for civil society, including the trade union movement.

The Croatian worker has lost the factory she worked in, her workplace, the possibility to ensure a decent life for herself and a future for her children. Workers are also bereft of the possibility to influence their own lives, sentenced to struggle for survival from one day to another. Thus, they become insensitive to the injustices, the repression, and the lack of freedom; they lose their self-respect and the dignity of existing through one's own work.

The basic interest of the ruling elite and the circles accompanying it— material gain and fast accumulation of wealth by any possible means—has created a social climate in which an injustice, an individual misfortune, or an accident becomes the private problem of the individual. The irresponsibility of the government brings about the irresponsibility of the individual, as well as apathy, anger, and withdrawal from social engagement, including in one's own trade union.

GENERAL ECONOMIC TRENDS

In Croatia in the past nine years, approximately seven hundred thousand people lost their jobs. The current gross national product (GNP), despite a slight increase in recent years, amounts only to 83.2 percent of the GNP in 1990. In 1998, GNP per capita amounted to $4,663, whereas in 1990 it amounted to $5,186. The level of production has only now reached the level of production of 1990.

The reality in which Croatians have been living the past nine years is reflected in the following: At least one in five potential workers is unemployed, one in nine workers does not receive a wage at the end of the month, and almost two-thirds of the population struggle to survive with incomes that have led them to the verge of poverty. Meanwhile, a small part of the population (2–3 percent) benefits from the transformation and privatization of the economy, all of which creates social tensions.

It is almost impossible to distinguish how much the current social situation in Croatia is a consequence of the transformation from communism to capitalism and how much of it is a consequence of the war—including the redistribution of public expenditures to finance the military, the burden of refugees and displaced persons, the lost markets, and so forth.

In Croatia the shock of transition on the labor market has been much more intensive than any other shock since World War II. The largest decrease in employment occurred between September 1990 and September 1991, when more than 248,000 of those employed in the state sector lost their jobs.[2] In that period, unemployment officially increased by 110,000 people, while 54,000 workers retired. That leaves 84,000 people who apparently either left the labor force or were employed in the informal economy. According to a survey on the labor force conducted in 1996 by the National Institute for Statistics, employment in the state sector decreased by 678,000 workers from 1990 to 1996. Unemployment rates increased from 8 percent in 1990 to more than 18 percent in 1998, whereas the unemployment rate in 1999 reached 19.6 percent (as of March 1999). If we included in the calculation of the unemployment rate workers who do not receive wages, the revised unemployment rate would amount to 29.4 percent. The consequence, according to trade union estimates, is that approximately 25 percent of the labor force works in the informal economy.[3]

WAGES AND NONPAYMENT OF WAGES

The transformation and privatization in Croatia has been accompanied by a number of individual strikes—as many as three hundred strikes per year, according to the Organizational Department of the Autonomous Trade Unions of Croatia (UATUC)—particularly strikes for nonpayment of wages. In a large number of companies, wages have not been paid or have been late, with delays ranging from a couple of months to several years. This has led to an increase in the number of workers not receiving wages. From 1993, when 4.4 percent of workers were not receiving wages, the percentage increased to more than 5.8 percent in 1994, to 8.4 percent in 1996 and 1997, to 12 percent in 1998, and to 15 percent in 1999. The period of wage delays has increased as well, from three months on average in the early 1990s to more than six months on average currently.

In 1991 and 1992, real wages decreased drastically, while in 1993 they decreased less. From 1994 to 1997, real wages increased. Official analyses on changes in purchasing power indicate that despite an increase in real wages in past years, wages expressed in terms of internal purchasing power reached only 80 percent of wages from the prewar period. However, signed collective agreements did result in an increase in wages, despite the fact that from 1992 to 1996 the government of the Republic of Croatia conducted a restrictive policy on incomes. The policies were characterized by the limitation of wage increases and related benefits. Until 1999, fourteen branch collective agreements, approximately six hundred collective agreements on the company level in industry, and four collective agreements in the nonindustrial sector

(that is, culture, health care, social welfare, education in elementary and secondary school, and science) were signed.

Given inadequate data, trends in earnings over the past nine years cannot
be precisely quantified. However, the data at our disposal indicate that
although average earnings have increased, this is largely the result of a small
number of employed people with high earnings (the ratio of the lowest to
highest earnings is 1:700, according to the data of the Money Transfer Institute). Even with this growing inequality, the increase in average wages is still
not sufficient to reach the level of the prewar years.

Before 1996 the average monthly worker's wage in Croatia did not cover
even half of the cost of living for a family of four. After 1996 the situation
improved somewhat, but at the beginning of 1998 it worsened again due to
the introduction of value-added taxes of 22 percent.

Over the past several years, only 1.7 percent of the number of employed
people had incomes higher than the minimum living costs of a family of four.
If we use the United Nations' criteria in determining poverty (according to
which, one person needs four dollars per day), we are faced with a grim fact
that almost 37 percent of the population of the Republic of Croatia—one person out of three—are poor. These data illustrate the economic and social
environment in which trade unions have been operating that have shaped their
choice of strategies and methods.

THE DIVIDED AND FRAGMENTED
TRADE UNION SCENE

Currently, there are some 350 trade unions in Croatia, some thirty trade union
associations,[4] and five trade union confederations.[5] From late 1989 to early
1990 a whole range of new trade unions appeared, particularly in transportation and education, even before the first democratic parliamentary elections.[6]
However, these new unions were established within the existing confederation of the Union of Trade Unions of Croatia. The constituent congress of a
new organization, the Union of Autonomous Trade Unions of Croatia, was
held May 12–13, 1990, in Zagreb, where after confrontations between old
and new trade unionists, reformers within the former confederation won elections for the leading positions. One result of these confrontations was the separation of several of the new trade unions and the establishment of a new
trade union confederation, the Confederation of Independent Trade Unions of
Croatia, on June 28, 1990. Some other trade unions remained unaffiliated
with any union confederations.

Meanwhile, some political parties, particularly the ruling party, tried to put some trade unions under their control. In response to the strike of metalwork-ers and textile workers (affiliated with the Union of Autonomous Trade Unions of Croatia) that was announced for December 1990, then–prime min-ister Josip Manolić attacked trade unions on national television, stating that they were working against the state. Manolić announced that a new union would soon be created as the only appropriate trade union with which the state would negotiate. The Croatian Union of Trade Unions (HUS), whose name was later changed to the Croatian Association of Trade Unions, was founded on December 29, 1990, under the auspices of the Croatian Demo-cratic Union, the governing political party in Croatia.

The ruling party also took advantage of the war and related suffering to manipulate people's feelings and shape public opinion about national and social priorities, that is, on whether the top priority should be the defense of the country or social concerns. Thus, it managed to weaken the trade union struggle and the whole movement, and it practically silenced the left wing of the political spectrum. Further fragmentation and changes on the trade union scene were mostly a result of conflicts of personalities, arrogance, and the financial interests of trade union leaders.

Trade unions in Croatia remained pluralist for a long time. According to estimates of the UATUC International Department, the total trade union membership, which in 1990 amounted to 90 percent of the employed (as in most socialist countries), decreased to 70 percent in 1994 and 55 percent in 1999. Further decreases in membership have been slowed by delays in the privatization process and the escalation of economic problems, which have caused high insecurity for workers.

The reasons for the decrease in trade union membership in Croatia include

- the continuous decrease in the number of the employed and the privatiza-tion and restructuring of socially owned companies
- the breakdown of large industrial complexes and of particular sectors (e.g., metal, textile, construction, wood industry)
- the consequences of the war (e.g., migrations, displacement, refugees)
- the privatization of smaller, socially owned companies and the establish-ment of new private companies in which private employers try to obstruct or avoid trade union organizing of their workers by means of blackmail and threats of dismissals
- the liquidation and bankruptcies of companies and other institutions
- the low incomes of workers and the massive late payments of wages, pay-ments in vouchers, and the refusal of some employers to have membership fees deducted from wages
- the members' disappointment with trade unions because of increased

expectations combined with the inefficiency of trade unions in the defense of basic labor rights
- the centralization and bureaucratization of trade union organizations and the past conception of unions as organizations that provide services to members instead of enabling members to fight for the defense of their rights and initiate changes on their own
- the lack of awareness of a part of the labor force of the necessity of trade union organizing
- the introduction of accurate records of membership in trade unions, whereby nonexistent members were removed from records

FURTHER OBSTACLES TO
TRADE UNION ACTIVITY

The postcommunist Croatian trade union scene has been characterized by radical changes in ideology, by the collapse of old institutions, and by the pluralism of trade unions. This pluralism led to a disintegration and dispersion of trade unions, weakening their power. This pluralism was caused by a number of factors, including the disintegration of the socialist system of production, efforts by the new authorities to control the trade union movement, a sudden rise in unemployment, negative connotations of the former monolithic trade union, and privatization. The most important obstacles faced by trade unions include the hostile policies of the government and private employers' associations toward union organizing, antiunionist public statements by politicians and the media, the establishment of "yellow" trade unions obedient to political parties, authorities, or employers, and the consequent internal union competition. Moreover, there has been decreased legal protection for shop stewards, and prominent trade union leaders and shop stewards have been dismissed, transferred, and even physically assaulted for their trade union activities.[7]

The war created a major disadvantage for trade unions because the defense of national sovereignty became the top priority, suggesting that trade unions should leave the struggle for labor and social rights for peacetime. The war, however, did not prevent employers from transforming ownership and rapidly changing labor and social legislation. Practically all such changes so far have reduced workers' rights. New legal provisions and measures were often unjust, and they have directly contributed to further the social division and poverty of the working population. Trade union confederations have almost always been *post festum* consulted by the government of the Republic of

Croatia, usually through the inefficient tripartite body, the Social and Economic Council.

Another disadvantage for trade unions is the legacy of socialism. Workers under the socialist system enjoyed a high level of job security, education, housing, and so forth. Yet it was the state that provided these rights, so workers and trade unions lacked the experience of fighting for workers' interests and the awareness that they needed to do so. Little was known about collective agreements and negotiation techniques in trade union circles at the beginning of the 1990s. Unionists learned from the odd piece of foreign literature and by intuition of the need for protective mechanisms for workers, whose well-being had become increasingly jeopardized. Those with opposing interests, the state and the Croatian Chamber of Commerce (which for a long time was only an extended part of the state) resisted collective agreements. They declared themselves in favor of a socially regulated labor market, but in reality they delayed finding solutions that would put that into practice. Because this was when an independent state was being created and ownership transformed, one could assume that the other side was also ignorant and that it feared the new and the unknown.

Moreover, the ideology and rhetoric of socialism also hindered union activism. For example, one of the numerous ministers of labor and social welfare, helpless at the shower of trade union arguments about the need for collective agreements in Croatia, asked trade unions to propose another name for these negotiations, because "collective agreement" sounded too "socialist-like."

The influence of the socialist legacy can also be seen in the case of strikes, which have been many and often intense but limited in impact. The ideology of the former system influenced the attitude of many workers toward strikes. The ideology of socialist self-management viewed the strike as a negative form of struggle, because the strike was not treated as a basic human and trade union right but rather as a destructive, revolutionary act contrary to the interests of the society. Under the ideology of the new state, the strike is treated as anti-Croatian and contrary to Croatian national interests. The ruling party claims that strikes, and even trade union demonstrations, only deepen the current social crisis. Through the manipulation of the war and nationalism, the large majority of workers have been transformed into a formless mass out of fear of repression or the loss of one's job (or the illusion of a job in cases where workers do not receive wages but still work).

Today, workers in Croatia know that collective agreements are the key to the defense and improvement of their rights. Yet until the adoption of the Labor Act in 1995, the Ministry of Labor sometimes refused to register national branch collective agreements for as long as two years, and only then after union protest actions. After the adoption of the Labor Act, the problem became the insufficient intervention of the government in collective bargaining, so employers avoided collective bargaining through the establishment of "yellow" trade unions, which then postponed negotiations or refused to negotiate altogether.[8]

Employers also took advantage of restrictions on the right to strike in many services and branches. When the right to strike is restricted, unions are compelled to pay the employer for the damage caused by the strike, while workers who organized and took part in the strike are dismissed. According to the Croatian Supreme Court, workers do not have the legal right to strike over late payments or nonpayment of wages because strikes are legal only in the case of a collective labor dispute. Instead, workers who face wage arrears may file suit instead. Such interpretations represent an extreme restriction of the right to strike.

The government of the Republic of Croatia, through the nationalization of trade union assets,[9] very slyly attempted to set the various trade unions against each other. Of course, trade unions are more vulnerable without their assets, especially given their weak financial position, and their ability to act collectively is limited, which was the government's ultimate objective. With the assets in the hands of the government, which can also set the criteria for their distribution to the various unions, we can see how the state could compel trade union obedience.

Given such conditions, the problem of trade union leaders' lack of skills and experience was acute. Thus, they had to learn fast and acquire the necessary skills and techniques of trade union struggle from the experiences of other countries. At the same tame, they faced the need to raise the awareness of workers about the need to organize and take their fate into their own hands. Yet, needless to say, trade unions in Croatia have been quite diverse in their strength, orientation, and willingness to struggle to achieve their demands.

CROATIAN TRADE UNIONS

UATUC/Autonomous Trade Unions of Croatia is the largest trade union confederation. It was founded jointly by dissident trade unions and reform-oriented trade unions from the once-official trade union confederation at the beginning of the 1990s. It is the only Croatian trade union confederation affiliated with the ICFTU/International Confederation of Free Trade Unions and the ETUC/European Trade Union Confederation. Branch unions affiliated with UATUC organized voting on voluntary affiliation with the federation among their workers in the summer of 1990, thus demonstrating

UATUC's independent and democratic nature. At the time of this initial affiliation, UATUC had 700,000 members, whereas today it has approximately 350,000 members. It is the largest Croatian trade union confederation. It has twenty-two affiliated branch trade unions and federations, mostly industrial but also from the public sector. UATUC is also independent of any political parties, employers, or the government. It cooperates with the Social Democratic Party, Croatian Populist Party, Liberal Party, and Croatian Liberal and Social Party on concrete common interests, such as lobbying and advocating in the Croatian Parliament.

URSH/Association of Workers' Trade Unions of Croatia was founded in 1994 by dissidents from UATUC who disagreed with its work, methods, and centralist approach. At the beginning, this new trade union confederation gathered only those employed in public companies, whereas today it includes approximately forty-four branch unions, some regional trade unions, and various trade unions at the company level. URSH states its total membership is 90,000, with 30,000 paying members. In addition, URSH is affiliated with the World Confederation of Labor and with the International/European Federation of the Employed in Public Services. Since 1998 it has been cooperating with two trade union confederations, HUS and the former KNSH (see below), and a large number of political parties: HDZ/Croatian Democratic Union, the conservative wing of the Croatian Peasants' Party, and some leaders of the Action of Social Democrats.

HUS/Croatian Association of Trade Unions was founded in December 1990 by HDZ leaders as a counterbalance to UATUC. It had some 220,000 members initially, whereas today it claims approximately 40,000 members. HUS includes fifteen trade unions, and only some of them are branch unions. After it conducted several political actions related to the war, such as the blockade of Ploče harbor and the petition against the agreement on the status of the harbor that would have placed it at the disposal of Bosnia and Herzegovina, this trade union confederation was excluded from the list of cooperation with ETUC and ICFTU. HUS has been closely cooperating with KNSH and the Co-ordination of Croatian Trade Unions of Public Service Workers and Employees, though recently it has undertaken joint actions with URSH. Because it was founded by the HDZ/Croatian Democratic Union, and as it propagates the social views of the Catholic Church, this confederation cooperates closely with the right wing of HDZ and operates as an extension of the ruling party.

Association of the Croatian Trade Unions of Public Services was founded in 1990 by dissident trade unions. This trade union confederation includes workers from five branch unions in science, the social sector, health care, and education. The membership of the association used to be 24,000, but

as of February 26,1999, it had 50,000 paying members after it had merged
with the Trade Union of Teachers of Croatia.[10] The confederation is not affiliated with any international organization, although its major trade unions, such
as the Trade Union of Sciences, are affiliated with international federations.
The association cooperates with UATUC on certain common issues of social
and labor legislation, and they—together with three other confederations—
make up the Croatian Bloc of Democratic Trade Unions. The association cooperates with the Social-Liberal Party and the Social Democratic Party.

Independent Croatian Trade Unions is a new trade union confederation
founded in February 1999 by the fusion of KNSH/Confederation of Independent Trade Unions of Croatia and the Co-ordination of Croatian Trade Unions
of Public Service Workers and Employees. KNSH/Confederation of Independent Trade Unions of Croatia was founded in June 1990. It had approximately
25,000 members and a Christian-Democratic orientation. Co-ordination of
Croatian Trade Unions of Public Service Workers and Employees was
founded in 1993 and had, at one point, 80,000 members. It represented a very
loose structure of a fluctuating number of trade unions, with several trade
unions leaving the Co-ordination during its six-year existence. With the foundation of this new confederation, the two former confederations were abolished. The Independent Croatian Trade Unions include twenty-five trade
unions with approximately 50,000 members. For now, they declare themselves independent of any political orientation. In explaining the unification,
they state the "wish to reduce the number of trade union confederations to
more easily reach inter-trade union agreements on the state level, without
unnecessary politicization and the creation of a cult of trade union leaders."[11]

UNAFFILIATED TRADE UNIONS

Some reputable and large trade unions remain unaffiliated. These include the
Trade Union of State and Local Government Employees of Croatia, the Journalists' Trade Union of Croatia, the Trade Union in Printing and Publishing
Industry of Croatia, the Croatian Post and Telecommunications Trade Unions,
the Trade Union of Locomotive Engineers of Croatia, and some three hundred other trade union associations on the company or the territorial level.
According to some estimates, these trade unions have at least one hundred
thousand members.

TRADE UNION ACTIVITY AFTER
COMMUNISM

Although workers are in a very weak position, trade unions have prevented
that position from being even worse. From 1990 to 1999 trade union confed-

erations organized numerous trade union activities in their fight for the protection of labor interests of their members, ranging from signing collective agreements to organizing petitions, strikes, protests, demonstrations, and hunger strikes and establishing workers' committees. A review of trade union activities by year follows.

1990

In December, two trade unions affiliated with UATUC, the metalworkers' trade union, and the textile workers' trade union, organized a general strike of sixty-three thousand workers against low wages and threats of massive redundancies without an adequate national social program.

1991

In April, UATUC and KNSH forwarded a public appeal to the Croatian Parliament regarding the postponement of the adoption of the bill on the transformation of socially owned companies, as the provisions proposed in the bill meant nationalization of the economy instead of real privatization. Despite the public appeal, the Croatian Parliament adopted the bill. In September, UATUC, HUS, and KNHS signed the Agreement on Co-operation and Operation in War Circumstances.

1992

In March, UATUC forwarded a public appeal to the government of the Republic of Croatia to fulfill its obligations of the so-called "war agreement." The demands included the signing of a tripartite national agreement, the registration of the signed branch collective agreements, the establishment of an independent labor judiciary, the introduction of participation in decision making, and the supervision of the work of enterprise steering committees in the process of the transformation of socially owned companies. Accordingly, in March, UATUC organized a three-day action among its membership called "Demands of a Social Labor Force," where a petition containing fifteen labor and social demands was signed. The demands included the indexation of wages to inflation, an increase in unemployment benefits, the abolition of profit taxes for children's products, the free distribution of shares to the population, the legal regulation of protection for shop stewards and workers' representatives, the registration of signed branch collective agreements, and the drafting and adoption of the Croatian social charter. Despite the ongoing war and the fact that the action lasted for only three days, 343,000 signatures were collected. At the end of March, three union confederations—UATUC, HUS, and KNSH—canceled the so-called "war agreement" with the government, pointing to its arrogant behavior. In July, the same three unions announced a joint warning strike aimed at the signing of a new collective agreement in industry. Under the pressure of trade union membership and the announced warning strike, the new General Collective Agreement for Industry was signed, and consequently the strike was canceled. In October, the government of the Republic of Croatia, UATUC, HUS, KNSH, and trade unions from the public sector signed the General Collective Agreement for the Public Sector. That same month, in front of the building of the Croatian Parliament, UATUC in cooperation with HUS and KNSH organized a distribution of brown bread and leaflets. At the end of October, UATUC held a public referendum on the organization of a general strike to be held on November 13. The cause was the decision of the Croatian government to annul the collective agreements and to adopt a provision on controlled wages. A day before the referendum, the Croatian government withdrew the provision, and the strike was canceled.

1993

In February, UATUC forwarded an initiative to the Croatian government regarding amendments to the act on the transformation of socially owned companies, demanding a part of the resources from the sale of socially owned companies be used to save jobs and create new employment. It also demanded that shares in the privatized firms be distributed to workers and pensioners. In March, UATUC undertook a four-hour general strike called "Bread for All," which was joined by KNSH and the Independent Trade Union of Higher Education. Consequently, they won the automatic index-ation of wages to the galloping rate of inflation. Thus, the decrease in real wages was stopped. After two years of appealing for the establishment of a tripartite national body, the constituency meeting of the Economic and Social Council was held in August 1993, with all three trade union confederations (UATUC, HUS, and KNSH), the Croatian government, and the Croatian Chamber of Commerce as partners. In September, UATUC organized protests in seventeen towns demanding exclusion of a package of labor and social legislation from the Parliament's agenda. The action was successful.

1994

In January, two trade union confederations, UATUC and KNSH, organized a joint protest against the new taxation act. In March, UATUC organized a pro-test against the impending adoption of the amendments to the act on indus-trial relations, the act on employment, and the provision on a wage freeze.

Trade unions in education organized a general strike in their sector. In May, UATUC, HUS, and KNSH signed the Agreement on Wages in Industry and Public Companies with the Croatian government and the Croatian Chamber of Commerce, whereby the government's provision on wages was annulled, a new fundamental national agreement was reached, and negotiations were opened for signing branch collective agreements. In September more than one thousand trade unionists and workers from branches affiliated with UATUC organized a peaceful protest in front of the Croatian Parliament against the difficult situation in their sectors. They called for a new act on cooperation with trade unions. In December a general strike of four railway trade unions was held because of inadequate health and safety provisions, low wages and Christmas bonuses, and the collective agreement. The government tried to break the strike, exerting different kinds of pressure such as compulsory work, but it did not succeed. The strike ended after twenty days, and most of workers' demands were met. UATUC also held a two-hour warning strike in December, protesting the government's avoidance of social partnership and dialogue. UATUC demanded the payment of a Christmas bonus and the signing of a basic national agreement and branch collective agreements. The protest was also against the Labor Act's abolition of meal bonuses. The strike was in solidarity with the rail workers.

1995

A five-day protest organized by four branch unions affiliated with UATUC was held in June in front of the Ministry of Labor. The workers' demands were

- the immediate payment of all late wages
- the improvement of the social welfare of workers who were not receiving their wages
- the stricter control of social insurance payments
- the implementation of the basic national agreement
- the urgent discussion of the announced new pension system

In December, the Trade Union of Textile, Footwear, Leather, Rubber Industry of Croatia and the Association of Employers in Textile and Leather Industry of Croatia (HUP) signed a branch collective agreement, the first branch agreement to be signed with the Croatian Employers' Association.[12]

1996

The Croatian Trade Union Bloc[13] adopted (for the first time) a "Joint Statement of Croatian Trade Unions," in which they forwarded a range of demands to the Croatian government. In February, UATUC undertook a Valentine's Day action, sending its large negotiating team of almost one hundred delegates to negotiations with the government. When delegates walked through the city center distributing leaflets, the prime minister ordered special police forces to harass the protesters. In February a one-day strike of three trade unions of the Croatian post and telecommunications industry was held with 70 percent of workers participating. The same month, UATUC organized a massive march in the center of Zagreb of some seven thousand UATUC shop stewards and activists from all over Croatia. On that occasion, the government sent thousands of policemen to the protest because all protests on the city main square were banned. In the same month, trade unions of railway workers organized a general strike. The complete blockage of rail transportation lasted for seven days until the Croatian Railways Management and the trade unions signed an agreement on an increase in wages and on working conditions. In October a protest was organized in several Croatian towns by the Metalworkers' Trade Union of Croatia, which was affiliated with UATUC. UATUC announced massive demonstrations in Zagreb for November 7, but they were canceled because UATUC and HUS succeeded in achieving an amendment to the taxation system and the creation of special committees to resolve labor disputes. In November, fifteen thousand members of the Retired Persons Trade Union of Croatia, affiliated with UATUC, protested in Zagreb against low and delayed pensions. At the end of November, a general strike was organized by the railway workers; however, it was banned on December 17 by the Croatian Supreme Court. A new general strike was announced for December 28, but an agreement to end the strike was reached on January 2, 1997.

1997

In February, UATUC organized a petition against the reduction of maternity leave benefits for almost eight thousand mothers, collecting some thirty thousand signatures. In April the Trade Union of Textile, Footwear, Leather, Rubber Industry of Croatia held a protest in Zagreb of two thousand shop stewards. In April the Trade Union of Locomotive Engineers of Croatia organized a protest by stopping all trains on Croatian railways for fifteen minutes. In October, UATUC undertook a petition of "Demands of Croatian Labor Force to the Croatian Parliament and the Government of the Republic of Croatia," collecting 315,427 signatures.

1998

In January, UATUC organized a protest in Zagreb called "Take Off Your Masks!" with the participation of five thousand shop stewards from all over the country. The rally of four thousand workers of Petrokemija (in Kutina) against the planned privatization resulted in the formation of the first workers' committee for the defense of the company.

On February 20, URSH in cooperation with the HUS, KNSH, and the Coordination of Croatian Trade Unions of Public Service Workers and Employees organized a protest meeting with twenty thousand protesters and representatives of political parties of the extreme right wing (Croatian Party of Right, or HSP 1861) and the extreme left wing (Association of Croatian Socialists, or ASH).

To increase the power and the credibility of the extremely fragmented trade union movement in Croatia, UATUC gathered three other democratic trade unions and founded the (fourth) Croatian Bloc of Democratic Trade Unions in April. A protest was held "For the right to work, for wages and decent pensions, against thieves and self-rule of the powerful," that was organized by the UATUC office in Sisačko-moslovačka County, featuring three thousand protesters.

1999

Trade union members (metalworkers, textile workers, and woodworkers) moved to the streets to protest the government's economic policies and demand the salvation of their sectors and companies. UATUC had continuously pointed out the catastrophic economic and social policy that was aggravated further by corruption, the insolvency of an alarming number of companies, massive job losses, long nonpayments of wages, and a drastic decrease in the living standard of the majority of population. As a result, UATUC established committees for the defense of companies as a means of both social dialogue and pressure. In 1999, some thirty committees were founded that aimed at protecting workers' rights, preventing bankruptcy and the loss of jobs, ensuring wages be paid, and initiating the revision of privatization in workers' interests.

CONCLUSION

In the pretransition period of the late 1980s, within what was then Yugoslavia, the Republic of Croatia had reached a level of development that placed it among the ten newly industrialized countries of the world, according to the United Nations. In 1989, GNP per capita amounted to five thousand dollars. However, the war, the transition crisis, and the loss of markets almost halved the GNP, tripled the unemployment rate, and reduced investment to the level of amortization. Mistakes in the process of privatization created monopolies and oligopolies, and they spurred corruption and organized crime in all areas of society. The grim picture of the economy is followed by an even more difficult social situation. At least nine out of ten people in Croatia have social difficulties of one sort or another. The Croatian social tissue is disintegrating daily, and in the past ten years the majority of the Croatian population has become impoverished. The gap between the few, new wealthy and the great majority of the impoverished is continuously increasing. We are witnessing the manifestations of "wild capitalism." The concentration of capital and wealth is not the result of hard work and honest entrepreneurship but rather political obedience and patronage.

The war created a major disadvantage for trade unions because the defense of national sovereignty and the care of refugees became the top priorities, leaving workers' concerns as issues to be dealt with in peacetime. The war, however, did not prevent employers from transforming ownership and rapidly changing labor and social legislation. Practically all such changes so far have reduced workers' rights. New legal provisions and measures were often unjust, and they have directly contributed to further social division and the impoverishment of the working population. In short, the war has been a facade for the ruling elite to conduct "primary accumulation" and to adopt antiunion laws that enable key figures to freely pile up wealth and prevent their opponents from acting.

Trade unions have been further weakened by being systematically pigeon-holed as a "socialist" concept, by the large rise in unemployment, and by their own internal differences and competitions.

One can find many answers to the question frequently asked by politicians, intellectuals, and trade union leaders in Croatia: Why have not progressive social forces—including autonomous workers' organizations—accomplished more in the fight for the protection of rights and interests of their members? However, it should be stressed that despite all the difficulties and obstacles to trade union activity, trade unions have attenuated the situation and prevented workers' position from being even worse and more difficult than it is. The new forms of trade union struggle that have emerged from 1990 on—such as public rallies and blockades instead of classic strikes—show that the demonstrators who go out into the streets are no longer helpless masses afraid of being fired upon or beaten by police. They are conscious individuals who will fight for their rights by any means possible.

NOTES

1. This chapter was completed prior to the Croatian elections of 2000—eds.
2. Sanja Crnković-Pozaić , *Stimulating Mechanisms of Labor Market Restructuring in Croatia*, 1997.

3. *Report on UATUC Activities between II and III Congress, 1998* (Zagreb: UATUC, 1998).

4. The minimum legal condition for registration of a trade union is to have at least ten members and for an association to have at least two trade unions with ten members.

5. Until recently, the Ministry of Labor and Social Welfare recognized six trade union confederations. As of February 19, 1999, there were five trade union confederations in Croatia: UATUC, URSH, Co-ordination of Croatian Trade Unions of Public Service Workers and Employees, Association of Croatian Trade Unions of Public Services, and Independent Croatian Trade Unions.

6. Jasna A. Petrović, *The Name of Solidarity* (Zagreb: UATUC, 1997), 42.

7. There is evidence that trade unionists in Croatia are victims of organized physical attacks and threats for their trade union activities. For example, in December 1992, Milan Krivokuća, founder and president of the Trade Union of Locomotive Engineers, was murdered at the threshold of his home. He was the leader of the first "real" strikes of railwaymen in 1989 and 1990 in the former socialist Croatia. A year later, Zoran Durić, head secretary of the Trade Union of Transport, was attacked. Following that, a bomb was planted in the car of Darko Pavičević, the president of the Trade Union of Croatian Railways Infrastructure. During these years, trade unionists were taken in for interrogation in the Ministry of Interior Affairs before organizing protest activities. In 1999 the number of threats and blackmail schemes increased. In May 1999 unknown assailants beat Ivan Tolić, president of the Trade Union of Locomotive Engineers of Croatia.

8. Jasna A. Petrović, *Trade Union Action* (Zagreb: UATUC, 1998), 32–34.

9. On January 12, 1998, the Republic of Croatia appropriated (temporarily) all trade union assets. These assets were the legitimate property of the trade unions because most of the real estate was purchased and built from membership fees, donations, and voluntary work immediately after World War I. In the socialist system, the state did not finance trade union activity in this regard.

10. The Trade Union of Teachers of Croatia has twenty-six thousand members and has been affiliated with Education International.

11. Information provided by UATUC International Department, November 1999.

12. The Croatian Employers' Association is a voluntary and interest employers' association founded in 1994 in Croatia. It includes some twenty-five hundred affiliates with some 250,000 employees.

13. The Croatian Trade Union Bloc consists of UATUC, HUS, KNSH, the Co-ordination of Croatian Trade Unions of Public Service Workers and Employees, and the Association of Croatian Trade Unions of Public Services.

Chapter Eight

Waiting for the Workers: Explaining Labor Quiescence in Serbia

Mihail Arandarenko

In Serbia's dramatic decade after 1989, labor stood at the center of public attention only once. Symbolically, it was labor's quiescence, not a spectacular industrial action, that attracted the attention. The moment was January 1997, at the time of large-scale civic protests against the Milosević regime. (On labor's role against Milosević in 2000, see the postscript.) The protests, which had begun when the regime had rigged local elections two months earlier, now reached a climax. Every day, hundreds of thousands of citizens demonstrated continuously in Belgrade and other large cities. The protesters consisted mainly of young, urban, well-educated, middle-class citizens. Their energy and eagerness, however, was just not enough. People had the sense that if only one new, powerful social force would join in, the end of the shaken and discredited regime would be at hand. Opposition politicians, tired and half broken, turned to labor. In desperation, they pleaded for workers to join the protest. A general strike, they said, would paralyze the system. However, they pleaded in vain.

Workers simply did not come. Some, to be sure, were among the protesters, just as they had been all along. However, they were there as individuals, not as workforces. They came after, not during working hours, and they were walking, not marching. The huge blue-collar suburbs of Belgrade, such as Rakovica, Zeleznik, and Zemun, remained silent.

Why did workers not deliver the final blow to a regime that, judging by hard facts, had ruined not just their jobs but their lives? Why had they not stood up against the regime earlier, such as during the terrible hyperinflation of 1993 that wiped out their savings? Was labor *able* to join the protests at any point in time? Were workers satisfied supporters of the ruling Socialist Party and its charismatic leader, Milosević, or were they just too weak and divided to stage an organized resistance? Can we use the term "labor" at all, or have there been several "labors" with different or even opposite interests and goals?

Some of these questions are rhetorical; some are essential. There is almost complete agreement among labor researchers, union officials, rank-and-file union members, and the general Serbian public that the working class in the 1990s was divided and disorganized and that trade unions were weak and without any real influence. Workers have simply been unable to organize collectively or decisively for any serious purpose, regardless of their individual preferences.

As to the essential question of *why* labor is so weak, a plethora of explanations has been offered so far. Some of these explanations are competing with one another; some are complementary rather than mutually substituting. However, the puzzle is yet to be solved.

The primary aim of this article is to try to explain this undisputed weakness of labor in Serbia. The first section reviews and develops some of the many hypotheses that have been offered so far. Then these hypotheses are articulated in the context of the social, political, institutional, economic, and specific labor-market and labor-relations changes since the late 1980s. Finally, an attempt is made to construct a synthetic explanation that is consistent with the evidence and has a sound theoretical foundation.

EXPLANATIONS

Nationalism, War, and the Authoritarian Regime

This explanation usually goes back to September 1987, when at the eighth session of the Serbian League of Communists, the nationalist faction led by Slobodan Milosević defeated the moderate faction and took complete control over the party. Since then, the ruling regime has maintained its position through consistently abusing, and producing, ethnic crises throughout the former Yugoslavia. In these circumstances, the explanation usually goes, political issues became much more important than economic ones, and national identity naturally overpowered and suppressed the emergence of class identity.

A variant of this explanation would argue that it is not necessary to decide who is responsible for the national clashes. Once the national question is at the forefront of political life, all other lines of division become less important.

After 1987, the Serbian party leadership soon secured the support of virtually the entire nation. Nationalist euphoria spread almost equally to the intelligentsia, farmers, and white- and blue-collar workers. Moreover, no alternative conceptualizations were available for mobilization. Self-management ideology was watered down in practice and compromised by failure. With the country's weak democratic traditions, serious ethnic divisions, and deep economic crisis, liberal individualism was also no match for the simple and easily understandable populist nationalism offered by the Serbian Communist Party. The party also enjoyed the full support of respected national institutions, such as the university community, the Serbian Academy of Sciences, and the Serbian Orthodox Church.[1]

Nationalist euphoria, however, cannot serve as the sole explanation for Serb labor quiescence since 1987. Euphoria is by definition something that cannot last too long. The culmination of the euphoric nationalist moment was probably the massive rally of June 28, 1989, in Gazi Mestan, Kosovo, marking the six-hundredth anniversary of the Serb defeat at the Battle of Kosovo. Attended by 1 million people, the real aim of that rally was to propel Slobodan Milosević to the leadership of "the Serb nation" and to celebrate the subjugation of the autonomous provinces of Kosovo and Vojvodina and of the Republic of Montenegro to Serb power.

The 1990s, however, brought little to further feed the euphoria. In 1995, after the destruction of the Serb enclave in Croatia (the so-called Republic of Srpska Krajina) and the Dayton peace agreement, the idea of a Greater Serbia was definitely defeated and buried. In 1999, even more painfully, Kosovo, the "heart of Serbia," was lost.

The proponents of the nationalist explanation, aware of the logical difficulty connecting euphoria with the series of defeats that would normally prompt a general sobering up, often add a sort of "path dependency" explanation. They claim that once the initial steps toward national clashes were chosen by the ruling elite and approved by almost all social strata, the rest of the story was dictated by the will of the ruling elite. Indeed, the elite has endlessly produced war after war, crisis after crisis, to prevent the different social strata and opposition political parties from organizing into an effective social and political opposition. This constant "state of emergency" has served as an almost perfect excuse for the consolidation of repression and authoritarian rule, which has further discouraged attempts to organize resistance.

Media Manipulation

This explanation is complementary with the previous one. It argues that workers (especially blue-collar workers) are a social group easily subjected to powerful official propaganda, because they are less educated and typically lack multiple sources of information. Instead, they rely almost exclusively upon state-television news programs, which are extremely biased against not only the established opposition political forces but are also against any genuine democratic, liberal, antiauthoritarian opinion. There is impressive documentation that illustrates the technology of manipulation that state-run and state-controlled media used in the 1990s.[2]

Even if propaganda is not fully successful in convincing workers of the wisdom and infallibility of the government, it is efficient enough in denouncing struggles for democratization as treason, manifestations of civic disobedience as rebellion, and industrial actions as unpatriotic sabotage. Even more important, it can be very efficient in producing and disseminating fear.[3]

Legacy of Self-Management

This explanation emphasizes the dysfunctional economic and social characteristics of the system known as self-management, which prevailed at the onset of transition and has survived even into the social reality of the 1990s. It argues that the internal and segmented labor markets so characteristic of the Yugoslav self-management system, with their huge intra- and interindustry wage differentials, continue to prevent the emergence and dissemination of class solidarity.

The self-management labor market was institutionally structured as a collection of many fragmented internal labor markets. In fact, each enterprise had its own labor market. In the economy as a whole, there were "good" (capital-intensive) and "bad" (labor-intensive) enterprises. Incumbent workers could not be removed from either of them, and promotion was governed by established internal rules. In "good" enterprises, new workers were employed according to political criteria or nepotism.[4] The basic features of these fragmented labor markets were secure pay, egalitarianism within the work organization, and huge disparities between the people doing the same work in different companies.[5] This led to economic and status differentiation within the working class and prevented the emergence of a unified class-consciousness. For these reasons, the argument goes, nothing like Poland's Solidarity ever emerged.

If research done by economists showed that at the beginning of the transition there were no unifying economic interests for the formation of all-embracing labor organizations, then sociological research—to be discussed in more detail later in this chapter— has shown that workers in the self-management system exercised no actual power even within their enterprises.

Permanent Worsening of Economic Conditions

According to this view, poor and consistently deteriorating economic conditions are to be blamed for the weakness of labor in Serbia. The constant rise in unemployment, the obliteration of savings (both gradually and in hyperinflation and/or pyramid schemes), and the loss of alternative sources of income have caused the rising dependence of the vast majority of workers on their shrinking current income and, in fact, on the state. As a consequence, they lose their self-confidence and self-consciousness. Thus, opinion polls typically reveal ambivalence and contradictions not only in the beliefs and attitudes of the working class as a whole but among individual workers as well. The rapid impoverishment of working people leaves them extremely risk-averse, which in turn weakens their bargaining power and action potential, as can be demonstrated analytically through game theory and the economics of information.

Delay in Privatization

This explanation emphasizes the importance of clear-cut property relations for the effective articulation of the interests of labor. If property relations are blurred and undefined or left in some temporary and tentative status, it becomes much more difficult for unions to formulate and coordinate effective short- and long-range goals and strategies or to mobilize members around them. Serb unions have been split both horizontally and vertically over the issue of whether privatization is good or bad, which type of privatization is best for labor, and so forth.

The Serb experience shows that collective bargaining can acquire some very unusual features in a nonprivatized economy. Unions are typically faced with abstract bargaining partners that are invisible and invincible. No serious harm can be inflicted by striking against an enterprise that is a product of social ownership, which is only an abstract legal construction, or against the supposed representative of that legal construction. Because strikes are economically harmful to workers and harmless to managers (whose property and income are not threatened at all), social ownership provides virtually insurmountable obstacles to effective industrial action.

Several privatization programs have been launched in the past decade, but public property still constitutes around 85 percent of total capital stock. State or "social" enterprises employ more than 80 percent of the formally employed labor force. In such firms, the illusion of self-management still arguably leaves workers confused about their real interests, goals, allies, and adversaries. When a slow-track privatization program was launched in 1998, the vast majority of workers, even in enterprises with the poorest perform-ance, showed great interest in insider privatization that could result in an employee-share type of ownership.

Forced Leaves, Grey Economy, and Multiple Sources of Income

This economic explanation is complementary with the previous two. During the 1990s the proportion of workers on unpaid leaves mushroomed to as many as 25 to 40 percent of the total number of employed. Many loss-making enterprises sent significant portions of their workforce—up to 90 percent—on unpaid leaves. Huge manufacturing companies (such as the Zastava car fac-tory in Kragujevac, the MIN machinery plant in Nis, and several metalwork-ing factories in the Belgrade suburb of Rakovica) have been among the hardest hit enterprises, sending tens of thousands of traditionally, or at least potentially, militant blue-collar workers out of their workplaces.

These workers have been tacitly encouraged to find additional sources of income in the informal economy (e.g., smuggling, flea markets, small garden-ing, and so on), while maintaining a secured pension, a small guaranteed wage, social and health insurance, and some other fringe benefits at their for-mal job. Having experienced a significant loss of their human capital during the prolonged forced idleness, many such workers lose all interest in return-ing to their former workplaces, and they seek only to retain their formal employment status.

Though one may claim that this pattern of unpaid leave combined with an "informal economy buffer" is no more than a harmless transitional restruc-turing of the labor market, in fact those workers who continue to work and those on unpaid leave are worse off in comparison with their initial position. Their reasons for expressing dissatisfaction still exist, but workers are less able to organize around this dissatisfaction. When workers are divided not only in terms of interests but also physically, it is very difficult for unions to organize a successful collective action.

EVIDENCE

Legacies: Power Relations in a Self-Management System

One of the popular myths about the former Yugoslavia was that the self-man-agement system provided workers with more rights and more power than elsewhere in the world. This myth was spread by people as diverse as neo-classical economists studying "Illyrian enterprises," leftist intellectuals whose promised land changed every year among Tito's Yugoslavia, Mao's China, or Shiad Barre's Somalia, and of course, by official Yugoslav propagandists.

Yet despite these pervasive claims of direct working-class power, Yugoslav self-management was essentially no different from the bureaucratic system of management in the Soviet-type socialist countries. It was a system imposed from above when the party-state leadership initiated a process of controlled decentralization of power. It was not the result of action by autonomous social forces.

In comparison to industrial relations in developed democratic countries, industrial relations in the self-management system were defective in a number of ways.

First, the protagonists of economic life undoubtedly had far more autonomy than in other socialist countries—but only to a degree that did not threaten the basis of the one-party state. As in other socialist countries, the League of Communists remained the ultimate and unchallenged arbiter in all important matters of social and economic life, including industrial relations.

Second, conflicts of interests within the work collective were not recognized. The unity of management and the workforce was supposed to create harmony in the collective, which could supposedly be threatened only by "anti-self-management forces" or "techno-managerial structures." Because officially there was no permanent conflict of interest between capital and labor, there was no institutional regulation of collective bargaining in social enterprises. The right to strike and other forms of industrial action went unrecognized, or rather ignored, as they were allegedly unnecessary.

Third, there were no genuinely autonomous unions. The sole official union organization was more an extended arm of the League of Communists than an authentic working-class organization. Even Marxist authors admitted this.[6] Union leaders were part of the ruling party *nomenklatura*. Hardly any were genuine workers. Most were professional politicians who rotated between posts in union backwaters and more influential and lucrative positions in the state and party leadership.

Many sociological studies have been published since the late 1960s on the structure of power in social enterprises. All authors basically agree that, despite their enormous formal powers, workers' councils played an insignificant role in the power structure. It follows that ordinary workers, for whom these councils were supposed to be the collective voice, had virtually no power in comparison with directors and managers. The management's dominant position in the hierarchy of power was based on connections with the party apparatus outside and above the enterprise, on control of the administrative apparatus, and on specialist services within the enterprise itself.

Starting from the assumption of two structures within which decisions were made—the self-management and the managerial, the first being an expression of workers' direct self-management democracy and the latter an expression of the hierarchical management structure—Zupanov showed in a pioneering study in the late 1960s that workers had very little influence on either substructure. The members of work collectives perceived directors and senior managers as the most influential group in each. In the managerial substructure, they were followed by middle and lower management with workers at the bottom. In the self-management representative substructure, directors and senior managers were followed by the workers' council and the board of directors.

A more recent study,[7] examining power relations within enterprises in the late self-management period, focused on the process of decision making in collectives with respect to four key concepts: distribution of personal incomes, allocation of housing, election of immediate superiors, and strategic investment. Respondents were asked to assess their influence in each of these areas, and an index was constructed of their self-management powers. Like earlier studies, this one showed that most employees felt impotent, poorly informed, apathetic, and marginalized. In contrast, the minority who held key party and self-management positions were excellently informed and strove consciously to conceal their dominant role in the decision-making process. The powerless majority performed routine manual jobs, had few qualifications, and tended not to be party members (or at least not in influential positions). The typical member of the power elite was a member of the management, had a university degree or higher education, and was simultaneously a party or self-management official or, less often, a specialist.

Power Relations at the Enterprise
Level in the 1990s

Very few studies were made in the 1990s of the internal structure of power in social enterprises or new mixed enterprises. Nevertheless, because there were no fundamental changes in ownership structure yet new legislation (enterprise and labor laws) increased the institutional power of directors and managers, it is reasonable to assume that the imbalance of power has further widened against labor.

Research by Molnar carried out in ten enterprises in Novi Sad, the capital of the Vojvodina province, confirms this intuitive assumption in a rather radical way.[8] Molnar hardly found any traces of real self-management structures in the enterprises he surveyed. In cases where they still formally existed, they were subjected to the direct control of managers, who were for their part directly controlled by Milosević's Socialist Party *nomenklatura*. Molnar identified four types of management–trade union relations: authoritarian cooperation, disregard, complete control, and persecution. The first three types were identified in relationships between management and the state-supported union, the Confederation of Serbian Trade Unions (SSS—*Savez sindikata Srbije*), while the fourth type prevailed in a few cases where an independent union existed. In *all* enterprises, however, it was the management (and more precisely, the director alone) rather than the relative strength of both sides that decided which style of industrial relations prevailed. This led Molnar to conclude that Serbian enterprises were experiencing the rise of the *führerprinzip*, or dictatorial rule.

General Economic and Labor Market Background

Economic Trends in the 1990s

The Serbian economy almost collapsed due to the bloody dissolution of the former Yugoslavia, United Nations sanctions, and economic policy misconduct that in 1993 led to one of the greatest bouts of hyperinflation in history. Between 1989 and 1993, GDP fell from around three thousand dollars per capita to one thousand dollars per capita. A slight recovery followed the introduction of a stabilization program in January 1994, with moderate rates of growth between 3 and 7 percent from 1994 to 1998, but without serious long-term reform efforts, the structural imbalances remained and even worsened.

Data about GDP, however, do not reveal the true proportion of collapse in the main economic sectors. Agriculture played the role of a main buffer, with an annual drop of only 6.4 percent over the critical 1991–94 period. On the other hand, sectors of vital importance for transition and modernization declined at a rate much higher than average. In the same three-year period, for example, GDP in the service sector declined at an annual rate of 23.1 percent, and in manufacturing by 23.9 percent per annum.

As a result of these trends, radical changes occurred in the economy's sector structure. The share of agriculture in 1991–1994 was 27.3 percent of GDP, or as much as 11 percent more than in 1987–1990. The share of services slightly dropped from 44.9 percent to 42.8 percent, and a drastic drop was experienced by industry (from 38.8 percent in the 1987–1990 period to 29.9 percent in 1991–1994).[9] Industrial output in 1994 was only 36 percent of its volume in 1989. Within this restricted framework, capital goods production, formerly the most favored segment of industry employing the bulk of blue-collar workers, dropped to only 13 percent of its former volume, and some of its segments went under 10 percent (e.g., equipment 9 percent, automobile industry 5 percent). Generally, changes in GDP and industry composition may be deemed very regressive, with a relative increase in the share of traditional sectors and a decline in modern ones.

While in the early 1990s external factors (that is, the dissolution of the country, war, and sanctions) could be blamed for the poor economic performance and delay in the transition process, in the late 1990s it was the lack of political will that caused the country's prolonged economic stagnation. This became clear only a few months after the United Nations sanctions were lifted (following the Dayton peace agreement) in the fall of 1995, when Dragoslav Avramović, the reform-minded governor of the National Bank who had brilliantly defeated hyperinflation, was removed. The dismissal of Avramović signified that the ruling elite had chosen to build its own "inner wall of sanctions" toward the external world, holding the economy *de facto* in prolonged isolation. Thus, the main characteristics of the Serbian economy in the late 1990s were

- the slow growth of GDP without structural changes
- an obsolete economic structure
- a delay in the privatization process (in 1998 more than 80 percent of total economic assets was made up of state and social property)
- a restrictive tax policy
- delays in banks' rehabilitation and restructuring, leading to a total absence of domestic savings
- an underdeveloped financial market
- volatility in the real exchange rate
- overall institutional instability
- widespread corruption and rent-seeking behavior
- high investment risk

Labor Market Trends in the 1990s

The steep downward trend in GDP in the last decade was followed by a much slower fall in formal employment. In the nonagricultural sector, employment fell from 2.65 million in 1989 to 2.15 million in 1998, while registered unemployment rose from 600,000 to 770,000. The rate of open unemployment is an extremely high 27.2 percent, the second-highest rate in Europe. More than 80 percent of the unemployed have been out of work for more than a year, and more than 40 percent have been unemployed for more than three years. A natural consequence of the much faster fall of GDP than employment is the huge amount of hidden unemployment (labor hoarding), which is now estimated at about seven hundred thousand formally employed workers. Between three hundred thousand and five hundred thousand of these, depending on seasonal variations, are already out of work on so-called forced leaves.

One of the many indicators of the failed transition is the increase in inter- and intraindustry wage differentials. In 1998, for example, the average wage in the highest-paid industrial branch (oil and gas production) was twelve times higher than that in the lowest-paid branch (textiles). At one point in 1998, the average monthly wage dipped to fewer than ninety dollars, with more than four hundred thousand mainly industrial workers receiving only a guaranteed wage of two hundred dinars, or less than eighteen dollars. As in Russia and elsewhere in the Commonwealth of Independent States (CIS) countries, wage arrears are widespread.

On balance, informal (unregistered) employment was estimated at more than five hundred thousand people in 1997. GDP in the informal economy is estimated to be about one-third of the formal GDP, providing more than a million mainly part-time jobs to youths, retirees, people on forced leaves, and so on. The informal economy is undoubtedly the country's most significant social buffer, employing wide masses of unemployed and even the working poor. It is, however, a costly and imperfect buffer with many harmful effects, particularly in the long term. It diminishes state revenues and leaves workers and consumers unprotected. However, it can also be a powerful political buffer, dispersing and disintegrating social strata and atomizing the entire society.

Comparing the huge decline in GDP with the moderate decline in employment, one may argue that labor has not been very weak. Even with the rapid decline in wages, this could signify a sort of "concession bargaining," with unions in times of deep economic crisis putting more value on employment security than wages.[10] If the share of labor (the total wage bill) in the GDP has stayed stable or even risen, this strategy could even be considered successful.

In the context of transition, however, this line of reasoning is completely misleading. First, the proportion between the two declines has little or nothing to do with labor strength. It mainly describes the speed of transitional restructuring. Between 1989 and 1995, GDP in Poland fell by 1.4 percent, while employment fell by 13.3 percent; in Hungary, GDP fell by 14.4 percent, while employment fell by as much as 27.4 percent. At the other extreme, during the same period in Russia, GDP fell by almost 40 percent, while employment declined by only 11.2 percent; in Ukraine, GDP fell by 57.1 percent, while employment fell by only 6.7 percent.[11]

The rise of labor's share of GDP can be ascribed to union power only if GDP is rising as well. Otherwise, the deeper the GDP decline, the higher probability for the labor share to rise in a market economy regardless of labor strength, simply because the demand for investment goods is much more flexible than the demand for consumption goods.

Labor and Social Stratification during the Transition

Abundant sociological and statistical evidence confirms that it is the weakness of labor, rather than satisfaction with its own economic position, that is the main reason for labor quiescence in Serbia. Since the early 1990s, workers have been the most radically affected by pauperization. Manual unskilled workers have suffered the most. As in many other transition countries, they are the main losers among the social strata. Although the position of skilled workers is somewhat more favorable, they also lost their relative position in comparison with other social strata. This is confirmed by economists' research on the objective economic position of workers[12] and sociologists' research on subjective assessment of people's own economic position.[13]

In general, the rural population has been far more successful than the urban population in coping with economic crisis. Rural poverty rates range from 14.6 percent in prosperous 1990 to only 16.8 percent in 1996, while the comparable urban figures range from 13.2 percent to 30.4 percent. Poverty is thus very much an urban phenomenon, constituting 77 percent of the total. Among the urban population, the hardest hit are families of blue-collar workers and miners. By 1996, half of them had incomes below the subsistence minimum.[14]

Empirical sociological studies support these results. In research done by Lazic et al. in 1993, 95 percent of the respondents said their living standards had deteriorated since the late 1980s. The ranking of members of individual social strata whose standards, according to their own views, have deteriorated the most is as follows:

- unskilled workers (87 percent)
- pensioners (77 percent)
- skilled workers (75 percent)
- managers (72 percent)
- unemployed (66 percent)
- professionals, clerical workers, and technicians (64 percent)
- peasants (54 percent).[15]

On the basis of this study, Lazic and colleagues constructed a financial position index for various social strata composed of accumulated resources and consumption levels. Those with a "very low" financial position included 30.8 percent of unskilled workers, 29.6 percent of pensioners, 16.2 percent of skilled workers, 14.5 percent of the unemployed, 11.4 percent of peasants, and single-digit percentages of clerical workers, technicians, managers, and professionals. Those with a "low" financial position were 49.2 percent of skilled workers, 48.6 percent of unskilled workers, and 43.8 percent of pensioners.

Old and New Trade Unions

The trade union scene in Serbia can be divided into two blocs, with the once-official union on one side and a diverse set of new independent union confederations and nonaffiliated enterprise unions on the other. The relations between the two blocs are confrontational rather than cooperative. Clashes are widespread also within the bloc of new unions, even though they mostly have common goals and programs and constitute no more than 10 percent of the employed labor force. Such conflicts, of course, weaken the alternative unions' potential for collective action.

The old official union organization, SSS, enjoyed strong state support during the entire 1990s. It has shown no serious desire to transform itself from the typical "transmission belt" into a real interest organization. With a leadership even more conservative than the Serbian party and state leadership, it played no significant role in the democratic changes that belatedly and partially occurred in 1990.[16] A strong reformist faction tried, and failed, to change the union's course in spring 1991. Since then, SSS has been firmly controlled by the ruling Socialist Party of Serbia. It claims a membership of about 2 million, but the real number of dues-paying members is probably about half that. Membership is loose, and most members appear to be almost exclusively interested in the unions' social functions.

The first independent unions since World War II were formed at the end of 1989, almost a year after new political parties emerged. In contrast to the new parties, the most influential of which quickly spread to the whole of Serbia, the new unions remained mostly local or even craft organizations. As in the case of the first unions a century earlier, these new unions were largely created by labor elites—the working-class aristocracy of white-collar workers, pilots, truck drivers, train engineers, and journalists. There was little attempt to unify these unions until 1991.

The new unions were mostly formed at the grassroots level in response to particular problems in the workplace, and they remained isolated and uncoordinated. They often stressed their nonpolitical character, contrasting this to the close relationship between the old union and the state. Paradoxically, their growth seems to have been limited by the proliferation of political parties. The parties appeared as a shortcut for political involvement, far more attractive than the slow, laborious process of building trade unions. Unions remained in the shadow of political parties for the entire 1990s.

The UGS Nezavisnost ("Independence") Confederation of Industrial Unions was the first independent trade union confederation, and it remains the most important. It began its activities in mid-1991, under extremely unfavorable political and economic conditions. While the state union defined the aims of the union struggle as the concrete, everyday interests of employees, Nezavisnost saw its goal as radical political, social, and economic change.[17] Organizationally, the main difference is that Nezavisnost is based on independent industrial and craft unions, whereas the SSS is organized predominantly on a territorial basis, mirroring the political organization of society, and has a strongly hierarchical structure in which the confederation dominates the individual unions.

By 1998, Nezavisnost consisted of thirteen industrial unions with a claimed (and probably slightly exaggerated) membership of 153,000. Many members do not pay dues, and some are simultaneously members of SSS. Fluctuations in membership are similar to those seen in the development of independent unions in other transition countries: An initial rapid growth is followed by stagnation, often accompanied by internal splits in the union leadership. The rival, and far less influential, independent unions—the Independent Union of Serbia, Association of Independent and Autonomous Unions of Serbia, and Free Trade Unions of Yugoslavia—were all formed predominantly by groups that broke away from Nezavisnost. Altogether, the new and independent unions act as a somewhat strange mixture of interest organization, social movement, and nongovernmental organization.

Unions and Politics

The old union has, though somewhat less overtly than before the transition, retained close ties with the ruling party. These ties become quite apparent, however, at key moments, typically before elections and in periods of civic or social unrest or ethnic crises.

Most of the newly formed democratic parties focused their energies on the national question or abstract democratic goals. They addressed people as members of ethnic groups or citizens in general, not as members of classes or social-interest groups. Nationalism proved far more successful than appeals to civic consciousness, which met with little response from the broad masses.

Almost ten years after the beginning of the democratic transition, Serbian political parties are still, like their counterparts in some other transition countries, predominantly conglomerate parties led by strong leaders.[18] Despite great expectations, the introduction of a democratic political system did not mean the sudden disappearance of the previous social structure, with its low level of class differentiation and lack of social groups with clearly defined sectional interests. Political parties were therefore obliged to appeal to the whole society instead of to their own "clients," and also to a broad category of the politically neutral, as is common in Western democracies. This led to the emergence of conglomerate parties or protoparties,[19] which were characterized by syncretic political programs, socially heterogeneous memberships, and extremely weak internal organizations that are constantly in danger of falling apart.

The lack of recognizable group and class interests forces most conglomerate parties to adopt nationalism as their chief means of mobilizing and consolidating members and supporters, particularly in ethnically mixed societies such as Serbia. These parties also need charismatic leaders whose personal image compensates for the lack of a clear program. The identification of parties with their charismatic leaders explains the frequent sudden changes in policy, which are unimaginable in parties with clearly defined programs.

In this context, it is no surprise that these parties have a complete lack of interest in trade unions. Some of the parties openly justify their dismissive attitude with the argument that unions are weak and without any real influence. Even the programs of Serbia's main political parties give little or no attention to union rights and freedoms, industrial relations, and the protection of workers' interests.[20]

The independent unions tried several times to cooperate closely with democratic opposition parties and coalitions, but they were never treated as equal and respected partners. Nezavisnost was part of the broad democratic coalition *Depos* in 1992, and the Confederation of Independent and Autonomous Unions entered the electoral coalition *Zajedno* (Coalition Together) in 1996. Both times, however, these unions were marginalized and even humiliated by their stronger partners. They are thus now very skeptical toward the idea of broad popular coalitions, and they choose to focus on autonomous action instead.

Institutional Framework of Industrial Relations

Three phases can be distinguished in the system of collective bargaining since its establishment in 1990. A centralized system, with the dominance of a national collective agreement (designed to include basic negotiated pay),

lasted from 1990 to mid-1992. From then till the end of 1994, the so-called
sanctions laws practically suspended the entire system of collective bargaining. In the third phase, from late 1994 onward, an intermediate bargaining
structure was established with pay negotiations transferred to the industry
level, despite its well-known negative consequences. In all phases and at all
levels, except in some rare local negotiations, the bargaining partners are
made up exclusively of representatives of the official chamber of commerce
and its industrial branches (acting in the place of nonexistent employers'
organizations), the state and its ministries, and SSS officials.

As for tripartite bodies, there were none at all until Serb National Bank
governor Avramović established so-called ad hoc commissions for pensions,
wages, and taxes in 1995. Since that year, a tripartite social council has
existed at the federal level (including Montenegro), composed of labor
experts, representatives of republican chambers of commerce, and official
Serbian and Montenegrin trade unions. This, however, is just an advisory
body, with members appointed by the federal government. It lacks any real
authority.

The Labor Relations Act states that national and industrial agreements are
binding not only for the parties concerned but for all employers and employees in the economy or, in the case of industrial agreements, in the industry
concerned. In practice, however, it is very difficult even for unions included
in the bargaining process to enforce some elements of the agreements, especially those concerning wage rates. This seriously undermines the very institution of collective bargaining.

The changes in the institutional setup of the industrial relations system
show that the power elite has learned rather quickly that the main threat to
its domination comes from nationwide collective bargaining and industrial
actions, where not only distributive but also institutional and sometimes
purely political issues could be raised. Accordingly, bargaining has been
decentralized (or rather atomized), and true, independent tripartite bodies
have never been established.[21]

Industrial Actions

For most of the old self-management period, strikes belonged to a grey area
of social life. The Constitution and legal code simply ignored the possibility
of strikes, which were therefore neither banned nor permitted, nor were they
properly registered. As the system gradually lost its political and economic
legitimacy, due to its inability to cope with the growing crisis, strikes were
accepted as a legitimate weapon of workers' power. At first glance, the second half of the 1980s can be seen as the golden age of the strike. Strikes

were numerous, tacitly accepted, very positively perceived by the public, and frequently successful, at least in the short term.

In 1988 and 1989, however, party hard-liners organized strikes for their own instrumental purposes, claiming them to be part of the "antibureaucratic revolution" and "happening of the people." The year 1989 saw a record number of strikes even though living standards increased by a double-digit percentage. When Serbia's new political leadership consolidated its position, it returned to more conventional methods. The number and intensity of strikes fell sharply from the second half of 1991 to the end of 1993. A number of factors discouraged strikes in this period, including the outbreak of war, the rise of nationalism, rapid inflation, high poverty and unemployment, United Nations sanctions, the practice of unpaid leaves, changes in the government's attitude toward strikes, and a new restrictive strike law.[22]

The most serious and best-organized strikes in this period took place in large public enterprises. Electrical-power workers, Belgrade bus drivers, railway engineers and air-flight controllers all organized protracted strikes. While the government showed little interest in strikes in the heavily impoverished social sector, typically leaving local management to deal with labor dissatisfaction, it reacted quickly and decisively to repress strikes in sectors under its direct control.

That double standard continues to be the rule. In recent years, only teachers, health-care, and a few other social-service unions have been able to organize coordinated nationwide strikes. While the government has tolerated isolated strikes, even wildcats, by those not seen as a danger to political stability, it has acted firmly and repressively toward strikes where the negotiating power of unions and employees was relatively great and where concessions might provoke a chain of new demands.

CONCLUSION

While the explanations offered early in this chapter reveal some important causes of labor quiescence, they do not all explain the problem of labor weakness. On first glance, the rise of nationalism and the prominence of media manipulation appear to be very persuasive explanations. If we reverse the line of causation, however, the puzzle remains unresolved. Perhaps it is not nationalism that caused labor weakness, but the weakness of labor (and of other social strata and interest groups) that led to the success of nationalism and to the atomization of the entire social structure. This brings us back to the features of the old Yugoslav system that might have caused social groups to be so fragmented in the first place. Another problem with the nationalism explanation is its implicit elitist approach, with its assumption that workers are less resistant to propaganda and more prone to irrational "blood-and-soil" type arguments than other social strata are.[23] In fact, vulnerability to an authoritarian demagogy seems to be a function of the level of education throughout the world. However, if this is universally valid, how can it explain the matter of labor weakness in this specific time and place? Moreover, an authoritarian orientation is often positively correlated with labor militancy, and it can thus constitute an important part of labor's strength rather than weakness.

Although the rise of ethnic nationalism and nationalist propaganda matter, they can be only a minor part of an explanation that assumes that workers are rational in their individual decisions. Rationality here means that each worker tries to improve his absolute and relative economic and social position. To achieve this goal in a rapidly changing and uncertain environment, he has to repeatedly make important decisions, always having in mind the costs and benefits of his actions. Specific complex structures of the environment, however, can often turn *ex ante* optimal (rational) decisions into *ex post* suboptimal (irrational) ones, as in the classical prisoners' dilemma framework. This is precisely what has happened with Serbian workers.

Our main thesis is, thus, that a complex set of structural factors—including the self-management legacy of segmented (balkanized) labor markets, the horizontal and vertical fragmentation of labor, the deep and prolonged economic crisis, the prevalence of unpaid leaves, the domination of social ownership and the delay of privatization, and the structure of collective bargaining—best explains labor's weakness and apparent ineffectiveness in preserving its relative and absolute position. From a classical Olsonian collective action framework,[24] all of the above-mentioned factors prevent unions from overcoming the free rider problem and organizing nationwide collective actions.

The vast majority of strikes in the 1990s occurred in individual enterprises, without any industrial or nationwide coordination. As a rule, they yielded no lasting results. Although there is no official statistical data about the number of strikes, the trend since 1993 has been steadily downward. This is consistent with the idea that repeated failed attempts produce discouragement and a sort of "learned powerlessness" among union leaders and workers.

To use Hirschman's exit-voice framework,[25] collective action is a form of voice. From the point of view of individual actors, voice is more costly and less attractive than exit if and when exit options are relatively easily available. Two types of exit are of special importance in the Serbian context. First there is literal emigration, which in the last ten years has drained Serbia of hundreds of thousands of mainly well-educated young people, many of whom first tried the voice option. Second, there is the informal economy option, which has the additional advantage for most workers in that it does not require severance of formal employment status. Eventually, however, they are trapped: After some time in the informal economy, voice becomes meaningless or even counterproductive for the workers themselves.

It is the extremely high level of uncertainty that prevents workers faced with unpaid leaves from raising their voice rather than accepting the exit option. In conditions of extreme uncertainty, people generally discount remote gains at a much higher rate than they do immediate ones. They also try to protect themselves from risk by creating a portfolio entailing as much security as possible. In the Serbian context, this can include preservation of formal employment status (which brings a small monetary wage and important fringe benefits such as health and pension insurance), membership in the state union (which provides occasional material aid, consumer discounts, and occasional access to union facilities such as health and vacation resorts), and participation in the informal economy (which often becomes the main source of current income).

This framework can also help us understand why the old unions are still not seriously threatened by the new ones. The new unions, with their orientation toward long-term gains that can only be achieved by raising labor's voice, are clearly less attractive to the average risk-averse worker than the old union, membership in which is an integral part of a risk-neutralizing exit option.

POSTSCRIPT: APRIL 2001

Has Serbian labor quiescence come to an end? After a decade of dormancy, Serbian workers emerged on the political scene in late 2000 to help topple the Milošević regime at last. Strong electoral support for opposition candidate Vojislav Kostunica in the industrial centers illustrated the extent to which labor had finally deserted the Milošević camp. Then, when Milošević failed to abide by the election results, it was a general strike that helped decide matters. Small shops were closed, as well as many large state enterprises. The powerful strike at the Kolubara coal mine struck a particularly painful blow to the regime. The inability—or unwillingness—of the police and army to crush that strike contributed, perhaps decisively, to Milošević's realization that he could no longer trust his coercive apparatus, not to mention his previous labor supporters. Soon after, he accepted his electoral defeat.

What caused the change for Serbian labor? It seems that at a certain point after the NATO bombing of spring 1999, workers realized that no economic improvement would be possible under the Milosević regime. A deteriorating economy, combined with tightened sanctions from abroad, meant that even previous exit options were closing off. In a desperate state of isolation, poverty, and hopelessness, and with exit options shrinking, labor, along with much else of Serbian civil society, finally found voice an attractive proposition. Whether it will hold onto this newfound voice, however, is quite unclear. For in the end, this was a voice directed *against* Milosević, not *for* labor itself. The latter development will still take time.

NOTES

I would like to express my gratitude to editors David Ost and Stephen Crowley for their guidance and helpful comments; to Collegium Budapest—Institute for Advanced Study for hosting me while preparing the final version of this article; and to RSS Prague for supporting related research, grant number 1065/1998, the results of which are used in this paper.

1. Nenad Dimitrijevic, "Serbian Nationalist Intellectuals," in *Intellectuals and Politics in Central Europe*, András Bozoki, ed. (Budapest: Central European University Press, 1999).

2. S. Milivojevic and J. Matic, *"Ekranizacija izbora"* [Broadcasting the Elections] (Belgrade: Vreme knjige, 1993); Z. Milivojevic, "The Media in Serbia from 1985 to 1994," in *Serbia between the Past and the Future* (Belgrade: Institute of Social Sciences & Forum for Ethnic Relations, 1997).

3. S. Mihajlovic, *Puls Srbije 1999* [The Pulse of Serbia in 1999] (Belgrade: Center for Policy Studies & UGS "Nezavisnost," 1999).

4. M. Stimac and V. Sonje, "Interna trzista rada: teorija, metodologija i empirijsko istrazivanja" [Internal Labor Markets: Theory, Methodology, and Empirical Research], in *Ekonomski pregled* 42, 1991.

5. N. Novakovic, *"Samoupravna moc u radnoj organizaciji"* [Power in Self-Managed Work Organization] (Belgrade: Institute of Social Sciences, 1992).

6. I. Jakupovic, "Eksploatacija i klasna borba u suvremenom jugoslovenskom drustvu" [Exploitation and Class Struggle in Contemporary Yugoslav Society], in *Marksisticka misao* 5, 1989.

7. Novakovic, *"Samoupravna moc u radnoj organizaciji."*

8. A. Molnar, "The Collapse of Self-Management and the Rise of *Führerprinzip* in Serbian Enterprises," in *Sociologija* 38:4, 1996.

9. *"Koncepcija razvoja Srbije do 2000"* [Development Perspectives of Serbia until the Year 2000] (Belgrade: Ekonomski Institut, 1996).

10. For a similar explanation concerning Russia, see R. Layard and A. Richter, "How Much Unemployment Is Needed for Restructuring? The Russian Experience," in discussion paper number 238 (London: Center for Economic Performance, London School of Economics, 1995).

11. M. Keune, "Introduction: Transition, Employment and Local Development in Cen-

tral and East Europe," in *Regional Development and Employment Policy: Lessons from Central and Eastern Europe*, M. Keune, ed. (Geneva: ILO, 1998).

12. A. Posarac, "Basic Facts about the Social Sector, Social Consequences of the Crisis and Employment and Unemployment in Yugoslavia," in *Challenges and Opportunities for the Economic Transition in Yugoslavia* (Belgrade: International Conference Proceedings, Economics Institute and USAID, November 1997).

13. M. Lazic et al., *Society in Crisis: Yugoslavia in the Early Nineties* (Belgrade: Filip Visnic, 1995); M. Lazic et al., *Delatni potencijal drustvenih slojeva* [Action Potential of Social Strata], unpublished research data (Belgrade: University of Belgrade, faculty of philosophy, 1997).

14. Posarac, "Basic Facts about the Social Sector, Social Consequences of the Crisis and Employment and Unemployment in Yugoslavia."

15. Lazic, et al. *Society in Crisis*.

16. M. Arandarenko, *"Trziste rada u tranziciji: Nastajanje industrijskih odnosa u Srbiji"* [Labor Market in Transition: The Emergence of Industrial Relations in Serbia], Ph.D. dissertation (Belgrade: Belgrade University, faculty of economics, 1998).

17. This is how Darko Marinkovic, one of Nezavisnost's leaders, put it. See his "Sindikalni pokret u Srbiji 1990–1993" [Trade Union Movement in Serbia 1990–1993], in *Srbija izmedju populizma i demokratije: politicki procesi u Srbiji 1990–1993* [Serbia between Populism and Democracy: Political Processes in Serbia 1990–1993], S. Antonic et al., eds. (Belgrade: Institute for Political Studies, 1993).

18. V. Goati, "Serbian Parties and Party System," in *Serbia between the Past and the Future*.

19. P. E. Mitev, "From Communism to Democracy: The New Elites in the Context of the Social Change," paper presented at conference on *New Elites, Social Stratification and Social Mobility in the Course of Antinomenklatura Revolutions* (American University, Blagoevgrad, Bulgaria, 1991); V. Goati, "Demokratska tranzicija u Srbiji" [Democratic Transition in Serbia], in *Gledista* 35:1–6, 1994.

20. S. Antonic, "Stranke i sindikati u Srbiji 1990–1998" [Parties and Unions in Serbia 1990–1998], in *Uloga sindikata u tranziciji* [The Role of Trade Unions in Transition] (Belgrade: Center for Policy Studies & UBTU "Nezavisnost," 1999).

21. M. Arandarenko, "Kolektivno pregovaranje i tripartizam" [Collective Bargaining and Tripartism], in *Uloga sindikata u tranziciji* (Belgrade: UGS Nezovisnost, 1999).

22. D. Marinkovic, *"Strajkovi i drustvena kriza"* [Strikes and Social Crisis] (Belgrade: Institute for Political Studies, 1995).

23. This, of course, is the famous argument of "working-class authoritarianism," put forth by Seymour Martin Lipset in *Political Man* (New York: Doubleday, 1960).

24. Mancur Olson, *The Logic of Collective Action: Public Goods and the Theory of Groups* (Cambridge: Harvard University Press, 1965).

25. Albert Hirschman, *Exit, Voice and Loyalty: Responses to Declines in Firms, Organizations and States* (Cambridge: Harvard University Press, 1970); Albert Hirschman, "Exit, Voice, and the Fate of the German Democratic Republic: An Essay in Conceptual History," in *World Politics* 45, 1993.

Chapter Nine

Workers and Unions in Postcommunist Ukraine

Włodzimierz Pańków and Evgienii Kopatko

The disintegration of the Soviet Union, the dismantling of the structures of the communist state, and the opening of domestic markets to world economic pressure threw tens of thousands of enterprises and millions of workers into disarray. In Ukraine, the changes have led to a dramatic social and material degradation of most workers.

This chapter is guided by the biblical principle that "by their fruits ye shall know them." We can know the position of labor in postcommunist Ukraine by looking at the conditions in which laborers live—not just industrial workers but people in labor communities. For this reason, this chapter focuses on the conditions facing workers in the southeastern industrial region known as the Donbass.[1] We hope both to provide the kind of close empirical account that is missing from most discussions on the subject of labor in postcommunist transformation and to suggest explanations for the general labor and union weakness that we identify. We begin the chapter with a discussion of the economic context of postcommunist Ukraine and of the specific actors in the contemporary Ukrainian labor movement. We then go on to report the results of survey research and fieldwork in the Donbass. We conclude with an explanation for Ukraine's poor record at economic reform and for the pervasive labor and trade union weakness that we find.

LABOR CONDITIONS AT THE STARTING POINT

At the time of independence, the Ukrainian economy was tightly linked with that of the other republics in a single, complex economic system. State ownership prevailed not only in industry but in agriculture and nonmanufacturing services. Production, investments, trade, and consumption were planned and controlled in a centralized fashion. Typical Soviet-type dysfunctions followed, such as price stability but perpetual shortages of goods and services, meaning a high level of suppressed inflation. On the labor front, employment was guaranteed for all but marked by low wages, low wage differentials, low employee motivation, and low productivity.[2]

The emergence of a new economy meant that new pathologies replaced the old ones. Shortages no longer appear as queues but as exorbitant prices that few can afford. As for labor, Ukraine's economic path has combined dramatic reductions in wages, production, and total labor costs with only limited official unemployment. Between 1990 and 1997, GDP declined by an astonishing 57 percent, but total employment declined only by 11 percent. By 1998, Ukraine's GDP fell to only 39.4 percent of the 1989 level, but official unemployment stood at only 4.3 percent. Naturally, productivity also plummeted, by some 51 percent, a decline offset by the drop in wages; real average monthly pay in 1997 was three times lower than in 1990. Total labor costs per hour came to 3 to 5 percent of the world price; forty cents an hour in Ukraine compared with $25.00 in Germany, $16.50 in Japan, $15.50 in the United States, $7.50 in South Korea, $3.00 in Mexico, and $2.50 in Malaysia.

One of the reasons for the low unemployment rate is that employers have other means of keeping labor costs down. Chief among these are delays in paying wages, forced administrative layoffs, and reduced working days. The first practice is the most pervasive, having grown exponentially since 1995 to the point where nearly 60 percent of the workforce in 1999 is not paid on time. Many have not had their wages paid in full in years. The other practices are also widespread. Some 22 percent of the total workforce was put on forced leave for at least some part of 1997, one-third of these for over a month, and about 16 percent worked a reduced day. These last two techniques are popular with employers and the state because they allow reductions in labor costs without the social tensions connected with permanent dismissals and without the payment of severance pay. At the same time, workers are available if and when the enterprise might need them. Official unemployment levels thus underestimate the problem. While official figures from late 1996 to 1998 hovered between 2 and 4 percent, independent analyses showed a real unemployment rate between 7.5 and 9 percent. Such practices, meanwhile, have drastically driven down real wages, which in 1997 were about one-third the levels of 1990.

The result of the poor allocation of labor in the old state firms is that the most competent and competitive workers are the first to leave, mostly to a nonunionized private sector, while those who stay behind tend to be the least skilled workers who need the social services still provided by the firm. In 1990, 78 percent of the workforce was employed in the state sector. This declined to 40 percent in 1997. The rest was divided between co-operative ownership (36 percent) and private ownership (24 percent).

While unemployment in Ukraine has always been low compared with other transition countries, it picked up considerably after 1995 as a result of tightening market pressures and state policy. State firms stopped hiring new workers. In 1998, there were thirty job-seekers for every posted vacancy. The average length of unemployment increased from year to year: from 6.8 months in 1996 to 8.5 months in 1997 and up to 10 months in 1998. In the western Lviv region in 1998, it exceeded one year.

In independent Ukraine, a large part of the population is simply uninvolved in productive labor. This leads to reduced flows to the state budget and an increased exit of capital from the country. People are losing their professional skills and their motivation for productive work. Perhaps the main danger is the pervasiveness of unemployment among youth. Excluding students, 32 percent of young people between the ages of fifteen and twenty-eight do not have a job. Needless to say, the unemployment compensation they are entitled to is also frequently in arrears. In 1999, total state indebtedness to citizens in the form of lagging wages, pensions, stipends, and welfare payments amounted to about 10 percent of the GDP. To survive, people grow food in small plots and, like so many others, seek to escape into the informal sector or abroad.

After a disastrous beginning, the situation seemed to improve briefly in the mid-1990s, at least in macroeconomic terms. In particular, the country achieved financial stabilization, as the hyperinflation of the immediate postcommunist years fell to a manageable 12 percent in 1997. Wages also rose, to an official average wage of about eighty-five dollars per month. Prices were approaching European levels, and many firms did not pay wages at all, so this was no great success, but it did seem to be a real improvement in the context of the poverty wages of 1992 and 1993. The Russian financial crisis of 1998, however, changed all that. The detectable improvement of public mood of 1996 and 1997 seemed to evaporate quickly.

In general, labor's situation is characterized by the following features:

- high unemployment
- low or absent wages
- lack of motivation for productive work
- poor health and safety situations
- inadequate social welfare protection

- declining life expectancy among people of working age
- outward migration of labor and intellectual potential

THE UNION ACTORS

In the Soviet era, there were actually two official trade union federations in Ukraine: the Ukrainian Republican Trade Union Council, with nineteen unions from enterprises under republican (Ukrainian) ownership, and the All-Union Central Trade Unions Council, which included forty-four sectoral trade unions from plants under central (Soviet) control. This bureaucratic diversification made little difference as far as union activities were concerned. Both unions acted as appendages of the state. Workers typically equated union authorities with the command economy.

Things started changing in the late 1980s following the pro-*perestroika* strike movement in the Donbass. By 1990 the official unions acknowledged that the old organizational structures were finished. Internal reformers created the Trade Union Federation of Ukraine (TUFU, from 1991 to 1992 called the Ukrainian Independent Trade Union Federation), which was open to members from both former union structures. TUFU quickly became independent Ukraine's dominant union organization. By its first postindependence congress, in 1992, it consisted of forty-one sectoral unions and twenty-six regional ones, with a total of 138,000 local enterprise units. By 1998, it counted 17.7 million members, thoroughly dominating employee interest representation in Ukraine. In enterprises where TUFU exists, 96.6 percent of the employees are members.

New trade unions—labeled "free," "independent," and "solidaristic" (after Poland's Solidarity)—were established mostly on the basis of the former strike committees and mostly in the western part of the country. A wide variety of such "free" trade unions have arisen since 1991, but few have gained much stability. The first to arise was the All-Ukrainian Organization of Strike Committees, in May 1991, which one month later changed its name to All-Ukrainian Organization of Solidary Workers. That union lasted till a split in 1995 that saw the formation of another federation: the All-Ukrainian Free Trade Union Organization of Solidary Workers. In 1994 other independent unionists created the Trade Union National Conference, and three years later a split led to the formation of yet another federation, called the Ukrainian National Labor Conference.

As should be clear from this record, the independent unions have thus far been unable to break the control of TUFU. For example, one of the most important of the new unions is the Independent Trade Union of Ukrainian

Coal Miners, which began as a strike movement. By 1999, estimates of its strength ranged from forty thousand to ninety thousand members, in comparison with the TUFU-affiliated miners' union with some six hundred thousand members.[3]

The only independent union formation to achieve some stability is the Trade Union Federation of Workers in Cooperative and Other Kinds of Enterprises. The cumbersome name refers to its aim of bringing together employees in the enterprises of new ownership forms, chiefly cooperative and private firms. Instead of acting as an organization defending the interests of employees against the new owners, however, this union seeks chiefly to defend the new range of enterprises and their small owners from state and bureaucratic intervention.

The various unions are not inactive. They tend to work on issues such as collective bargaining, legislation, protest actions against state policy, and trade union education projects. They have, however, been totally unable to stem the catastrophic economic collapse, and this explains why membership and influence are declining. According to a 1997 Socis Gallup survey, the level of trust in traditional and independent unions is down to 15 percent and 20 percent, respectively.

It is on legal matters that unions have made their greatest advances. Under the old system, unions did not have the right to negotiate with employers or to strike, and they could sign collective agreements only at the lowest level. In independent Ukraine, all the basic union liberties have been explicitly confirmed. Article 36 of the Constitution gives citizens the right to join trade unions regardless of management permission, and it grants all trade unions equal rights. Article 44 guarantees citizens the right to strike. Several subsequent laws have expanded the legal framework for trade unions, giving unions the right to participate in firm-level and national discussions on labor relations. Legally, labor has received a good deal of favorable legislation since 1991. More problematic is the extent to which unions actually use these rights. The country has a tripartite commission, the Social Partnership National Council, where diverse interests are supposed to discuss state programs, bills, and budgets, but unions have not had much influence there. Parliament contains pro-union voices, who have managed to push through some legislation and make changes to some 360 bills. Overall, however, direct union influence is in inverse proportion to its political level. In 1998 more than four thousand unionists were elected to district and village councils, but only seventy-one were elected to the regional councils, and only eight were elected to the national Supreme Council.

Practically all trade unions have accepted an ideology of social partnership (consultation and negotiation) as the civilized way of reconciling the diverse interests of the state, employers, and employees. In 1998 collective agreements were signed at fifty-five thousand enterprises embracing more than 10.3 million people, or 65.5 percent of the working population. These agreements usually included basic provisions on conditions of employment, pay, work and rest schedules, employee protection, and social conditions. While the number of employees covered by such agreements is high, the changing structure of the economy means that less than 10 percent of all firms are covered. Almost all the agreements are in large state enterprises. In private and small firms, unions are largely absent. There are still considerable difficulties defending workers' rights in private and small businesses.

LIVED EXPERIENCES OF
UKRAINIAN WORKERS

Yet how do Ukrainian workers actually experience work and the unions that represent them? To answer this question, we refer in the following sections to survey research and to our own fieldwork in Ukrainian enterprises.

The first survey data come from two 1995–1996 surveys conducted by the Institute of Industrial Economics of the Ukrainian Academy of Sciences. One survey is from a sample of eighty trade union leaders from eighteen different regions and thirty-five trade unions, and the other is a sample of 1,165 rank-and-file unionists in twenty-two regions of the country. The goal of the studies was to understand the activities of TUFU-affiliated unions and the causes of general union ineffectiveness.

Why do people join trade unions? The most common response, selected by two-fifths of the respondents, was that they joined because "so far it has been considered normal that one should join the trade unions." Others said they did so "to enjoy the privileges to which union members are entitled," while a smaller number said they "consciously chose the unions to defend their rights and interests." This suggests that the extremely high union density in Ukraine is largely the consequence of old habits and inertia.

The respondents had a general perception of union weakness. Asked about factors restricting unions from fulfilling their duties, they pointed to the following reasons (multiple selections were permitted):

- the shortage of funds (58 percent)
- the industry's difficult economic situation (53 percent)
- the subordination of the unions to enterprise management (47 percent)
- the difficult overall national situation (43 percent)

The surveys show a high incidence of industrial conflict. In fact, only 5 percent of rank-and-file members and 7 percent of leaders said that there had *not* been conflict at their enterprise. A third of rank-and-file respondents and a fourth of the leaders confirmed that conflicts erupted frequently. The chief causes of conflict, according to the leaders, are management ignorance of the law, lack of general management "culture," management hostility to unions, ability to violate the law with impunity, and weak legislation protecting employees.

Altogether, the surveys show union weakness due to unfavorable legacies (e.g., continued administrative interference, management hostility to independent unionism) and the devastating economic crisis. About one-fourth of the respondents blamed the unions themselves for problems, saying that the lack of action and solidarity was the main reason for this ongoing weakness.

Other surveys from the Donbass region, the most prosperous in the country and the site of many important new union activities, indicate the extent of general distrust of trade unions. In a 1996 survey[4] only 4 percent named trade unions as an institution that citizens can count on to defend their general welfare. This was the lowest for any institution except political parties (2 percent). In a 1997 survey, unions were not mentioned at all as such an institution, nor were they mentioned as institutions providing citizens with information about job retraining or finding new employment. (Most respondents said they could not count on anyone to defend them.) Asked to assess trade union activity in general (in the 1996 survey), 44 percent were highly critical, 24 percent said it didn't matter, 20 percent were unsure, and only 12 percent gave a positive reply. It should be noted that most of this criticism was directed at the quasi-official TUFU. Few had even heard of the independent unions. Only 24 percent were aware of the activities of the Independent Workers Union, though 5 percent regarded it as the most influential organization in the Donbass region. While critical of trade unions, most respondents cited the economy as the main problem facing labor. Two-thirds reported that the economic situation had greatly deteriorated in the last year.

We will now more closely explore the 1997 Donbass region survey, insofar as this survey throws a great deal of light on the existential and socioeconomic situation of the region's employees.[5] As noted previously, the Donbass is Ukraine's most heavily industrialized area. The survey was conducted by a joint Ukrainian-Polish research team in May and June 1997. Six hundred heads of households were interviewed in four Donbass cities: Donetsk, Makeyevka, Stakhanov, and Brianka. Of the six hundred respondents, 42 percent were working in the region's enterprises. The 58 percent who were not employed included retirees, the disabled, and a larger number of working-age unemployed than the official 2 percent figure would suggest. Of the employed respondents, 72 percent worked at state enterprises, 9.2 percent worked in collectively owned firms, 9.6 percent worked in private firms, and 0.4 percent were self-employed. Even accounting for the large informal economy, these figures show that ownership transformation in Ukraine has not progressed far. It is about the same level as in nearby Georgia, far lower than in more distant Kyrgyzstan, and incomparably lower levels in the so-called Visegrad quadrangle (that is, Czech Republic, Hungary, Poland, Slovakia). Particularly notable is the paucity of "founder privatization," or the establishment of new, small, private firms. Only one of every four Ukrainian employees works in a small enterprise (defined as up to one hundred employees), compared with two-fifths of all Polish employees. The level of restructuring appears to be mixed. We found several cases of propitious and substantial restructuring, along with many stagnant firms and some decaying ones (often the very biggest ones). The financial and economic situation of most firms is dismal, and the prospects look dim.

What is the lived experience of the employees of the Donbass? In findings that illustrate a typical and chronic problem in contemporary Ukraine, about 80 percent of our wage-dependent sample[6] reported difficulties in getting their due wages. About one-third of these were owed more than six months' wages, and another third were due four to six months' back pay. State and cooperative firms are the worst offenders. Three out of four employees owed back wages work in those sectors. By contrast, two-thirds of those employed in private firms report no delays in wage payments; only one-ninth of state employees could say that. Private firms, however, employ only a small proportion of the workforce.

It is chiefly workers in large and medium firms that face these problems. Three out of every four employees who do not get their wages on time work for enterprises employing more than one hundred people, and a majority of those work in firms employing more than one thousand people. Three-fifths of those who get paid on time work in firms with fewer than one hundred employees. Like private firms, however, small firms are few; only 28 percent of our employed sample work in one.

Nonpayment of wages is far and away the chief cause of industrial conflict in Ukraine. In 1997 there were 1,162 strikes with 116,000 participants, resulting in 9.8 million hours lost (an average strike length of three and a half days). Almost all of these strikes, which occurred chiefly in the coal and transportation sectors, were directed at nonpayment of wages, a violation of employees' constitutional right to due payment.

Almost three-quarters of our employed respondents considered the economic condition of their firms to be unsatisfactory, compared with 5.6 percent who thought it was good and 17.9 percent who thought it was adequate.

Broken down by ownership, about 80 percent of state employees and 70 percent of cooperative employees said their firms were unsatisfactory, with only 4.4 percent believing the situation was good. Only one-fourth of private employees, however, said their firms were unsatisfactory, with an equal number saying the situation was good and 37.5 percent saying it was satisfactory.

We thus have a linear relationship between company size (that is, the number of employees) and employee perception of economic health. The percentage of those feeling they work in poor firms grows as we move from firms with the lowest employment to those with the highest, and from private firms to state firms.

Asked about the possibility of losing their jobs in the near future, 40 percent rated this as high or very high, 40 percent rated it moderately high, and only 20 percent thought the possibility was low. Once again, the responses are strongly related to size but in a different direction. Those saying "very high" are likely to work in medium-size firms, which have between fifty and one thousand employees. In the largest firms (defined as those with more than one thousand employees), nearly half rate the risk of losing a job as moderate, and about 25 percent consider it low. Interestingly, they believe this despite their belief that their firms are in poor economic health. Evidently, they believe that big firms will not be allowed to collapse. Another striking finding is the relatively high sense of security in the very smallest firms (defined as those with up to fifty employees), with about one in three regarding the risk of unemployment as low. This could reflect the greater adaptability of small firms to customers' needs and, consequently, their greater capacity for survival or growth.

Significantly, the perceived probability of losing one's job was not related to ownership status. The stereotypical picture of the brutal capitalist employer ruthlessly disposing of redundant labor is not borne out in this sample. From the point of view of employees, the private owner does not seem greatly different from the state employer. The decisive criterion appears to be the economic health of the firm. The state firm is judged more likely to lay off workers because it is in poor economic health, not because it is a state firm. The private owner is seen as less likely to do so because it is likely to be in better health.

Our respondents were relatively pleased with physical working conditions and job safety (54 and 52 percent satisfaction, respectively) but highly dissatisfied over low wages (79 percent), poor protection of employee interests (74 percent), and low benefits (70 percent).

As for physical working conditions, those working in small and very small firms expressed the highest satisfaction (three-fourths and two-thirds, respectively), while only one-third of state employees expressed satisfaction. In short, work is toughest for those in huge enterprises, typically coal mines and steelworks, the traditional bastion of "really existing socialism."

The assessment of job safety also depends on enterprise size, with about 70 percent of employees in small firms (defined as those with twenty to one hundred employees) seeing safety as satisfactory, compared to fewer than a third in the large firms. This, of course, relates to the generally dangerous conditions prevalent in mines and steel mills.

Satisfaction with wages, meanwhile, is strongly connected both to ownership status and to firm size. Seventeen percent of state firm employees are satisfied with their pay, compared with 58.3 percent of private employees. Paradoxically, the worst assessment of wages comes in the "intermediate" forms of ownership status (e.g., "leasing" arrangements, where 100 percent expressed dissatisfaction with their wages), which were supposed to offer a gradual move from state to private ownership. As for size, nearly 50 percent of those in very small firms (that is, twenty to fifty employees) and 25 percent of those in small firms (that is, fifty to one hundred employees) regard their pay as satisfactory, compared with 8 percent of workers in the largest firms and 14 percent of workers in medium-size enterprises.

Few employees anywhere were satisfied with the benefits they receive, though the number, surprisingly, relates inversely to size. Only 10 percent of state employees expressed satisfaction with their benefits (nearly two-thirds were openly dissatisfied), compared with about 20 percent satisfaction in medium-size firms and 25 percent in small firms. (Perhaps they understood wages to be part of their benefits.) In any case, smaller, mostly private firms seem on the whole to be better able to provide for their employees.

Finally, in assessing the protection of employee interests, size again seems to matter, though in ways that defy common assumptions. Only one out of ten employees in large enterprises—that is, in workplaces where trade unions were likely to be present—thought their interests were well protected. This compared with some 37 percent of those working in the smallest firms and 17.2 percent of those in small enterprises. Dissatisfaction with the quality of protection was voiced by a staggering 85 percent of employees of the largest enterprises, with 72.1 percent "highly dissatisfied."

Similar to benefits, however, it appears that no one is very satisfied with how their interests are represented. In medium-size firms, more than three-quarters of employees expressed dissatisfaction on this score, with about two-thirds "highly" so. In small and very small firms, dissatisfaction runs to 65.5 percent and 62.1 percent, respectively. These figures say a great deal about trade union weakness. There is a clear crisis in the system of interest representation in the Donbass region, particularly in the large enterprises. In practice, a great majority of employees have been deprived of any protection or defense, opening the door to systematic abuse. This inability of unions or anyone else to defend employee interests is one of the main factors behind the negligence and stagnation of Ukraine's economy.

Besides weak trade unions, a large part of the problem for labor is its limited opportunity to escape. There are few available jobs anywhere, and travel abroad, typical for Central European unemployed youth, is highly difficult for Ukrainians due to visa problems. The great difficulty of escape, combined with the great desire to do so, is reflected in the hundreds of thousands of Ukrainian women who have been lured into prostitution abroad. Typically, the women are recruited to be hostesses, then robbed of their documents abroad and told how they can work off the debt. With good employment opportunities scarce for men and rare for women, the situation is unlikely to get better soon.

Immobility is reflected in our respondents' answers to the question of why they worked in enterprises that were not paying them. Sixty-one percent said they had no choice, 26 percent said they were still hoping for a paycheck, and 10 percent replied "old habit." Habit seems powerful in a number of ways. When asked what form of ownership they would like to work for, 44 percent chose state enterprises (that is, those that don't pay wages) while only 15 percent chose private firms. It seems that the past decades generated a powerful stereotype of the state as the guarantor of employment that even today's disastrous crisis cannot shake.

Our survey included a large number of unemployed people. The main reason for not working was retirement (66 percent) or dismissal connected with plant closure (14 percent). Two-thirds of the unemployed had been out of a job for more than a year. Twenty-two percent said they were prepared to take any job, but 41 percent acknowledged making no effort to find employment. Insufficient interest and a loss of hope appear to be the chief causes of this. Eighty percent of our unemployed sample said they received no job-placement assistance, which can certainly contribute to the growth of social apathy.

It is often said that in the so-called normal societies, most people consider themselves somewhere near the middle of the social ladder. In our sample, four-fifths of our respondents considered themselves poor, even though most of them received some form of welfare aid. Almost all said their standard of living had declined in the 1990s. Ninety percent said their own financial situation was worse, 80 percent mentioned a deterioration of health care, 83 percent complained of weaker employment guarantees, and 76 percent pointed to a deterioration in environmental conditions. As noted before, many families supplement wages and/or pensions with auxiliary food growing, typically small rented orchards and gardens (42 percent), personal allotment gardens

(9 percent), and vegetable beds at dachas (4 percent). Vending, seasonal, and additional jobs were mentioned by 2–4 percent of respondents, while welfare handouts are an important part of the budgets of 10 percent of the families. The range of sources of income is fairly wide, but not enough to meet needs. Sixty-three percent of our respondents reported denying themselves basic material needs because of a lack of money. A third barely managed to make ends meet. Only 3 percent reported that they could save money, and then only from time to time.

Most of our sample had guaranteed shelter, either an autonomous apartment (43 percent), a house (26 percent), or part of a house (29 percent). In the mining housing estates, however, living conditions are particularly hard, with only 6 percent regarding their housing as good and 36 percent as satisfactory. Eighty-eight percent of respondents said their accommodation required repairs; for 20 percent, a thorough overhaul was needed. Three-quarters of respondents do not expect change for the better in the near future.

Apart from housing, more than two-thirds of the respondents believe that their lives will get worse during the year ahead. Also notable is a rapidly growing individualization of society. Mutual aid and solidarity are declining fast. Only a fifth of the respondents expected assistance from relatives, and a mere 4–5 percent hoped for help from other sources (e.g., friends, neighbors, acquaintances). Eighty-nine percent saw the problems in their lives as likely only to get worse. Most respondents said they could not count on anyone to defend them. It seems we are dealing here with the syndrome of a deserted society. Even mass organizations such as trade unions do not alleviate the problem to any degree.

What does all this mean for union effectiveness? On the one hand, density rates are clearly impressive, having changed little since communist times. Yet it is difficult to find any aspect of working or living conditions that could be assessed positively. In this sense, unions have not been effective at all. All the available information indicates that conditions for Ukrainian working people are bad and getting worse all the time. Our survey, after all, was taken *before* the financial crisis of 1997 and 1998.

TRANSFORMATION UKRAINIAN STYLE

Ukraine is not, alas, one of the leaders in terms of the depth, speed, and durability of postcommunist transformation. It is the second most populous of the former Soviet republics and third largest in area, but it lags behind many of its smaller neighbors. In terms of market transition, it lags far behind Russia or even Transcaucasia, to say nothing of Estonia or Lithuania.[7] Only Belarus provides a backdrop against which Ukraine looks favorable.

There seem to be several reasons for this relative lack of reform. First, there has never been a consensus on the vital *need* for reform. Ideas are important. In our numerous interviews with Ukrainian enterprise managers, local political leaders, and even some scholars, we found few who shared a conviction that deep socioeconomic reform is necessary and possible. The difference between Ukrainian and Polish elites is quite striking. The latter have been telling their citizens from the very start of the transition process that the economy and society were in a very difficult, if not altogether lamentable, shape and that Poland was far, far behind even the least developed Western economies. We had the impression that the Ukrainian elites lacked awareness of the country's critical situation, especially the widening gap between Ukraine and the leaders of structural transformations. In Ukraine, even those who have traveled the world tended to tell us that the gap between them and more developed economies was merely "some two to three years." Domestic leaders seemed to be lulling society to sleep rather than mobilizing it to deep and rapid transformation. We also detected enduring elements of what might be called the "post-imperial syndrome." Ukrainians were well represented in the political and economic elite of the USSR, and, similar to Russians, they (specifically *eastern* Ukrainians) tended to regard themselves as coarchitects of the Soviet empire. Our interlocutors frequently emphasized the size of the Ukrainian contribution to the economic and military might of that empire. In this way, they perpetuated a "Soviet pride" that made it easy to dismiss the achievements of other countries and downplay the need for change.

Ukraine seems also to have been lulled into inaction by its initial economic situation, which seemed better than it really was. Taking into account its size, its large populace, and the fact that it had at lease some energy sources (coal and nuclear power plants), Ukraine appeared to be in not-so-dire straits after the fall of the USSR. Its market did not shrink as in Estonia, Georgia, or Kyrgyzstan. Its industrial capacity seemed intact. Russia seemed to need it too, if only as an outlet for goods. Ukraine's decision makers did not have to make immediate radical decisions, such as finding new markets or alternative sources of supplies. When the situation proved to be worse than initially anticipated, the country had already frozen into a stagnant pattern.

Finally, the newly independent country was burdened by the pressures of state building and had few resources with which to accomplish this.[8] It had to establish Ukraine's international presence in the face of considerable initial opposition, first from the United States (there was Secretary of State James Baker's admonition against independence in spring 1991) and continually from Russia, which has not reconciled itself with Ukrainian independence to this day. Ukraine had to build new central and local governments, a diplomatic corps, an army, a national bank, and a national finance system. And it had to do these things in the context of the formidable brain drain from the Slav republics to the federal administration in Moscow.

EXPLAINING LABOR WEAKNESS

Reform or no reform, workers have paid a great price for the collapse of the Ukrainian economy. Trade unions have not been able to defend them. Why has there not been more protest? One key reason is a pervasive sense of hopelessness. To most Ukrainian people, protest seems futile. Most enterprises are uncompetitive institutions with poor prospects and an unresolved ownership status. Firms are either dismissing workers or artificially maintaining them. These are not conditions in which workers believe they can win concessions. With less and less to divide, it appears to even the most militant union leader that no form of pressure, from strikes and hunger strikes to demonstrations and marches, can produce significant results. This does not mean there are no strikes. However, when they occur (as noted earlier, almost exclusively in coal and transport), they tend to be aimed solely at clearing up wage arrears. Though such demands are hardly an expression of militant unionism, in the mid-1990s such strikes were alternately repressed, with some union leaders thrown into jail or ignored. On the whole, the unionist who wants to engage in protest against management is the rare one. Our research acquainted us with several union leaders who were co-opted and corrupted by management and never sought to challenge anything.

With conditions for successful protest so few, most workers have substituted personal survival strategies for collective action. One such strategy is, of course, the informal economy. In the face of enterprise insolvency, employees take up myriad kinds of unofficial, ad hoc productive, service, and commercial jobs, which together with the lingering benefits of the official jobs, make survival possible despite the nonpayment of wages. Petty trade, based on the import-export business from the "near abroad" (that is, Poland, Hungary, Turkey, or Germany), is particularly popular among young workers as well as secondary-school and university graduates—people who might otherwise be leading protests. Operating on the borders of the law, they fall prey to crooked customs officers and gangsters, and they often set up rival gangs themselves, if only for self-defense. At the same time, they amass capital and become the kernel of a new middle class. Either way, they eschew collective class action.

Another, even more widespread, phenomenon is the return of industrial workers, often first- or second-generation migrants from the countryside, to the land. The families of employees deprived of wages and other sources of income spend many spring, summer, and autumn months in small allotments assigned to them by local authorities. The crops grown on those small plots, of several thousand square meters at most, are crucial for many Ukrainian diets. The one potential benefit of this development is that it lays a possible basis for the emergence of a highly productive fruit- and vegetable-growing sector, which was sorely lacking in the communist era.

The widespread resorting to such personalized strategies of survival (and we have presented here only the most accessible and relatively legal ones) draws millions of workers away from the unions, weakening the latter's organizational and mobilization potential and eroding even more the low attraction of collective action.

Union action, of course, is often also political action. Ukrainian unions, however, have been marginalized politically as well. They have been unable to find genuine allies on the political scene. In most market economies, trade unions ally with parties on the left, but the left-wing parties in Ukraine are those with communist roots, whose main focus is defending the interests of the embourgeoised *nomenklatura*. These are the ones who delay payment of wages to invest the funds in legal or illegal get-rich ventures; they also appropriate, with the central and regional bureaucracies, much of the foreign funds allocated ostensibly to restructuring. The interests of these parties thus clash very clearly with the interests of labor, and union cooperation with them can produce no good for most workers. The leadership of these parties are certainly willing to accept labor's support in their election campaigns in return for verbal commitments. On the whole, however, the relations between these two groups are full of mistrust. The parliamentary elections of March 1998 strengthened the position of the Communist Party but not the position of labor.

The center and right-wing parties, meanwhile, do not trust the main Ukrainian unions because of the latter's old-regime legacy. Then there is a geographical problem too. The unions are particularly strong in eastern and southern Ukraine, while the right-wing and center parties are strong in western Ukraine. Thus, distrust permeates this potential political configuration as well. In short, there seems little chance of real cooperation with any of the existing political parties leading to a better situation for labor.

Finally, union weakness is a result of labor's own reluctance to stir up trouble in a country that has just won an historic but still insecure independence. The problem is particularly acute insofar as union potential is concentrated in the east and southeast, the same regions dominated by Russian ethnic and language ties. In present circumstances, large-scale union actions could be viewed as anti-Ukrainian moves designed to weaken the already fragile independence of the country. Ukrainian unions appear to be intent on avoiding activity that could be construed as contrary to the interests, or at least the values, of the young Ukrainian state, and this too contributes to union weakness.

APPENDIX

Trade-union movement of Ukraine (most important unions): Name of organization, founding date, approximate membership, (name of president).

Trade Union Federation of Ukraine, 1990, 16.5 million members, 41 sectoral trade unions, 26 regional trade union formations, (A. Stoyan).

Trade Union Federation of Cooperative and Other Forms of Property Workers, 1990, 250,000 members, (N. Koshevina).

National Confederation of Ukrainian Trade Unions, 1994, 3.2 million members, (U. Pivovarov).

Joint Trade Unions of Ukraine, 1990, 130,000 members, (O. Sheikin).

Trade-Union Formation "Nashe Pravo," 1996, 150,000 members, (F. Sudnitzin).

All-Ukrainian Organization of Workers Solidarity (AUWS), 1991, 50,000 members, (O. Dshulik).

Formation of Free Trade Unions of Railway Workers of Ukraine, 1995, 5,000 members, (T. Nedviga).

Trade Union of Engine Drivers of Ukraine, 1992, 4,000 members, (S. Karikov).

Independent Trade Union of Ukrainian Coal Miners, 1991, 40,000 members, (M. Volinetz)

Trade Union of Railway and Transport Builders of Ukraine, 1992, 760,000 members, (A. Chornomaz).

Maritime Trade Union Federation of Ukraine, 1992, 35,000 members, (E. Izotov).

Trade Union of Ukrainian National Academy of Science Workers, 1991, 50,000 members, (A. Shirokov).

Trade Union of Ukrainian Tax Offices, 1998, 60,000 members.

Trade Union of Ukrainian Customs Bodies, 1993, 15,000 members, (A. Pavlov).

NOTES

1. While the research was largely carried out in Donets Oblast, we refer to the region throughout by the more popular (and geographically broader) name of the Donbass. While

we make no claims that this is a representative or average region in Ukraine, it is the most heavily industrialized and, hence, where labor issues have the most impact.

2. Sources used for this analysis of the Ukrainian economy include A. Bazyluk "Social Partnership as a Means of Socio-economic Problem Solving"; M. Biloblotskyj, "The Current State of the Labor Market and the Prospects for Its Development"; and I. Bondar and O. Kuznetsova, "The Labor Movement as a Reflection of the Socio-Economic Situation in Ukraine" all (in Ukrainian) in *Ukrajina: Aspekty truda* 1, 1997. Also H. Stojan, "The Impact of Trade Unions on the Social Direction of Economic Reform in Ukraine," in *Ukrajina: Aspekty truda* 1, 1998; and S. Ukrajinec, "Social Partnership in Ukraine from the Viewpoint of Legal Regulation," in *Ukrajina: Aspekty truda* 2, 1998. Other sources include H. Mimandusova, "The Unemployment Rate and Categories of Unemployment in the Population Structure in Ukraine" (in Ukrainian), in *Sotsiolohiya: teorija, metody, marketynh* 4–5, 1998; H. W. Osnowyj, "The Trade Union Movement in Ukraine: A New Social Role, the Search for Optimal Organizational Structures" (in Ukrainian), in *Profspilki Ukrainy* 4, 1998; and "Trud w Ukraini w 1997h: Statystyczeskyj sbornyk," in *Hosudarstwennyj Komitet Statystyki Ukrajiny* (Kiev, 1998).

3. In a pattern typical of other Eastern European countries (and in Western Europe and North America not long ago), coal is an unprofitable industry that the government is trying to close—but slowly because of the huge social costs involved. Output fell from 165 to 90 million tons between 1990 and 1997, but the industry still employs close to one million people, including a vast bureaucracy in 257 mines (mostly in the Donbass region).

4. Sample of 780 inhabitants, discussed in *Socio-political Profile of the Donbass* (Donetsk: Donetsk Information-Analytical Centre, 1996).

5. Report on the survey and research project in Aleksandr Lach and Włodzimierz Pańków, eds., *The Future of Old Industrial Regions in Europe: The Case of the Donets Region in Ukraine* (Warsaw: Fundacja Edukacji Ekonomicznej, 1998). See especially the chapters by E. Kopatko and V. Korshunov, A. Mokrzyszewski, B. Gąciarz, and W. Pańków.

6. As already noted, this was only a minority of our sample. The majority of our respondents procure income from old-age or disability pensions, gardening, or help from relatives.

7. Marek Dąbrowski, "Liga reformatorów," in *Polityka* 19, 1999, 64–66.

8. On these and other objective factors delaying economic reform, see M. Dąbrowski and R. Antczak, eds., *Ukrainskij put' k rynocznoj ekonomikie, 1991–1995* (Warsaw: Centre for Social and Economic Research, 1996).

Chapter Ten

The Social Explosion That Wasn't: Labor Quiescence in Postcommunist Russia

Stephen Crowley

There is a paradox concerning labor in Russia. One constantly hears phrases like "social explosion" or even words like "revolution" being uttered. Yet despite conditions that are nearly catastrophic, there has been no social explosion, and a few dramatic exceptions aside, there is little sign that it is about to appear.

From the perspective of workers in particular, the conditions in Russia are distressing. Between 1991, when Russia began to move from central planning to a market system, and 1999, the Russian economy experienced a downturn worse than the Great Depression. By official statistics, the GDP was reduced by almost half since the start of "reforms" in 1991; in other words, factories and other economic units produce about half the goods and services they did prior to the collapse of communism.[1] According to the government's accounting, in 1999 some 35 percent of the population received a monetary income below the officially defined subsistence minimum, and most of these people were "working poor."[2] There has been a chronic problem with wage arrears: Many workers simply are not getting paid for months at a time. While there has been some recent improvement in wage arrears, especially since the collapse of the ruble in August 1998, the value of those wages has dropped in real terms. In fact, in March of 1999, Russia's average hourly labor costs, including benefits, were fifty-six cents an hour—less than half the labor costs in Guatemala.[3]

Yet, one wants to know, where is the protest? Most would expect that under such conditions workers would protest. Yet relative to this grim social and economic picture, there have been very few strikes. The Federation of Independent Trade Unions of Russia (FNPR), Russia's main trade union federation and the successor to the communist-era trade union, has proven largely impotent against wage delays and other crucial working-class concerns. Nor does it have any significant rivals that might better defend Russia's workers. Indeed, aside from some strike activity in limited sectors of the Russian economy, workers in Russia have remained remarkably quiescent.

The question is not only one of workers' social and economic well-being. Politically, labor as an organized interest is practically nonexistent in Russian society. Besides ineffectual trade unions and despite the large number of political parties that have appeared, virtually none, including the Communist Party (KPRF), has targeted its appeals at this large and grievance-filled social group. If this significant social actor is not able to defend its interests and has no real representative institutions through which to articulate its grievances—and there are real ones—what kind of civil society and what kind of democracy is being consolidated in Russia?

By looking at a number of possible explanations, this chapter will address the question of why Russian workers have seemed so quiescent. We will then turn to the central question of trade unions in Russia in an attempt to understand their ineffectiveness to date. We will conclude with the prospects of Russian workers overcoming their difficult situation.

Let us first address the question of whether Russian workers have indeed been quiescent. This question first appeared in 1989, when political conditions under Gorbachev's perestroika made workers' collective action a possibility. Then four hundred thousand coal miners throughout the Soviet Union, from western Ukraine to Sakhalin in the far east, went on strike, occupied city squares, and articulated demands that ranged from more provisions of consumer goods to the deepening of political and economic reforms. They organized themselves into strike committees, and they later created independent trade unions. Yet meanwhile steelworkers in the same towns seemed, in the words of one observer, to be "in another world."[4]

Indeed, the question was a compelling one. Why did steelworkers—in the same communities, sometimes living literally right next door—not join the coal miners in striking?[5] This question has persisted for more than ten years. Miners remain militant, but most other industrial workers are hardly heard from at all. This is in conditions where, at the risk of understatement, grievances have become much more compelling since 1989.

Yet there certainly are strikes in Russia. From 1992 to 1996, a total of 24,185 strikes were reported in Russia, for an average of 4,837 per year.[6] When we break down these figures by sector, however, a different picture emerges. Teachers lead the large majority of these strikes. More precisely, fully 87 percent of all strikes in Russia from 1992 to 1996 took place in the education sector, and these figures have remained largely consistent since.[7] Manufacturing and mining combined account for less than 5 percent of the official strike figures; almost certainly most of these strikes took place in the strike-prone coal industry. This means that since the start of the painful "transition," very few strikes have occurred in any industry other than coal mining.

Yet when protests do happen, especially in coal mining and education, workers display a tremendous amount of anger and frustration. Examples include the large proportion of overall strikes that are wildcat strikes; the miners' "rail wars" of 1998 when they blockaded the Transiberian and other major railways; the hostage taking of managers; the seizure of factories by work collectives contesting privatization; and the hunger strikes and even the self-immolation of those not getting paid. All this suggests that despite the lack of organized collective action on a wide scale, Russian workplaces are ridden with conflict.

What might explain the inability of Russian workers to defend their interests in a time of such wrenching hardship? Several explanations are possible:

- individual "exit" strategies and the extremely weak labor market
- the nature of the postcommunist "liberal transformation"
- continued enterprise paternalism
- Russia's trade unions
- the role of the state
- postcommunist ideologies

We will discuss these in turn.

"EXIT" AND THE LABOR MARKET

In explaining the lack of worker protest in Russia, some point to workers' use of survival strategies. For instance, workers in formerly state-supported enterprises are often engaged in paying work in the informal economy in addition to their official job. Some would go so far as to argue that Russian workers on the whole are not doing so badly but that their real income is not captured in official statistics.[8] Others argue that because workers spend their free time growing food and engaging in other means of simple survival, there is little time and energy left for organizing.[9] In either case, in Hirschman's terms, workers are engaged in individual-level "exit" strategies rather than using collective "voice" to improve their well-being.[10] Yet it is difficult to sustain the optimistic version of this argument—that Russian workers are doing relatively well but that their well-being comes from informal employment and is hidden from view—given the rather desperate lengths workers and others have taken to survive.[11] One must ask whether workers are choosing individual exit options in preference to collective options as a conscious strategy, or whether they are adopting this approach out of desperation because collective options are so difficult to bring about. If the latter, then we still need to explain why collective action is so difficult in this context. While individual-level strategies might explain why people in Russia are not going hungry, this factor on its own cannot explain why there is so little real protest.

A related, yet more persuasive, factor can be summarized as follows: How to strike when there is no work? Though the Russian economy has begun a modest recovery, for some time industrial output, according to official statistics, was cut almost in half. It is difficult for workers to shut down production when they are being sent on unpaid leaves, as has often been the case.[12] Many workers in Russia have not been working, and many are not getting paid. While the extent of wage arrears has recently declined, by late 1998 approximately two-thirds of Russian workers reported overdue wages, with those affected reporting close to five months' pay in arrears on average.[13] Often, workers would not be paid in rubles but would be paid in kind—in products the enterprise had obtained by barter or in consumer goods the plant produced, including matches, bras, coffins, and in one case, manure.[14] This phenomenon gives new meaning to the Soviet-era aphorism "we pretend to work and they pretend to pay us," once a clever witticism and now a sad lament.

This difficulty in striking when not making anything would explain why, if there are not many strikes in the traditional sense, there are cases of hunger strikes, the blockading of rail lines, and other nontraditional, more desperate collective actions.

This dramatic change in the demand for labor—moving from labor shortage to labor surplus—has certainly been the greatest single shock that workers have faced in the transition from communism to capitalism. Under the old shortage economy, workers could use the excess demand for labor by moving from enterprise to enterprise, bidding up their wages and benefits. They are now faced with the very real threat of unemployment. Returning to Hirschman's analogy, workers in the past had the ability to "exit"; in theory, given unprecedented political freedoms, they should now have "voice." Yet they appear to have little of either.[15]

This lack of collective action combined with workers' weak position in the labor market fits with the traditional economic theory of strikes—that strikes take place not when labor is weak but when it is strong, such as in conditions of low unemployment. We will return to this issue in the concluding chapter to this volume, but for now suffice to say that were this theory true, we would expect to see an even modest increase in labor activity with the beginning of economic recovery in Russia. Yet there is little evidence that this is the case.

LIBERAL TRANSFORMATION

One reason this is so (and another factor in the overall inaction of Russian workers) is not simply the degree of economic decline and its impact on the labor market but the nature of the postcommunist transformations—in particular, the abandonment of central planning and the privatization of state enterprises.[16] Under the old regime, instead of the invisible hand of the market, the very visible hand of state planners acted as a lightning rod for labor conflict, quickly politicizing it. For example, when coal miners in the Siberian Kuzbass region first struck in July 1989, initially in a single mine over local issues, the strike soon spread to the entire industry. Miners in the Ukrainian Donbass region struck after the strike in the Kuzbass region ended, just to make sure, despite promises from top state officials, that the strike agreement covered them too.[17] The question of why other workers did not join the miners' strikes, then and subsequently, has been examined elsewhere.[18] However, in this first strike, miners were united by the coal industry, or more precisely the Coal Ministry, which was handing out the concessions. That is, the strike followed the institutional channels that the state set up.

With the advent of market reform, the role of the state has changed significantly. It is no longer the central employer. The importance of this is evident if we compare the protest actions that took place in Indonesia and Russia, both of which, in 1997 and 1998 respectively, suffered a severe economic crisis.[19] The conventional explanation for the lack of protest in Russia has been the purported stoicism of the Russian people. As the *New York Times* glibly put it, the ability to withstand suffering is in Russians' "genetic code."[20] However, Indonesians also had a reputation for subservience before authority. Yet in Indonesia we witnessed student protests and riots that brought down the Suharto regime in 1997. In Russia, by contrast, a "day of protest" called by the main trade union federation and opposition parties in October 1998—just months after the August collapse—was even weaker than the ineffective attempts at such protest in the past.[21] The FNPR, Russia's main trade union federation, did manage to up the rhetoric—from "a change in the course of reforms" to "Yeltsin resign," but with Yeltsin's popularity rating in low-single digits, in so doing they were not exactly going out on a limb.

The difference, or at least one major one, between these two countries is the role of the state in the economy. In Indonesia, the state has maintained direct control over much of economy, not unlike the Soviet Union. Indonesians popularly perceived control of the state and the economy as focused on one individual and his family, who then served as a target for economic protests. By contrast, in Russia, control over the economy was perceived as dispersed and diffused, and no longer under the direct control of the state.[22]

This factor helps explain which sectors are the ones that engage in strikes in Russia. As mentioned earlier, while few strikes take place in manufacturing, a large number of strikes occur in the public or "budget" sector—besides teachers, health-care workers, and others paid (or until quite recently, most often not paid) directly from the state budget. Coal miners are also still largely part of the state sector. This factor alone cannot explain why so few industrial workers went on strike even before their firms were privatized. Nevertheless, that so few strikes take place outside the budget sector strongly suggests that the state has succeeded in no longer being perceived by workers as directly responsible for their well-being; or perhaps workers in the "privatized sector" simply are not sure against whom to strike.

ENTERPRISE PATERNALISM

Another factor, and one that is less part of the postcommunist transformations than the communist past, is the continuing impact of enterprise paternalism. The Soviet welfare state was largely administered through the workplace. The typical Soviet factory not only provided employment but also provided housing, day care, vacations, and often a wide range of consumer goods to workers and their families. With shortage a pervasive feature of the Soviet economy, the workplace typically provided goods and services that workers could not buy elsewhere. These goods and services were also used to prevent skilled workers from using the labor shortage to leave for another, better-provisioned enterprise. The goods and services were also distributed on a discretionary basis to ensure worker compliance. This paternalism created multistranded dependencies on the workplace.[23]

Do enterprises still distribute such goods and services, and if so, does this continued paternalism still have a significant impact on workers' actions? As to the first question, one would expect that as market pressures increase and as profit becomes the motivating force, managers would stop providing day care, vacations, housing, and consumer goods to their workforce. These provisions are simply too costly, and without the shortages of the past, in theory such items can be provided more efficiently by markets. Yet while greatly diminished, the benefits provided by Russian enterprises are still present.[24]

When their wages were in arrears, workers would not be paid cash but would often be paid in kind—in products the enterprise had obtained by barter or in consumer goods the plant produced. However, even when wages were in arrears or even when on unpaid leave, workers continued to receive other benefits as well. For instance, workers might eat a hot dinner in the plant cafeteria that could be the main meal of day. Though they might not receive a regular salary, workers could sometimes obtain goods at the factory store with "chits" or "company credit cards." Though they might be laid off, maintaining even formal employment meant the eventual possibility of a pension. Such services as child care, while much more expensive than in the past, were still cheaper within the enterprise than outside it.

The Russian state has officially transferred such social assets from enterprises to local government, but they have not provided sufficient funds to pay for them. To the extent these services exist at all, they are still paid for and administered through the workplace. While the level and quality of the benefits provided at the workplace has declined significantly, they take on increased importance given the struggle of so many people to escape poverty.[25]

Why should managers bother to provide such services any longer? After all, the main incentive in the past was the labor shortage—enterprises provided goods and services to retain workers who could "exit" for a better deal somewhere else. The answer is partly the paternalistic mentality of the past—workers expect these benefits, and managers are used to providing them. More important, it would seem, was the process of privatization in Russia, where in most enterprises the majority of shares went to the "labor collectives," at least on paper. In these conditions managers still need the tools that worked in the past to keep the labor force quiescent, so as to keep themselves in office—and with control over ownership the ultimate goal, the stakes are even higher than before. Even when property rights have formally shifted to management, as they typically have, a strong stakeholder mentality still exists among the workforce. Should the employees succeed in striking against management, however remote the prospect, they might well force out the management team, signal their vulnerability to outside takeover, or perhaps invite the renationalization of the firm by regional governments.[26]

This continued dependence of the workforce on the enterprise for more than a monetary wage helps explain an otherwise curious phenomenon: Why, when the economy has shrunk by as much as half, have unemployment levels remained so low? During the Great Depression, real wages remained stable, while unemployment rose to between 20 and 25 percent. In Russia the opposite has happened. Unemployment levels have remained low relative to the fall in output, but real wages have been cut by about half.[27] Put differently, in the Great Depression, workers bore the brunt of the crisis through unemployment; in the postcommunist depression, workers took the hit through wages.

In Russia this has taken the extreme form of workers being officially kept on the payrolls, even though there is no work and they are not being paid. In this context it is worth recalling a standard definition of corporatism: wage restraint in exchange for full employment.[28] From this perspective, Russia seems to be a case of corporatism gone mad!

The Russian government has taken a number of very large steps along the road of structural reform. It has liberalized prices, dismantled central planning, opened to the world market, and privatized enterprises. Yet given the continued dependence of workers and their families on these workplaces, the Russian government could not get past the step, so crucial for a capitalist economy, of removing workers from unprofitable enterprises and shutting them down. In short, there appears to have been an implicit deal between the state and industrial enterprises: Companies might not pay their workers, their bills to creditors, or their taxes to the government, but they should continue to take care of the "collective."[29] The state thereby loses revenue, but it prevents social unrest. There are additional factors to help explain Russia's non-payment crisis and its relatively low level of unemployment, but this is clearly a crucial one.

As of May 2000, unemployment in Russia was more than 11 percent.[30] This is low only relative to the deep economic contraction that Russia has experienced. The relationship between the state and workplaces in Russia is something like a war of attrition. To use a historic metaphor that Russians would understand, the situation is something like the siege of Leningrad. Enterprises are starved of cash and credit. Managers are implicitly permitted to use whatever means they can, legal and otherwise, to induce workers to quit without massive firings.[31] The government hopes these factories will not explode but instead will wither away, as workers eventually leave of their own volition.

RUSSIAN UNIONS

Where are unions in all of this? That the Soviet welfare state was administered through the workplace explains much about unions in post-Soviet Russia. Unions in the communist period were not only an arm of management but were essentially social welfare agencies. A worker would go to the trade union not with a complaint about the boss but for a voucher to the plant's vacation resort, for a place in summer camp for one's kids, or perhaps for a television distributed by the plant's consumer network.

Polls show that the demands trade unions raise are popular. People's greatest concerns are often unemployment and delayed wage payments.[32] Yet poll after poll shows that the FNPR, and unions generally, are among the least-respected public institutions in Russia.[33] Put differently, unions—the organizations that in theory should be the most capable of achieving the goals of most people—are among the least trusted institutions in society and have proven themselves largely incapable of mobilizing their members in support of those goals.[34]

Why have Russian unions been so ineffective? The once-official, now independent trade unions are having a hard time becoming truly independent—but not for lack of trying. Unions remain doubly dependent on both management and the state. At the factory level, managers in many cases are still trade union members, as they were in the communist era. In 1993, 95 percent of union leaders saw themselves as part of management's team.[35] A more recent survey found that two-thirds of trade union presidents and the same number of enterprise directors think it is normal for workers and managers to be members of the same trade union because "this helps to avoid conflict."[36] Moreover, unions continue to serve as the distributors of social services and in-kind benefits, which were once funded by the state and now, if they exist at all, are provided by management. A 1995 survey found that more than twice as many people turn to the union with questions about social benefits than with questions about pay—and this in conditions of growing wage arrears.[37] In her in-depth study of one coal mine and its trade union, Ashwin reported that "days spent observing events in the trade union office revealed that union officers unquestionably spent most of their time dealing with *sotskul'tbyt* [social, cultural, and daily life concerns] and related issues."[38]

Russian unions face a paradox. Given the unions' long and continued legacy of being an arm of management for the provision of goods and services, workers do not look to them to defend their rights. However, given the dire economic and social conditions in Russia, workers more than ever need what goods and services unions can provide. Still, because it is managers who provide the resources for such services, union leaders are effectively prevented from taking a tough stance against management because they can easily be cut off from these resources and, thus, further lose their standing with their members.[39] In these conditions, it is not surprising that there is little evidence of unions being viewed by workers as real defenders of their interests.

At the national level, the FNPR remains dependent on the state.[40] While social insurance is supposed to be administered by a government agency, a large part by default is still administered by the FNPR.[41] The union federation inherited an enormous amount of property from the communist period, including revenue-generating concerns like vacation resorts and other real estate. The continued control over these and other resources gives the unions what power they have, and it helps explain the continued high (although declining) rates of membership, especially in comparison with the new trade unions that do not have access to such resources. Yet, as the newspaper *Izvestia* put it, "Being one of the greatest landlords in Russia, the FNPR is not interested in confrontation with the state. The government may decide to privatize its property at any moment."[42] The Russian government has used this dependence successfully to keep the FNPR in line. The removal of such resources from union control was explicitly threatened after the union sided with the defenders of the Russian White House in October 1993.

This explains the impotence of the main union federation in pressing demands against the state. Another telling example was the March 27, 1997, national "day of protest" called for by the FNPR. Although a large portion of its members had not been paid in months, the union leadership refused to put forth any political demands at all, merely calling for "a change in the course of reforms."[43] As mentioned, only after the August 1998 collapse of the ruble, when it became clear that Yeltsin's popular support was virtually nonexistent, did the FNPR strengthen its rhetoric for its October 1998 "day of protest" to include demands for Yeltsin's resignation.[44] In short, the state has managed to keep the FNPR dependent on the good will of the Russian government. While there are some small independent unions in some sectors like coal mining, for the most part, the FNPR is the only union that matters.

LABOR AND THE RUSSIAN STATE

Despite, or perhaps because of, the dependence and impotence of Russia's unions, the state has sought to integrate labor and employers in a tripartite arrangement of "social partnership," modeled roughly on the corporatist arrangements of Western Europe.[45] One monograph-length study on this topic called the attempts at tripartism a "sideshow," among other things, and there seems to be little reason to substantially revise this conclusion.[46]

One obvious problem with setting up an arrangement whereby the state mediates labor conflict between unions and employers is the continued problem of differentiating interests in a society still experiencing radical economic transformation. We have already seen that at the plant level, unions and managers often see themselves as working on the same side. This phenomenon is also evident at the national level. In tripartite negotiations, unions and industrialists do not look to the state as a neutral body to help them settle their conflicts; instead, they unite along sectoral lines to lobby the state for more resources. Furthermore, it is not always clear whom the state represents. This is especially obvious in branch tariff agreements that cover a given industry. Because there is typically no employers' organizations for a given branch, branch unions fill this role, as do industrial ministries. In other words, unions and branch ministries, in the absence of an employers' organization, work out and sign an agreement that is typically aimed at extracting more resources from the rest of the state.[47]

As an example of how unions differentiate between "their" ministry and other parts of the state, consider the September 1998 meeting of the central committee of the health-care workers trade union. Union leaders at the meeting stated sharply, "We demand the president step down," a hardly surprising demand given that many members had not received their meager salaries from the government in the last six months. Yet according to a correspondent for *Nezavisimaya Gazeta*, "Interestingly enough, after blasting the president, union activists uttered hardly a single word of reproach for the Public Health Ministry officials attending the plenum."[48]

Unions remain committed to tripartite bargaining in large part because they are so weak in the workplace. Tripartite negotiations give the unions an additional reason for existing beyond the provision of goods and services. However, these negotiations are nearly meaningless. Most striking is the level of the minimum wage. Generally the most basic function of corporatist negotiations is to establish an effective minimum wage—for a given industry and for society as a whole. Yet the minimum wage in Russia, as of July 2000, was 132 rubles, or about $4.65 a month. This is a tiny fraction of the state-defined physiological subsistence minimum.[49] The average wage in Russia, at about sixty-two dollars a month, was itself not much higher than the subsistence minimum.[50]

Then–first vice-premier Mikhail Kasyanov summed up the ineffectiveness of attempts at corporatist social partnership by bluntly stating that "the government has not discussed this problem [of low wages] for nine years. The state has, in fact, lost hold of the instruments to influence the level of earnings in the nonstate sector . . . such a mechanism as social partnership was not used at all."[51] Clearly, then, Russia's attempt at "social partnership" is an abject failure.

Ironically, to capture the degree that the state has failed to meet its basic obligations to working people (and by implication, the failure of trade unions to force them to do so), one need look no farther than the Russian government's own human rights commissioner's report for 1999.[52] The report noted that with the financial crisis of August 1998, real wages plunged to less than half their level in 1991, the last year of the Soviet Union. Partly as a result, "Russia is now among the bottom 20 percent of the world's nations in terms of the 33 indicators the United Nations uses to determine the standard of living." The report also noted that "the payment of wages in the form of enterprise credit cards and vouchers is becoming a common practice, putting Russia in the same position as countries with the most primitive distribution systems." The report charged that the chronic delays in the payment of wages were a violation of basic human rights.[53]

The report also described widespread violations of the law, including "more frequent incidents of unlawful dismissals, mandatory leaves without pay, and other violations of the Labor Code of the Russian Federation. Close to 20,000 illegally dismissed workers are reinstated in their jobs each year by court order." Furthermore, the report stated that "The working conditions of more than 43 percent of the laboring public are inconsistent with public health standards," and "the rate of industrial accidents has risen sharply."[54]

With such widespread violations of the law, unions and workers have increasingly turned to a legal strategy. The number of wage complaints handled by public courts rose from nineteen thousand in 1993 to 1.3 million in 1998—an almost seventy-fold increase.[55] Such legal efforts would seem to make sense because, despite tremendous changes elsewhere in the political economy, much of the extensive (though then largely formal) Soviet-era legal code remains intact. Yet such a legal strategy diverts scarce union resources into the courtroom rather than into organizing. Moreover, such cases can take a long time to resolve, and even when decided in the union's favor, there is still the problem of enforcement. Some factory directors claim to have piles of unenforced court orders sitting on their desk.[56]

The legal protections that Russian workers enjoy, even if rarely enforced, may soon narrow. At present, among the legal protections in the Soviet-era Labor Code is the trade unions' traditional right to prevent firings without union approval. However, the Russian government is currently trying to pass a new labor code. Critics charge that the law as proposed would not only make dismissals easier; it would also mean that such issues as work discipline, shift working, the length of the workday, holidays, norms, and pay cuts would no longer require the agreement of the trade union. Workers could have damages taken from their wages as a result of illegal strikes or protests. The eight-hour workday and the five-day workweek would no longer be mandatory, as employers could extend the workday to twelve hours and the workweek to fifty-six hours. Needless to say, if the proposed labor code is passed by the Duma in such a form, it will be yet another sign of the inherent weakness of Russian unions, especially on the national level.

LABOR AND IDEOLOGY IN POSTCOMMUNISM

Given the ineffectiveness of the main union federation (and of such national institutions as federal labor law and tripartism), the conflict that has erupted has been local, typically confined to the enterprise. Partly because of the reticence of union officials at higher levels and partly because Russia's strike laws make legal strikes quite difficult, many of these enterprise-level strikes are wildcat actions.[57]

Moreover, a lot of the enterprise-level actions have recently switched from a focus on wage arrears to the issue of ownership.[58] The entire process of privatization remains widely unpopular in Russia because of widespread corruption, the enrichment of a few "oligarchs," and the ideological commitment of many Russians to such communist-era notions as the labor collective and workers' control.[59] As a result, particularly when plants are threatened with closure, workers in a number of cases have entered into the struggle over control of the enterprise.

Emblematic of these conflicts has been the struggle over the Vyborg Pulp and Paper Mill outside Saint Petersburg. Privatization of the plant by a British firm and fears of resulting layoffs were contested by the plant's trade union committee, which organized the seizure of the plant. This led to a bloody confrontation between workers and OMON troops. The case has apparently inspired workers elsewhere.[60]

Yet it remains unclear in many of these cases whether workers are acting on their own or are being mobilized by one management faction to further its bid for ownership. Moreover, in the absence of some organizational connection between these disparate enterprises, it is unlikely that the gains that workers might win will reach beyond the local level.

But these cases of militant action by "labor collectives" are not only lacking organizational unity; they also lack a unifying ideology or discourse. While they may attack what they see as illegal privatization in the name of collective ownership, in so doing they lack a language that is distinct from that of the old regime. In this they are similar to Russia's coal miners, who for a crucial time pushed for the "market" and even "privatization" but did so with the labor theory of value and workers' control in mind. Yet while the miners understood their social situation in class terms, they were without an ideological framework to organize these notions because they were fighting the injustices of the old system, and for them the language of socialism (and even social democracy) was the language of the enemy.

For evidence that workers face continuing problems with the legacy of the Soviet regime's appropriation of socialist ideology and working-class identity, consider the electoral strategies of Russia's major political parties. In conditions of extensive wage arrears, illegal privatization, declining living standards, and even declining life expectancies, the most rational electoral strategy would seem to be an appeal to the large number of impoverished workers. Yet out of the large number of parties that have appeared, virtually none have directed their appeals specifically to labor as an aggrieved group. The Communist Party has shifted its rhetorical focus from labor to nationalism and Russia as a "great power."[61] When the main union federation, FNPR, made a major push to enter party politics for the December 1995 parliamentary elections, it did so by reaching across class lines to form the misnamed Union of Labor with industrialists. Not surprisingly, it was trounced in the polls.[62] This lack of coherent class language and class identity goes a long way in explaining why labor as an organized interest does not really exist in Russian society.

FUTURE PROSPECTS

There is still much talk in Russia of the threat of a "social explosion," but the threshold for that explosion has been raised dramatically. In Soviet times it was argued that simple price rises were enough to set it off.[63] Now, it would appear, the Russian state is no longer perceived as being directly responsible for individuals' well-being, and thus it is no longer a lightning rod for labor and other conflicts. There is labor conflict and protest, but it has been dispersed, fragmented, and localized.

Now the question has become, what (if anything) could bring about this social explosion? It would seem the Russian government and many others believe that the threshold would be crossed by massive bankruptcies, factory closures, and widespread and open (as opposed to hidden) unemployment.

The Russian trade unions and the state have clearly failed to protect labor in the most basic sense by raising the minimum wage to the physiological subsistence level and by enforcing laws on the timely payment of wages. The resulting outcome has been virtually costless workers being kept on the books and given access to the only part of the welfare state that exists: the workplace.

Leaving workers' welfare to the mercy of enterprises and their managers has so far prevented massive unemployment and, perhaps, ensuing social unrest. On the other hand, it is here that economic reform comes to a halt— just short of closing unprofitable firms and forcing workers to find employment elsewhere.

Perhaps most troubling for the future is the failure of effective trade unions or other institutions that might effectively channel the grievances of workers and others in a time of wrenching social change. As Simon Clarke has argued, this "underlies the dual fear that the bulk of the population will, in its passive moment, vote for the authoritarian leader who can make the most radical promises and, in its active moment, take to the streets in outbursts of mass civil unrest."[64]

At present, the prolonged depression of the Russian economy appears to have reached its end. The economy is growing, and industrial production is up. While more than one in three Russians remains impoverished, wage delays are declining, and real wages are beginning to rise after a precipitous decline. What impact might such trends have, should they continue, on the lives of Russia's workers? If the crisis in Russian society is indeed over, would it remove the grievances of workers that could lead to the long-expected social explosion? If anything, the Russian case underscores the observation that grievances do not easily lead to collective action. As we have seen, Russian workers have been burdened with grievances for some time, and the end of the Russian depression will not remove most of those anytime soon. On the other hand, the end of the economic crisis would seem to weaken some of the explanations of workers' quiescence that focused on the dire economic circumstances. Will growth in the economy provide workers with sufficient resources to enable their collective action? Increased levels of production, for example, would presumably make strikes in manufacturing a greater possibility. Unemployment has dropped slightly; perhaps some further tightening of the labor market will strengthen workers' bargaining position. This does not seem very likely however. First, it is more likely that if Russia travels farther down the road of capitalist transformation, unemployment will grow still higher, as currently hidden unemployment becomes open.[65] Second, as other chapters in this volume have shown, greater reform elsewhere, even if combined with economic growth, has not resulted in an increase in workers' collective action. If anything—as the economy becomes less state centered and more private, and as the strategies and the mentalities of working people become more individualized and less collectively oriented—the possibility for a strengthened workers' movement in Russia or even a social explosion may decline even further.

NOTES

1. While official figures may fail to capture informal economic activity, other measures put the decline at only slightly lower levels. See Branko Milanovic, *Income, Inequality, and Poverty during the Transition from Planned to Market Economy* (Washington, D.C.: The World Bank, 1998).

2. Beyond the official statistics, a poll carried out by the National Institute for Social and Regional Problems revealed that seven out of ten Russians considered themselves poor, only 14 percent said they could pay for necessary medical treatment, and just 8 percent took a holiday in 1999. President Vladimir Putin conceded that Russia occupied

seventy-first place in world rankings for its people's standard of living. See *Agence France Presse*, February 28, 2000. On the large number of "working poor" in Russia and other postcommunist societies, see Milanovic, *Income, Inequality, and Poverty.*

3. *The New York Times,* March 18, 1999.

4. Author's transcript of a talk by Theodore Friedgut, given at Georgetown University, Washington, D.C., October 1989.

5. Stephen Crowley, *Hot Coal, Cold Steel: Russian and Ukrainian Workers from the End of the Soviet Union to the Post-Communist Transformations* (Ann Arbor: University of Michigan Press, 1997); Stephen Crowley, "Barriers to Collective Action: Steelworkers and Mutual Dependence in the Former Soviet Union," *World Politics* 46: July 4, 1994.

6. International Labor Organization, *Yearbook of Labour Statistics: 1997* (Geneva: International Labour Office).

7. Of the 169 strikes that took place in April 1999, for instance, 5 were in industry, 1 was in transportation, 6 were in "other," and 157 were in the education sector. For an extensive list of strike and demonstration activity by Russian workers, see "Russia Campaign: Strikes and Protests," *ICEM*, http://www.icem.org/campaigns/nopaycc/protests 0001a.html, May 18, 2000. This may be partly a result of the way strikes are counted. When one looks at the intensity of strikes—not only the number of strikes but the number of strikers and the strikes' duration—the disparity between strikes in the budget sector and those in mining and manufacturing is not quite so great. Even with this correction, however, one finds very few industrial strikes outside coal mining.

8. For example, according to a meeting report of the Kennan Institute, Anders Aslund argued, "It is important to note that there has been little to no labor unrest in Russia, which may be proof that the situation is not so dire." See "Achievement and Failures in Russian Reform," *Meeting Report, Kennan Institute for Advanced Russian Studies* 14:13, 1997.

9. Nor have such "survival strategies" always been successful. As Guy Standing notes, one factor concealing the extent of unemployment has been "the real disappearance of workers—in premature death. Since the late 1980s, average life expectancy at birth has declined by over five years," and for males it declined from about sixty-five in 1987 to fifty-eight in 1995. He argues further that while declining public health care played a role, "it seems that economic insecurity and stress have been the main factors." Between 1990 and 1995, the number of working-age people who died from alcohol-related causes more than tripled, while in the same period the number of registered disabled rose by 1.4 times, the number of murders more than doubled, and the number of suicides rose by 1.6 times. See Guy Standing, "Reviving Dead Souls," in *Structural Adjustment without Mass Unemployment*, Simon Clarke, ed. (Cheltenham, U.K.: Edward Elgar, 1998) 154.

10. Albert Hirschman, *Exit, Voice and Loyalty* (Cambridge: Harvard University Press, 1970). An argument that extensive use of exit options explains the lack of labor protest in Eastern Europe is made forcefully in Bela Greskovits, *The Political Economy of Protest and Patience* (Budapest: Central European University Press, 1998).

11. In one case of informal economic activity, young men have been stripping copper wire from utility poles to sell as scrap. Unfortunately, in a number of cases the wires were live, and this has led to some rather gruesome injuries. However, this has not deterred others, and sometimes the very same individuals, from taking such action. See "Power Line Thieves Loot Russia, Often Risking Death or Maiming," *The New York Times*, April 18, 2000. Another example would be the alarming rise of sex workers working in, and often illegally exported out of, Russia and other former Soviet republics.

12. The term "unpaid leave" is used here instead of "layoff" because workers still maintain ties to their workplace, as we shall see.

13. These figures come from the Russian Longitudinal Monitoring Survey, as analyzed in John Earle and Klara Sabirianova, "Equilibrium Wage Arrears: A Theoretical and Empirical Analysis of Institutional Lock-In," draft paper, 2000.

14. Teachers in Voronezh oblast were offered fences and tombs from a local cemetery instead of cash wages. In Tula oblast, authorities in the town of Kimovsk, having received manure from collective farms to pay off the farms' debts, redistributed the manure to teachers in place of back pay. The teachers received some one thousand tons of manure, but 125,000 tons were required to pay off all their back wages. See *Izvestiya*, November 26, 1999, as reported in "Russia Campaign: Strikes and Protests."

15. Again, there is an "exit" of the informal economy, but given the dramatic turn-around in the labor market (both formal and informal), workers had much greater freedom to choose jobs in the past.

16. The role of the state in labor relations in Russia is more fully explored in Stephen Crowley, "Liberal Transformation: Labor and the Russian State," in *Building the Russian State*, Valerie Sperling, ed. (Boulder: Westview Press, 2000).

17. Crowley, *Hot Coal, Cold Steel*; Theodore Friedgut and Lewis Siegelbaum, "Peres-troika from Below: The Soviet Miners' Strike and Its Aftermath," *New Left Review*, summer 1990; Simon Clarke and Peter Fairbrother, "The Origins of the Independent Workers Movement and the 1989 Strike," in *What about the Workers? Workers and the Transition to Capitalism in Russia*, Simon Clarke et al., eds. (London: Verso, 1993).

18. Crowley, *Hot Coal, Cold Steel*; Crowley, "Barriers to Collective Action."

19. Between June 1997 and December 1998, the value of the Indonesian stock market declined by 80 percent, and the Russian stock market declined by 86 percent. More pain-fully for average citizens, both local currencies were sharply devalued. *The New York Times*, February 17, 1999.

20. *The New York Times*, September 6, 1998.

21. *Nezavisimaya Gazeta*, October 8, 1998. *Segodnya*, October 9, 1998.

22. On this point see also Paul T. Christensen, "Why Russia Lacks a Labor Movement," in *Transitions*, December 1997. While many blamed the handful of economically powerful Russians, the so-called oligarchs, it was unclear how to target them and their offshore bank accounts for protest.

23. Crowley, *Hot Coal, Cold Steel*; Crowley, "Barriers to Collective Action"; Sarah Ashwin, *Russian Workers: The Anatomy of Patience* (Manchester, U.K.: Manchester University Press, 1999).

24. For a range of viewpoints on the extent of such benefits, see Standing, "Reviving Dead Souls"; Ashwin, *Russian Workers*; Scott Thomas, in *Social Policy and Social Safety Nets in the Post-Communist Economies*, M. Mandelbaum and E. Kapstein, eds. (Armonk, N.Y.: M. E. Sharpe, 1997); Simon Commander, Une Lee, and Andrei Tolstopienko, "Social Benefits and the Russian Industrial Firm," paper presented at the conference *Russia: Economic Policy and Enterprise Restructuring* (Saint Petersburg, June 12–13, 1995).

25. See Standing, "Reviving Dead Souls."

26. On the struggle of labor collectives over privatization, see Paul Christensen, "After Communism, What's Left: Analyzing Radical Politics in Post-Soviet Russia," paper presented at the Kennan Institute for Advanced Russian Studies, Washington D.C., February

28, 2000. In the example of the Krasnoyarsk Aluminum Plant, workers were said to support the existing director in a privatization struggle, because the plant was one of the few that "retained its Soviet-era wealth of social benefits, ranging from medical services to kindergartens." This was despite the fact that the director was being held on money-laundering and murder charges. See *Moscow Times*, April 28, 2000.

27. Milanovic, *Income, Inequality, and Povery*, 28–29.

28. Kathleen Thelen, "Beyond Corporatism: Toward a New Framework for the Study of Labor in Advanced Capitialism," in *Comparative Policies* 27:1, October 1994, 110.

29. Guy Standing points to the "considerable financial incentives to induce firms to put workers on layoff rather than make them formally unemployed," such as avoiding severance payments. See Standing, "Reviving Dead Souls," 153.

30. The figures were calculated according to International Labor Organization methods. *Agence France Presse*, May 30, 2000.

31. Clarke, "The Development of Industrial Relations in Russia: Report for the ILO Task Force on Industrial Relations."

32. For example, a September 1998 poll by the Institute of the Sociology of Parliamentarianism found that to the question of what problems in your personal life anger you the most, 60 percent answered wage arrears, and 55 percent answered low wages. *Izvestia*, September 23, 1998.

33. One survey found that the new independent unions had less trust than even the former communist-led trade unions. Respondents placed them second from the bottom of trusted social institutions, just percentage points above "Westerners advising the Russian government." See Richard Rose, Stephen White, and Ian McAllister, *How Russia Votes* (Chatham, N.J.: Chatam House Publishers, 1997). A more recent survey, conducted by the Agency of Regional Political Studies in 1999–2000, shows no improvement. While the majority of respondents did not trust a single institution, labor unions were less popular than any other organization. *Nezavisimaya Gazeta* May 5, 2000.

34. Interestingly, a survey conducted by the All-Russian Center for the Study of Public Opinion in February and March 1998 found that respondents placed trade unions at the very bottom of institutions that "have influence" (with only 4 percent of those surveyed saying unions had influence). However, when asked "who ought to have influence," unions came in second place (below the intelligentsia) with 64 percent of respondents saying unions ought to have influence. *Obschaya Gazeta* 29, July 23–29, 1998, as translated in *The Current Digest of the Post-Soviet Press* 50:29, 1998.

35. Clarke, "The Development of Industrial Relations in Russia." At the Kuzbass coal mine she investigated, Ashwin found that mine managers remained apart from the trade union until 1998. Ashwin, *Russian Workers*, 95, n. 15.

36. Clarke, "The Development of Industrial Relations in Russia."

37. T. Chetvernina, P. Smirnov, and N. Dunaeva, "Mesto profsoyuza na predpriyatii," in *Voprosi Ekonomiki* 1995, 6; Clarke, "The Development of Industrial Relations in Russia." That workers would not approach union representatives about wages is quite rational because, as Guy Standing reported in an extensive survey of Russian enterprises, the presence of unions appears to have little to no impact on wage levels in Russian workplaces. See Guy Standing, *Russian Unemployment and Enterprise Restructuring* (New York: St. Martin's Press, 1996), 210–11.

38. Ashwin, *Russian Workers,* 90. She also found that even this "militant" trade union had difficulty separating its interests from those of management.

39. Clarke, "The Development of Industrial Relations in Russia." For an example of a trade union in a steel factory being cowed by management in just such a fashion, see Crowley, *Hot Coal, Cold Steel,* 164–71.

40. Even President Putin joined the denunciation of unions along these lines. In what was billed as his "State of the Nation" address, besides accusing the unions of "bureaucratization," he argued, "In the new conditions the trade unions should not be taking upon themselves state functions in the social sphere. What the people of Russia need is not just another middleman for distributing social benefits, but professional monitoring to see that labor contracts are just and their conditions properly observed." Putin's remarks, while on target, are certainly ironic. Some ten years after Russian trade unions declared themselves "independent," they are being lectured to by the head of state on how to defend workers' interests. See "Russian President's Address to Federal Assembly," in *BBC Monitoring,* July 8, 2000.

41. Sue Davis, *Trade Unions in Russia and Ukraine* (London: Palgrave at St. Martin's Press, 2001).

42. *Izvestia,* April 9, 1998; *Izvestia,* August 24, 1999.

43. *Kommersant-Daily* March 29, 1997; *Moscow News* 13, March 30-April 6, 1997. In several regions, mayors and governors were directly involved in organizing this protest, and enterprise managers appeared to support such union "days of action" as well. Ashwin, *Russian Workers,* 86.

44. *Nezavisimaya Gazeta,* October 8, 1998.

45. Tripartism refers to centralized and formal negotiations between representatives of labor, employers, and the state.

46. Walter Connor, *Tattered Banners: Labor, Conflict and Corporatism in Postcommunist Russia* (Boulder: Westview, 1996), 170.

47. Clarke, "The Development of Industrial Relations in Russia." On the dearth of employers' associations with whom labor might negotiate, see Viktor Komarovsky and Ye. Sadovaya, "Ob'edineniya rabotodatelei v sisteme sotsialnogo partnerstva: opit razvitikh stran i Rossii," in *Mirovaya Ekonomika i Mezhdunarodnie Otnosheniya* 5, 1997.

48. *Nezavisimaya Gazeta,* September 18, 1998.

49. *The Saint Petersburg Times,* June 13, 2000; *Segodnya,* June 19, 1998; Standing, "Reviving Dead Souls," 151; Tatyana Chetvernina, "Minimum Wages in Russia: Fantasy Chasing Fact," in *Minimum Wages in Central and Eastern Europe,* Guy Standing and Daniel Vaughn-Whitehead, eds. (Budapest: Central European University Press, 1995). As this last volume makes clear, this situation is similar in most postcommunist societies.

50. Itar-Tass, February 24, 2000. With the officially defined subsistence minimum of thirty-four dollars a month, a worker with one dependent could not survive on the average wage.

51. Itar-Tass, February 24, 2000.

52. "The 1999 Report of RF Human Rights Commissioner," in *Rossiyskaya Gazeta,* April 4, 2000.

53. "The 1999 Report of RF Human Rights Commissioner." The report continued, "People in the northern regions and regions with a high rate of unemployment have to work for a limited variety of food items, which essentially constitutes forced labor." It cited workers on a collective farm that had not received any wages for twenty-one months—but instead got one loaf of bread a day and one kilogram of sugar and two or three kilograms of cereal grains a month.

54. "The 1999 Report of RF Human Rights Commissioner."

55. "The 1999 Report of RF Human Rights Commissioner." In 1997, 6 percent of the total Russian workforce sought redress for the nonpayment of wages through the courts. *Izvestiya,* January 6, 1999; Christensen, "Why Russia Lacks a Labor Movement."

56. *Russia and Commonwealth Business Law Report,* November 18, 1998.

57. For further discussion of the strike law, see Clarke, "The Development of Industrial Relations in Russia"; Crowley, "Liberal Transformation." Being illegal, these wildcat strikes would be subject to additional fines under the government's proposed labor law.

58. Christensen, "After Communism."

59. On the continued unpopularity of privatization, see Christensen, "After Communism." Ashwin places much emphasis on the notion of the "labor collective" as a source of unity between workers and managers and an explanation for workers' "patience" (Ashwin, *Russian Workers*). Yet it would seem that the continued viability of the idea of the collective requires certain obligations on the part of management, and therefore suggests limits to workers' patience.

60. A meeting of "labor collective representatives" took place near Vyborg, and a meeting of the Kuzbass Congress of Working People invited representatives from the Vyborg plant. *Segodnya* December 29, 1999; *Nezavisimaya Gazeta,* October 27, 1999.

61. Christensen, "After Communism"; Veljko Vujacic, "Gennadiy Zyuganov and the 'Third Road,' " in *Post-Soviet Affairs* 12:2, April-June 1996, 118–54.

62. Boris Kagarlitsky, "Russian Trade Unions and the 1995 Elections," in *Labour Focus on Eastern Europe* 52, autumn 1995, 64–69.

63. While such open protests were rare, so were price rises. The most dramatic confluence of the two phenomena was the violent repression of protesting workers in Novocherkassk in 1962. Regardless of the empirical validity of the claim that price rises in the Soviet Union led to protest, this perception was widespread, inside and outside of the Soviet Union.

64. Clarke, "The Development of Industrial Relations in Russia."

65. By one estimate, "in 1996 suppressed unemployment in Russian industry was over a third of the workforce." See Standing, "Reviving Dead Souls," 174.

Conclusion

Making Sense of Labor Weakness in Postcommunism

David Ost and Stephen Crowley

We began our research with a hypothesis of labor weakness in postcommunist society. In the preceding chapters, authors from diverse academic disciplines confirmed and gave shape to this hypothesis in a variety of ways. In every case, they reach the conclusion that labor has indeed been a weak social and political actor throughout the region since 1989. They provide clear and consistent evidence of union weakness throughout the region, regardless of its diverse economic, political, and institutional particularities.

This weakness consists of a low capacity to shape public policy or to win material benefits on behalf of their members, an inability (and an even more significant unwillingness) to organize the newly important private sphere, and a general decline of labor's social and cultural standing. Far from being recognized as guarantors of broad citizenship, which was crucial to the consolidation of trade unions as powerful actors in the West, they are more usually seen as relics of an obsolete past not really relevant for a capitalist future.

In this concluding chapter, we try to clarify what we mean by "weakness" and examine the overall evidence in support of this finding. Then we explore explanations that might account for labor as a weak actor in Eastern Europe, and we highlight the importance of ideological legacies of the communist period. Finally, we address the issue of how and why this matters for the building of democracy.

INDICATORS OF LABOR WEAKNESS

We understand labor weakness to mean that workers and trade unions have been unable to shape conditions of work or public policy in accord with their interests. They have been on the sidelines, watching passively (or angrily and sometimes even enthusiastically) as new elites restructure the national economies in accord with fashionable neoliberal trends, cutting back on government regulation, union participation, and commitments to equality. The diverse internal reactions to these developments suggest that labor is still not clear where its interests lie. Which policies should it support and which should it oppose? When and where should it support restructuring or privatization (and then which kind of each?) and when and where should it oppose them? At different times labor has taken quite different positions, thus making it an uncertain actor, which only reinforces its subordinate status. Workers in postcommunist societies are weak not because they have failed to derail reforms, but because they have had surprisingly little influence in shaping reforms, whether on the national level or in the workplace. Labor is weak in that it has been the object and not the subject of postcommunist reform, and it finds itself ten years after lacking the will and the resources to make much of a difference.

The chapters document this weakness in a number of ways:

- declining trade union membership
- increasingly hierarchical management
- toothless collective bargaining
- redundant agreements
- low and ineffectual strike action
- ineffective or nonexistent political alliances
- minimal union influence over public policy
- declining material outcomes for workers

While many observers anticipated Eastern European capitalism to be hobbled by the legacy of workers' power, postcommunist marketization has instead produced a capitalism able and anxious to marginalize labor.

First, as already noted, there has been a dramatic drop in union membership. Density rates, starting from nearly universal membership in the communist period, have dropped precipitously. Various estimates of union membership conflict, and exact numbers are impossible to come by. However, roughly speaking, union density has dropped to about one-third of the workforce in Poland, Hungary, and the Czech Republic, two-fifths of the workforce in Bulgaria, Romania, Slovakia, and Croatia, one-half of the workforce in Serbia, and some two-thirds of the workforce in Russia and Ukraine. (In the latter cases, however, membership frequently means little more than maintaining connections to institutions and firms that still supply benefits, which have been indispensable in the face of wage arrears.) Given the membership rates of the communist period, the overall decline is not surprising. Reasons for the decline in union membership include the growth of the tertiary sector and the exit of professionals (that is, those with higher education such as designers, engineers, accountants, and marketing specialists), some of whom no longer work in large unionized enterprises and many others who simply no longer believe in unions or see any use for them. Aside from the health and education sectors, very few educated workers have joined trade unions. Since 1989, factory unions have become almost completely blue-collar throughout the region, depriving them of much of the social capital that always helps unions bargain with elites.

Union membership is now concentrated in the public sector and in state-owned or recently privatized heavy industry. The new private sphere, where most of the growth has taken place in the last five years, remains almost completely unorganized throughout the region. Unlike in Western Europe, it is not just small private firms that emerge union-free but even large manufacturing ones. This means that not only are old members leaving, but unions hardly try to replace dropouts with new recruits. New private firms would be the logical place to try, but for the most part unions in Eastern Europe have been unwilling to do so. They are accustomed to thinking of unions as institutions dealing with the state sector, and they often express the view that the private sector does not really need unions. Private owners will frequently oppose efforts to unionize their firms, and they will fire the activists. Union leaders deplore this but have yet to organize campaigns in defense of unionization in private firms.

Even where unions exist, most Eastern European unions do little additional recruiting. Rather than fight for members, they take membership as an institutional legacy of the past, and they take it for granted. Eastern Europe's union activists remain somewhat embarrassed about recruiting, as it reminds them of Communist Party pressure from the past. Western European and U.S. unions have been increasingly developing innovative strategies of organizing. They respond to lean times and weakening class identities by organizing in new sectors (e.g., technology or service) or by treating traditional workers like "customers," offering membership incentives such as credit cards or free legal council.[1] In contrast, the chief way Eastern European unions try to gain members can be captured in what one Polish unionist told one of us: "We go about our usual activity, and if they like what they see, they'll join." It is little wonder that membership has stayed down.

This disinterest in unions affects both the old official unions and the new independent ones, which, with the exceptions of Solidarity in Poland and Podkrepa in Bulgaria, have hardly prospered. Interestingly, the successor trade union confederations, first established by the Communist Party, remain some ten years into the transitions not only the largest union in each country but the largest civic organization of any kind.

Labor mobilization as reflected in strike activity, while lower than many anticipated given the painful economic decline, has certainly not been absent. As a whole, it seems to be fragmented along familiar sectoral lines: a militant coal sector (as is common throughout the world) followed by transportation and the public sectors of health and education. Except for Poland and Romania, there have been almost no strikes in the last ten years in the manufacturing sector. Strike activity is rare in small firms, in new private firms, and in foreign-owned firms. Even where there are strikes, moreover, one point stands out: They are used chiefly to block the further decline of labor conditions rather than achieve a real advance. Most strikes since 1989 have been strikes of despair, where conditions have gotten so bad that workers feel they have little to lose. Miners and rail workers strike to keep their jobs or to get paid back wages, not to increase their pay. Health and education employees strike because their wages have become poverty wages, not because they seek a well-deserved increase. It is also important to note that most strikes tend to be triggered by spontaneous anger at the workplace rather than coordinated by trade unions as part of some overall strategy. Unions for the most part feel so battered down by postcommunist reality that they go on strike only when the workforce demands it and only on behalf of very limited goals. We see, in other words, signs of weakness even at moments of labor mobilization.

The preceding chapters also speak of the decline and fragmentation of collective bargaining. The complaints on this score are widespread. Either there are no collective agreements, or they tend to be powerless. Tóth notes that fewer than one-fifth of Hungarian manufacturing firms were covered by union contracts as late as 1997, while collective agreements were virtually absent in the textile industry. Pollert reports that collective agreements in the Czech Republic frequently do no more than reiterate legally binding rules. Arandarenko notes that collective bargaining has been decentralized and even atomized in Serbia, and those contracts that are reached are often unenforceable. Pańków and Kopatko note a high percentage of formal agreements in Ukraine, but insofar as they also report massive nonpayment of wages, it is clear such agreements are not worth much.

In a further indication of labor's weakness, many of the chapters note the weakening of labor law, which was often quite extensive in the communist period. A 1998 law in Hungary recognizes unions' rights of collective bargaining, yet it does not allow unions to intervene in cases of the breach of the collective agreement or in a dispute arising from it. In other cases—such as in Serbia, Russia, and Ukraine—formally strong communist-era laws persist, but they are often (or even typically) ignored with impunity.

Nor are the signs of labor's weakness confined to the spheres of the economy and industrial relations. Politically, in what is both cause and effect of labor's fortunes, there is the lack of reliable political partners, particularly political parties. Almost without exception and despite the large number of parties that have sprouted after communism, *unions have failed to create political alliances with parties that will defend labor interests.* This is closely related to the problems of class identity and ideology that we will return to shortly. As Arandarenko argues about Serbia, "the lack of recognizable group and class interests forces most parties to adopt nationalism as their chief means of mobilizing." It is in this context, he argues, that "the complete lack of interest in unions" by these parties should be seen. Even in a more fully developed party system, as in Hungary, Tóth notes that when the new unions tried to find political allies, they were treated as junior partners and even "marginalized and humiliated" by these parties. The old union MSZOSZ appeared to join the ruling coalition when the socialists came to power, only to find union interests ignored with the imposition of austerity measures. The current center-right government in Hungary is openly hostile to labor.

Kideckel discusses a thoroughly politicized labor movement in Romania, where confederations split into rival unions not out of disagreement over strategy but because leaders opt for different political alliances, with little success for workers' interests. It might also be noted that the "old" left also provides scant support for workers. In Ukraine, as Pańków and Kopatko argue, the communists and the socialists are too busy defending the interests of the old *nomenklatura*. In Russia, as Crowley points out, the Communist Party defines itself as a defender of "great Russia," and it rarely mentions workers at all. In Poland, an exception to prove the rule, the two major parties have strong union contingents, but time and again the parties isolate labor after the electoral campaign, offering union deputies little more than promises and continued parliamentary seats.

Even the discussion of apparent successes drives home the argument about minimal labor power. For Pollert, Czech unions win when they defeat a bill for the introduction of works' councils, while for Stein, a new tripartite law gives Slovak unions "symbolic esteem." For Tóth, getting the Hungarian government to return to tripartite negotiations, after having violated them earlier, constitutes a sign of strength. Gradev notes that over time the liberals in Bulgaria learned how to marginalize labor more "subtly," continuing to ignore labor's views but integrating them more in the process. Kokanović, meanwhile, sees "strength" in Croatia in the mere fact that unions have survived. One is hard pressed to find examples of clear labor victories since 1989.

EXPLAINING LABOR WEAKNESS

By a wide variety of measures, then, workers and unions have little influence in postcommunist Eastern Europe. What might account for this weakness? In the introduction, we raised several possible explanations: resource problems, economic factors, adverse legacies, and ideas and identities. The chapters offer little evidence for the first thesis. On the contrary, they show that unions survived the fall of communism with their resources intact, and they were able to take advantage of communist-era legislation that gave them continued access to funds and paid staff.

Economic factors, however, appear to affect unions in diverse ways. *Neither economic growth nor economic hardship appears to have much effect* on labor's strength or weakness in the region. The evidence runs contrary to the view of those economists who argue that workers are more likely to strike when times are good.[2] Greskovits argues that "improved macroeconomic performance may release pent-up demands."[3] Yet countries that are experiencing improved performance, such as Poland and Hungary, see no noticeable change in the activity of workers or their relative power in society. Hungary's economy is considerably stronger than neighboring Romania's, its workers are better off than Romanian ones, but Romanian labor still remains more active than Hungary's. The chapters here show that recent governments in both countries have tried to cut back on union influence. Even if we look more narrowly at the level of unemployment and hence, presumably, at workers' relative bargaining power, we do not find any patterns between unemployment levels and strikes or other activities, whether comparing across countries or within a single country over time.

Yet it would be mistaken to disregard entirely the importance of weak labor markets on workers' relative power. For there is another component of the labor market that is not captured by unemployment statistics: the existence of the informal economy and other individual "exit" options. Some have argued that workers in the region have opted for individual "exit" strategies rather than more costly collective "voice" strategies to improve their situations.[4] In this view, the opportunity for exit is another cause of labor weakness. This explanation appears plausible given the level of informal activity and individual-level survival strategies in the region. Several of the authors here note the presence of such activity and its impact on labor relations. Arandarenko, for example, argues that the informal economy is undoubtedly the most important buffer against class opposition in Serbia. However, unlike some scholars who see the informal economy as a positive way to reduce social discontent, the authors here underscore the negative consequences of such phenomena. In Serbia, Russia, and Ukraine the extensive use of unpaid leaves forces workers to seek whatever employment they can, while maintaining their formal employment and their trade union membership to maintain their benefits. This means, Arandarenko wryly notes, that trade unions facilitate "exit" strategies rather than "voice." The employment that workers find in the informal economy is far from desirable. The black market for labor includes sexual harassment, forced prostitution, the need to pay agents for hiring, and the lack of recourse for violations of rights. Informal work does not make workers prosperous, argues Arandarenko, and it compounds problems of collective action as workers become physically separated from their old workmates.[5]

That these negative phenomena from the informal economy appear concentrated in a few cases points to a certain clustering of outcomes that is visible in the chapters gathered here. While in the countries farther to the west and the north the economies are generally growing, to the east and the south one finds continuing and severe economic problems, affecting workers in particular. In Croatia, Serbia, Russia, and Ukraine, wage arrears have been a significant source of distress for working families, and as mentioned, in the last three of these countries workers have also been subjected to unpaid leaves. These countries and Romania, our authors note, also have a more pervasive informal economy, where workers have little protection whatsoever. In the case of Serbia, Russia, and Ukraine (but notably not Croatia), the once-official trade union retains a near monopoly on what worker representation exists, and transformation of the old union has been limited. Together with these factors, there is significant poverty in these countries, and there is more pervasive use of individual strategies for survival.

These same countries, one hardly needs to add, are also the least "reformed" from the communist past. One might hypothesize that as these countries develop more "normal" capitalist relations, unions will reorient themselves and prove better able to defend members' interests. Moreover, moving further away from communist-era institutions might erode the pathological effects of communist legacies on the relative strength of labor, such as workers' skeptical relationship to trade unions themselves. In this view, as property rights become clearer, interests will become better defined, and unions will be better able to defend workers. In other words, another hypothesis might be that union weakness is a product of the underdevelopment of capitalist institutions, not low per capita GDP. The chapters on Serbia and Ukraine, probably the two least-reformed countries among the book's cases, explicitly make the argument that workers are weak because reform, and especially privatization, has not progressed far enough. Indeed, as we have seen, unionists throughout the region make the case for bringing about the very reforms that threaten workers' livelihoods. They do so, they argue, because "real capitalism" will eventually strengthen workers and unions.

The evidence thus far, however, suggests that this is not the case. Instead, these studies suggest that *the more private the economy, the less the union representation*. Hungary, for example, is certainly one of the most "reformed" countries in Eastern Europe. As privatization has proceeded apace, Tóth notes that "drastic deunionization took place in the private sector" (the largest union saw its membership drop from 1.2 million to five hundred thousand in just two years), and there was a growing number of nonunionized greenfield plants. The inability of unions to penetrate this most vibrant sector of the economy (the sector of the future!) raises serious questions about the ability of unions to survive, let alone prosper.

Perhaps the most interesting finding of this volume is that we see similar outcomes despite the wide cross-national variation in public policies and institutional arrangements. For example, union activity in the private sphere cannot be explained by the mode of privatization. Whether done by vouchers in the Czech Republic, foreign buyouts in Hungary, employee leasing in Poland, or personal appropriation in Russia, unions are weak throughout the new private economy. Nor is the involvement of international financial institutions a crucial factor. They have intervened more directly in Bulgaria than elsewhere, but this has not made Bulgarian unions any weaker (or any stronger) than anywhere else.

Not only do various economic reform programs not appear to make labor any less (or more) weak but neither do union strategies, at least those attempted by Eastern European unions so far. It does not seem to matter much whether there is a pluralist union movement (e.g., Poland, Hungary, Bulgaria, and Romania) or a largely centralized one (e.g., the Czech Republic, Slovakia, Serbia, Croatia, Russia, and Ukraine); whether new unions are more influential (e.g., Poland and Bulgaria) or old ones prevail (everywhere else); or whether there are works' councils (e.g., Hungary) or not. Union density does not seem to matter either. It remains high in Russia and Ukraine but low in Hungary and Poland, without any significance for the national power of unions.

One strategy that clearly has not succeeded, though it has been attempted everywhere, is that of corporatism. Tripartite boards have different rules and different outcomes in each of these countries, but nowhere have they brought about an inclusive neocorporatist arrangement.[6] Indeed, in what would appear to be the two strongest cases for successful corporatism in the region,[7] the authors here are categorical. Tóth argues that the attempt to build a social-democratic model in Hungary ended in failure, while Pollert describes the "fragile shell" of Czech corporatism.

Obviously, the degree of openness of the political system makes a difference to labor's very ability to organize, and there is a wide range of political outcomes in postcommunist societies. The countries of East Central Europe—Poland, Hungary, and the Czech Republic—have had several turnovers of government and few restrictions on civil liberties. The situation elsewhere is more problematic—assaults of unionists in Croatia and Serbia, periodic repression in Russia and Ukraine, and much more labor repression in the post-Soviet countries of Belarus and Kazakhstan, which are not included in our study. Yet while political opportunities in the more liberal countries obviously make it easier for labor to organize, the evidence suggests that they are hardly able to take advantage of it.

Labor's voice, of course, is not nonexistent—unions are relatively easy to form, some sort of enterprise negotiations usually take place, and tripartite bodies in most countries provide limited opportunity to interact with top decision makers—but it is consistently minimized as governments ardently pursue their vision of proper market economies. We cannot use the material here to find which institutional arrangements or policy options best help labor. On the basis of this evidence, virtually nothing has helped so far.

The chapters thus show unions to be weak regardless of the institutional specifics of each country. The union movement can be pluralist or concentrated, dominated by new unions or once-official ones, with high or low density, pervasive or rare collective bargaining, or with centralized or decentralized unions. The economy can be privatized by citizen voucher or capital market, and GDP or unemployment can be high or low. Regardless of these factors, unions have little influence on enterprise decisions or on public policy outcomes.

Does this mean that unions were destined for marginalization, regardless of the strategies they pursued? Certainly a more militant Eastern European union movement could not have averted the economic decline of the past decade or made the necessary processes of restructuring and market reform into a net gain for labor. However, a more assertive labor movement could have forced the consideration of alternative strategies (as it arguably did in the Czech Republic, where unemployment was initially kept quite low),[8] or it could have insisted, at the least, on *negotiated* restructuring plans instead of the *faits accomplis* issued by the various finance ministries. By consistently articulating an alternative vision, it could have kept long-term goals alive, thereby preparing to reassert itself after the initial transition crisis had passed. Instead, unions find themselves sinking even after the economy has begun to expand. That they haven't become stronger even in better times suggests that the unions' own attitudes and strategies, resulting in large part from the communist past, have been a big part of the problem.

One might argue that labor appears weak and its response is so limited in all the cases we have examined not because of factors unique to postcommunist societies, but because workers throughout the world are on the defensive. Downward pressure on wages brought on by globalization, structural changes stemming from technological innovation and the advent of a service economy (which in turn trigger changes in class identity), and the power of transnational corporations and international lending agencies to set agendas and limit room for maneuvering are all certainly factors contributing to union weakness in Eastern Europe as in much of the world. Yet there are good reasons to believe that globalization cannot fully explain the dilemmas faced by labor in Eastern Europe, nor the way in which unions have thus far responded to those dilemmas. Not all new global institutions are biased against labor. The first wave of multinational corporations (MNCs) investing in the region, for example, maintained their unions and sometimes even got unionists involved in the company's transnational supervisory board. It is only the second wave of MNC investment, the giant greenfield sites based on new "cooperative" management styles, that prefer to do without unions. Of course, other international institutions also have an adverse effect on labor. Global lending institutions have imposed harsh restructuring criteria that have contributed profoundly to domestic recessions that reduce labor's clout and options.[9] However, whereas in other countries subject to many of the same pressures, workers and unions try to resist global pressures through unrest or innovative recruitment strategies,[10] the response from Eastern European labor movements has been muted, as if such global pressures are just more proof that nothing can be done.

Of course, the new global economy is commonly identified as a powerful explanation for union decline in Western Europe too,[11] arguably the best reference point as so many former communist countries seek membership in the European Union. Yet while there are common factors in both cases, the position of labor in Western and Eastern Europe is not identical.[12] We know from institutional theory that institutions, once created, have a tendency to persevere. Unions may be declining in Western Europe, but their long and deeply institutionalized presence there means they are likely to survive as strong social actors.[13] The point in Eastern Europe is not so much that labor has been *weakened* since 1989 (it is difficult, after all, to say that a movement without the right of independent political representation was strong), but that it has been *created* as a weak actor. Thus, unions in Eastern Europe confront the new global economy not from an initial position of strength but of weakness. To understand why, we need to look more closely at those who are doing the creating. In particular, we will look at the contexts in which union leaders act and the ideas that guide their activity.

THE IDEOLOGICAL LEGACY OF
COMMUNISM

That this finding of labor weakness has held up across a broad variety of cases and circumstances leads us to the factor that they all have in common: the institutional and ideological impact of the communist period. While specific paths in "building socialism" differed, what all the countries had in common was that unions were on the same side as management. Their chief role was in performing social functions, particularly distributing benefits such as social security payments, sick pay, vouchers for factory vacation centers or summer camps for children, and consumer goods through the workplace. Given this, workers were much more likely to approach their immediate supervisor than their union representative when a grievance arose. Union officials were approached when one needed a particular benefit. When communism collapsed, the trade unions inherited a large amount of property and assets. Control over these assets helps explain, beyond simple inertia, the continued high membership of the successor unions. However, these resources—*pace* resource mobilization theorists—have not allowed unions to mobilize their members. Eastern European unions still have far to go in reorienting themselves from the delivering of social functions to defending their members' interests against management and private owners.

Much of this reflects the uncertainty, on the part of both unionists and potential members, of what a union's job should be. Here we come to ideas as a crucial factor in explaining labor weakness. In the introduction, we speculated that labor's own ideas might lead to the crisis of unions in postcommunist society. The chapters here offer considerable evidence of just that. Labor seems to have developed an overdose of skepticism about unions from its experiences with communism and from the dominant ideologies of the new elites. Whether liberal in East Central Europe or nationalist in the southeastern countries, the new elites have led the struggle against communism with conceptual narratives that identified communism's exaltation of the working class as part of the problem that needed to be redressed. Many Solidarity unionists in Poland accepted the neoliberal discourse that marginalized unions, while Croatian and Serbian workers frequently imbibed nationalist paradigms presenting other nations rather than other classes as labor's vital opponent. In other words, *the crisis of socialist ideas is itself a key factor explaining union weakness*, as this has helped delegitimatize class cleavages in favor of illiberal, identity-based cleavages.[14]

The chapters compiled here indeed offer ample evidence of an unwillingness or inability to think in terms of class differences and a decreasing identification with unions. We see, for example, the frequency with which the

problems of capitalism are blamed on communism. Even the social-democratic parties, wary of being tied to the past, do not offer a socialist narrative
that blames capitalism. Yet it is easy to find unions with right-wing or neo-
conservative ideologies, as in Hungary and Poland. In describing the Czech
case, Pollert well describes the general ideological dilemma facing unions in
postcommunist society: Not only must these unions relegitimate themselves
as genuine defenders of workers' interests, but they must carve "a space
between opposing the old system and ambiguously both supporting and
opposing the recently restored market economy." As one Czech union leader
put it, this ambiguous stance toward capitalist transformation makes unions
"schizophrenic."

As we have seen, there is very little unionization in the new private sphere,
and the demise of socialist ideas and the rise of a new pro-market narrative
help explain this as well. To use Offe's language, unions may have become
"market actors," in that their fate will be determined in the context of a market economy, but they still tend to act like "policy-takers," relying on the
state for their survival.[15] (Their members come from state-dominated sectors,
and laws give them rights that most collective bargaining merely reaffirms.)
They do so not so much because they are prevented from doing otherwise,
either by capital or the state, but because union leaders do not yet understand
their new role and are not united about where their interests lie. Ideas and
interests are, of course, shaped by institutions, economic possibilities, and
political conjunctures. These may not be conducive to unionism today. However, successful union organization, like any movement, requires coordination and mobilization not just in propitious times but in unpopular times too.
Such activity remains lacking, and it has been so for most of the last decade.
While unions in the West are trying to counteract the tendencies weakening
unions, Eastern European labor seems to believe that weak unions are precisely what capitalism is all about. They tend to see unions as rearguard institutions for the weak, relevant chiefly for obsolescent state sectors, rather than
as vital representatives of labor against capital, let alone as agents of
expanded citizenship.

WHY DOES IT MATTER?

Finally, what is the significance of all this? Why does it matter that labor is
barely included in contemporary political decision making, particularly if
protest is limited? After all, as Pollert notes, labor always occupies a weaker
position in relation to capital. So what does it matter if unions are weaker in
the East than elsewhere?

The problem, in short, is that democracies have historically had to incorporate rather than marginalize labor to stabilize their rule, but it is precisely attempts at marginalization that prevail in postcommunist society. Labor needs to be stronger to successfully mediate pervasive social conflicts in a democratic society. We still do not know any workplace institutions other than unions that can do this. As noted in the introduction, labor weakness can be dangerous to democracy because it deprives an important and sizable part of the population of political influence, and it can lead to class differences being expressed in nonclass and illiberal ways. We have indeed seen labor's problems being exploited by political illiberals and intolerants in several countries—most successfully in the former Yugoslavia and, for several years, in Slovakia. It is evident also in the support for populists like Zhirinovsky in Russia or Csurka in Hungary and partly in the appeal of Solidarity in Poland.

Clearly, however, it is not the case that the Right has been able to ride this dissatisfaction to power in the way that it did during the Great Depression of the 1930s. That this movement toward extremism has not (for the most part) happened may of course just mean that it has not happened yet. Right-wing mobilization may still capture working-class anger for antidemocratic ends (though this does not mean it will succeed in coming to power, given the formidable international pressures against it). It might also mean that safety-net policies and pro-market ideological hegemony have worked thus far to deflect or reduce that anger. It might also mean that class structures have changed so much that labor is just not politically important anymore. Maybe labor needed to be incorporated, in the way that Luebbert so persuasively argued, only in the early modern period when class was a powerful identity and people learned about politics from parties.[16] Postcommunist Europe has been a television democracy instead, in that people learn about political options mostly from talking heads on the screen. With part of the working class having become an underclass, irrelevant to the success of the economy, perhaps society just does not need labor anymore.

Greskovits seems to agree. Besides pointing to the importance of "exit" through the informal economy, he argues that Eastern European workers have been quiescent because they "protest" by voting rather than using collective action.[17] At first glance, the importance of protest voting seems quite valid. Still impressed with their newfound ability to express their views through the ballot, voters express their displeasure by waiting for elections to throw out the bums. Pendulum swings in electoral results thus far seem to bear out this argument. The problem with this view, however, is that the political system is likely to stabilize soon. Protest voting works best when there are several parties to switch to and vote against, not the same two parties over and over again. Here, too, this seems a reason why protest has thus far been avoided, not why it is likely to remain so. In the end, we are left with the observation that the marginalization of labor in Eastern Europe remains a major political problem. Until labor is successfully incorporated as an influential and rewarded player, the stability of liberal democracy will remain in question. This is why labor weakness in Eastern Europe is more of a problem than it is in the West, where union influence is more solidly entrenched and unionists more determined to defend it.

The chapters also show that labor weakness presents a continual problem—not just as a moral indictment of actually existing capitalism but as a potential political minefield for existing democracies. As we enter the twenty-first century, the "social question" that so affected the twentieth century still seems unresolved.

NOTES

1. George Ross and Andrew Martin, "Through a Glass Darkly," in *The Brave New World of European Labor: European Trade Unions at the Millennium*, George Ross and Andrew Martin, eds. (New York: Berghahn Books, 1999), 382. On new organizing strategies in the United States, see Kate Bronfenbrenner et. al., *Organizing to Win* (Ithaca, N.Y.: ILR Press, 1998).

2. John Kennan, "The Economics of Strikes," in *Handbook of Labor Economics,* vol. 2, Orley Ashtenfelter and Richard Layard, eds. (Amsterdam: Elsevier Science Publishers, 1986), 1091–1137. For critical discussion of the economic theory of strikes, see P. K. Edwards and Richard Hyman, "Strikes and Industrial Conflict: Peace in Europe?" in *New Frontiers in European Industrial Relations*, Richard Hyman and Anthony Ferner, eds. (Oxford, U.K.: Blackwell, 1994); Michael Shalev, "The Resurgence of Labor Quiescence," in *The Future of Labour Movements*, Mario Regini, ed. (London: Sage, 1992), 102–32.

3. Bela Greskovits, *The Political Economy of Protest and Patience* (Budapest: Central University Press, 1998), 113.

4. See Greskovits's chapter on, "The Social Response to Economic Hardship," in *The Political Economy of Protest and Patience*, where he uses Albert Hirschman's language of voice and exit to explain the absence of labor unrest.

5. While the informal economy certainly helps explain labor's relative lack of collective action, just how much it does so is questionable. If this were a truly significant factor, we would expect to find a negative correlation between the level of informal economic activity and labor mobilization. Yet this does not appear to be the case. Romania is a particularly vexing example for this hypothesis. Its labor force is probably the most assertive in the region, and yet as Kideckel (in chapter 5 of this volume) demonstrates, informal labor relations appear particularly widespread there.

6. David Ost, "Illusory Corporatism: Tripartism in the Service of Neoliberalism," in *Politics and Society* 28:4, December 2000.

7. Melanie Tatur, David Stark, and Laszlo Bruszt speak of the Czech Republic as the

dominant corporatist country, while Anna Seleny votes for Hungary. See Tatur, " 'Corporatism' as a Paradigm of Transformation," in *Poszukiwaniu Paradymatu Transformacyjnego*, Jadwiga Staniszkis, ed. (Warsaw: Instytut Studiów Politycznych, 1994), 93–130; David Stark and Laszlo Bruszt, *Postsocialist Pathways: Transforming Politics and Property in East Central Europe* (Cambridge: Cambridge University Press, 1998); and Seleny, "Old Political Rationalities and New Democracies: Compromise and Confrontation in Hungary and Poland," in *World Politics* 51, July 1999, 484–519.

8. In "Can Unions Survive Communism?" in *Dissent*, winter 1997, David Ost compares Czech unions favorably to Polish unions in this regard, though Bela Greskovits (*The Political Economy of Protest and Patience*) counters that better Czech labor-market policies were due to that country's better macroeconomic conditions.

9. See, for example, Peter Gowan, *The Global Gamble: Washington's Faustian Bid for World Dominance* (London: Verso, 1999); and Janine Wedel, *Collision and Collusion: The Strange Case of Western Aid to Eastern Europe 1989–1998* (New York: St. Martin's Press, 1998).

10. On unrest resulting from structural adjustment policies, see J. Walton and D. Seddon, *Free Markets and Food Riots: The Politics of Global Adjustment* (Cambridge, Mass.: Blackwell, 1994). On unions' new recruitment strategies, see Kate Bronfenbrenner et al., *Organizing to Win*; and George Ross and Andrew Martin, *The Brave New World of European Labor.*

11. On Western Europe, see Frances Fox Piven, ed., *Labor Parties in Postindustrial Society* (New York: Oxford University Press, 1992); and Ross and Martin, *The Brave New World of European Labor.*

12. See, for example, the much lower strike rates in Eastern Europe as compared to Western Europe in Stephen Crowley, *Class Dismissed?: Labor Quiescence and Its Implications for Post-Communist Europe,* manuscript.

13. Indeed, the extent of union decline in Western Europe and the OECD countries generally has been questioned. As one recent study concludes, "our data support the view that industrial relations institutions and trade unions have by and large proved quite resilient in the face of considerable domestic and international economic pressures in the past two decades." Miriam Golden, Michael Wallerstein, and Peter Lange, "Postwar Trade-Union Organization and Industrial Relations in Twelve Countries," in *Continuity and Change in Contemporary Capitalism*, Herbert Kitschelt et al., eds. (Cambridge: Cambridge University Press, 1999), 223.

14. On the democratic nature of class cleavages, see David Ost, "Labor, Class, and Democracy: Shaping Political Antagonisms in Post-Communist Society," in *Markets, States, and Democracy: The Political Economy of Post-Communist Transformation,* Beverley Crawford, ed. (Boulder: Westview Press, 1995).

15. Claus Offe, "The Attribution of Public Status to Interest Groups," in *Organizing Interests in Western Europe*, Suzanne D. Berger, ed. (Cambridge: Cambridge University Press, 1981).

16. Gregory Luebbert, *Liberalism, Fascism, or Social Democracy: Social Classes and the Political Origins of Regimes in Interwar Europe* (New York: Oxford University Press, 1991).

17. Greskovits, *The Political Economy of Protest and Patience.*

Index

AFL–CIO, 94n12
Alliance of the Democratic Left (SLD, Poland), 86–88
Ashwin, Sarah, 207
Avramović, Dragoslav, 168, 174

Baker, James, 193
Belarus, 193
black market. *See* informal economy
Bujak, Zbigniew, 82

Catholic Church, 88
Central Council of Bulgarian Trade Unions, 124, 126
Christian democracy, 113, 126
Ciorbea, Victor, 97, 102, 103–104
Civic Democratic Association (ODA), 20
Civic Democratic Party (ODS), 20
civil society, 4, 91, 120, 138, 142, 200, 222
collective agreements. *See* collective bargaining
collective bargaining, 222; Bulgaria, 136; Croatia, 143–144, 147, 151, 153; Czech Republic, 14, 21; Hungary, 37, 45, 48, 50; Russia, 208–209; Serbia, 163, 174; Slovakia, 70, 72; Ukraine, 185–186
corporate governance, 92, 96n38
corporatism. *See* tripartism
Cosma, Miron, 98–99, 110–111
Czurka, Istvan, 231

Dawson, Jane, 6
Democratic Union (Poland), 87, 88
democratization, 4–5, 10, 82, 200, 231–232

Ekiert, Grzegorz, 93
Estonia, 193
European Union, 91, 114–115, 139
European Trade Union Confederation, 148, 149

farmer-workers, 195
Frasyniuk, Władysław, 82
Freedom Union (Poland), 87, 88

Gardawski, Juliusz, 89
Gazeta Wyborcza, 83
General Motors, 95
Georgia, 188, 193
Germany, 194
globalization, 1, 7, 228
Great Depression, 1, 5, 205, 231
Greskovits, Bela, 224, 231

Habsburg legacy, 14, 15, 20, 61
Hayek, Friedrich, 83, 94n9
Hirschman, Albert, 176, 201, 202

ICFTU. *See* International Confederation of Free Trade Unions

About the Contributors

Mihail Arandarenko received his Ph.D. in economics in 1998 from Belgrade University. He has been a research fellow with Collegium Budapest, Institute for Advanced Study, and he is currently a research fellow at the Institute of Sociology, Hungarian Academy of Sciences, as well as a research associate with WZB Social Science Research Center Berlin. He is also a founding member of Group 17. (arandarenko@ceu.hu)

Stephen Crowley is associate professor of politics at Oberlin College. He is the author of *Hot Coal, Cold Steel: Russian and Ukrainian Workers from the End of the Soviet Union to the Post-Communist Transformations* (University of Michigan Press, 1997), as well as a number of articles on the politics of labor in Russia and the former Soviet Union. He is currently writing a book on the comparative study of labor in postcommunist societies. (steve.crowley @oberlin.edu)

Grigor Gradev's main area of research includes industrial relations, organizational design and development, and politics. Until 1999 he was director of the Institute for Social and Trade Union Studies and executive secretary of the Confederation of Independent Trade Unions in Bulgaria. Currently, he coordinates a project of the European Trade Union Confederation on foreign direct investment in the accession countries, the Balkan part of a project on social dialogue, and the ETUC task force on the Stability Pact for southeastern Europe. (T&K-hold@mobikom.com)

David A. Kideckel is professor and the chairperson of the Anthropology Department at Central Connecticut State University. Along with writing many articles and reviews, Kideckel is the author and editor of *The Solitude of Collectivism: Romanian Villagers to the Revolution and Beyond* (Cornell University Press, 1993); *East European Communities: The Struggle for Balance in Turbulent Times* (Westview, 1995); and *Neighbors at War: Anthropological Perspectives on Yugoslav Ethnicity, Culture, and History* (coedited with J. M. Halpern, Penn State University Press, 2000). His current research is a comparative study of labor, politics, and treatment of the body among Romanian chemical workers and coal miners. (kideckel@ccsu.edu)

Marina Kokanović has worked as a project adviser and analyst and as an adviser in economic and social issues for union members in the Croatian Trade Union Confederation UATUC/SSSH, Zagreb. She is a researcher and analyst for several women's organizations in Croatia in the field of legislation and economy. She is also a lecturer at the Centre for Women's Studies and at the Trade Union School. She has published several reports and research studies on the economic and social situation in Croatia and on the status of women. (mak6361@yahoo.com)

Evgienii Kopatko is the director of the Donetsk Information-Analytical Center in Donetsk, Ukraine. Since 1991 he has been leading the center's efforts in conducting public-opinion surveys and studying social policy, strike and union activity, and the processes of social adaptation to the new economic conditions in Ukraine. (Diac@skif.net)

David Ost is professor of political science at Hobart and William Smith Colleges and a frequent visiting professor at Central European University. He has written widely on labor, politics, and postcommunism, including recent articles in *Politics and Society* and *East European Politics and Societies*. He is currently completing a book on class, anger, and democratization in Poland. (ost@hws.edu)

Włodzimierz Pańków is professor at Collegium Civitas, a docent at the Polish Academy of Sciences in Warsaw, and the author of a large number of publications on industrial sociology and postcommunist transformations. His recent publications include *Modernization of Enterprises in France and Poland* (in French, 1996), *Transformation of Industrial Firms* (in Polish, 1998), and *Fall of the Bastion?: Trade Unions in a Privatized Economy* (in Polish, 1999). (wpankow@ifispan.waw.pl)

Anna Pollert is professor of employment relations at the University of Greenwich, London. Her work on gender, class, and work, and on post-command economy transformation, includes *Girls, Wives, Factory Lives* (1981), *Farewell to Flexibility?* (1991), and *Transformation at Work in the New Market Economies of Central Eastern Europe* (1999). (a.pollert@gre.ac.uk)

András Tóth, Ph.D. in sociology, is a senior research fellow at the Institute of Political Sciences, Hungarian Academy of Sciences. He has published a series of articles on Hungarian trade union development. Currently, he is doing comparative research on the car industry and union development in Spain and Hungary. (tothand@mtapti.hu)

Jonathan Stein is a research associate at the East-West Institute in Prague and an editor at the Economist Intelligence Unit. He is also the editor of *The Politics of National Minority Participation in Post-Communist Europe: State-Building, Democracy, and Ethnic Mobilization* (M.E. Sharpe, 2000). (jstein@iews.cz)